THE DIAGNOSIS AND TREATMENT OF ALCOHOLISM

THE DIAGNOSIS AND TREATMENT OF ALCOHOLISM

Second Edition

By

GARY G. FORREST, Ed.D., P.C.

Licensed Clinical Psychologist
Executive Director, Psychotherapy Associates and
The Institute For Addictive Behavioral Change
Colorado Springs, Colorado

JASON ARONSON INC.
Northvale, New Jersey
London

THE MASTER WORK SERIES

First softcover edition 1994

Copyright © 1975 and 1978 by Charles C Thomas

Library of Congress Cataloging-in-Publication Data

ISBN: 1-56821-330-1
Library of Congress Catalog Card Number: 94-72312

Manufactured in the United States of America. Jason Aronson Inc. offers books and cassettes. For information and catalog write to Jason Aronson Inc., 230 Livingston Street, Northvale, New Jersey 07647.

TO MY PATIENTS

PREFACE TO THE SECOND EDITION

THE various reviews of the first edition of this book have been most encouraging. During the past three years, I have received numerous letters as well as a great deal of verbal feedback indicating the clinical usefulness of the text. This general response has certainly reinforced my personal need to be involved in the field of alcoholic treatment and rehabilitation. Likewise, I have felt a need to continue my writing efforts in the alcoholism field.

Shortly after the publication of the first edition, I realized that I had omitted the very important areas of marital and family therapy involving the alcoholic. This was an omission which was easy to make in view of the marked dearth of clinical information in these specific areas of alcoholic rehabilitation work. The new chapter in this edition entitled "Marital and Family Therapy" will, in all probability, be perceived by the reader as a major contribution to the overall subject matter of the book. In fact, this particular chapter, although only a beginning point, may well be an important addition to the overall field of alcoholic rehabilitation. Unfortunately, any substantial clinical research or theoretical data dealing with the treatment of the alcoholic marriage and the alcoholic family system would represent, in my opinion, a most welcomed contribution to the alcoholism field.

The new material included in the "Behavior Therapy" chapter will add to the merit of this second edition. I believe that all strategies of psychotherapy and "rehabilitation" are, in the final analysis, behavioral. Behavior therapy with the alcoholic is certainly not limited to the aversion treatment strategies. I must thank Larry "Frank" Wellman, M.S. and Dr. Jim Evans, both behavioral psychologists, for their scholarly additions to the "Behavior Therapy" chapter.

vii

The other major additions to this new edition are in the form of a chapter dealing with many of the sexual issues associated with alcoholism and the five year follow-up data included in the final chapter of the book. I think the new data presented in the "Alcoholic Rehabilitation: For Better or For Worse?" chapter should be a source of encouragement for all involved in this very difficult profession. The many interrelated facets of alcohol addiction and sexual pathology have long been avoided and poorly understood. In this respect, the new material touching upon these issues represents but another beginning point.

Alcoholism and problem drinking continue to be major health and social problems today throughout the world. No new or significant "breakthroughs" have taken place in the field of alcoholic treatment and rehabilitation. Efforts at prevention and education appear to be as futile as ever. A poorly informed segment of our society seems to believe that the "drug and alcohol crisis" is over. To the contrary, I feel that the many individual and collective problems associated with chemical dependency and addiction are only beginning to become manifest in Western culture. It seems as though we will eventually collectively decide to either deny, accept and live with the addiction dilemma or do "something" about this spector.

G.G.F.

PREFACE TO THE FIRST EDITION

THE writing of this book was precipitated by numerous factors, but in actuality, I am not at all convinced of the primacy of any one or two individual factors as determinants of my need to create the manuscript. However, a few rather specific factors or needs seem to come to the fore in this respect. First, and perhaps foremost, has been my desire to communicate to rehabilitation personnel involved in the treatment of individuals experiencing difficulty as a result of their drinking behavior a global treatment approach which I have found successful. While a great deal has been written to date regarding specific rehabilitation strategies relative to such individuals, little has been done with regard to a more comprehensive treatment approach. In this text I have attempted to convey to the reader an approach to the rehabilitation of the alcoholic which encompasses a total process of interaction. In many respects this amounts to a "nuts and bolts" approach to the work of alcoholic rehabilitation. What to expect, what to do and what not to do and similar guidelines are central to my approach. This type of format has been applied to the multiplicity of rehabilitation strategies typically employed within the confines of an alcoholic rehabilitation facility; individual and group psychotherapy, residential treatment, behavior therapy, Alcoholics Anonymous, etc. Total engagement and ongoing "treatment" are the ever-present red thread of the text. Successful rehabilitation of the alcoholic patient seems to be contingent upon total systems of reinforcement of sobriety.

In chapters 1-4 a number of the primary issues relative to the development of a basic understanding of what pathological drinking entails are discussed. Needless to say, this information is incomplete. Yet is it hoped that this material will provide the reader with a "feel" for the complexity of the personal and social issues surrounding alcohol addiction. In addition to the factual data presented in this section, a good deal of clinically oriented information specific to pathological drinking behavior has been covered. Hopefully the reader will find the scope and depth of the material covered in section one germane to the global treatment process delineated in section two. In reality, understanding and treatment can only be one in the same. Academically, treatment certainly presupposes understanding. Clinically, I have found this to be the case.

The remainder of this book is directed specifically at alcoholism and problem drinking treatment strategies. The basis for this approach will be explored in chapter five. The particular strategies presented in the remainder of the text in no way exhaust the treatment regimen relative to alcohol addiction. While each treatment approach is presented individually on a chapter-to-chapter basis, it should be emphasized that successful rehabilitation is the product of an integration of various treatment strategies geared to the particular needs of the individual patient experiencing difficulty as a result of his or her drinking behavior. Individual psychotherapy may represent the most promising treatment approach with certain patients. Alcoholics Anonymous or residential treatment may represent primary treatment strategies with other patients. Determining appropriate individual treatment strategies is often most difficult. In this section I have attempted to look at a multiplicity of treatment strategies, from both the more traditional viewpoint of theory as well as "nuts and bolts" approach as to the employment of these strategies with addicted patients. I should stress that the various strategies of "treatment" work for me as presented. I am not sure the same "effects" will be the product of the reader's attempt to implement these procedures. In this general sense, I would encourage trying out some of the therapeutic behaviors advocated, while at the same time allowing oneself the freedom to experiment and find those personal strategies of intervention which work best. While we must all seek to enhance our repertoire of therapeutic skills, we at the same time should become aware of our particular strengths and weaknesses and behave accordingly with our patients. As change agents we must accept the risk of trying out new behaviors within the field of alcoholic rehabilitation.

The clinical readings section will hopefully provide the reader with a more in-depth understanding of both clinical and theoretical issues found to be germane to the treatment process with alcohol-addicted patients. The material presented in this section covers a broad spectrum of clinical issues. It is my feeling that a basic understanding of the issues discussed in this section is of crucial importance to successful clinical work with individuals experiencing interpersonal and social difficulty as a result of their drinking behavior.

During the past four or five years we have witnessed an unprecedented emphasis upon the interpersonal and social problems caused by alcohol addiction. In part, the Vietnam war with its drug-related social issues helped facilitate the current interest in alcoholism. The magnitude of the problem of alcohol addiction is such that it seems to have dictated social attention as well as rehabilitation and preventative efforts.

Behavioral scientists have speculated that the growing complexities of modern society have made the process of daily living so stressful that more and more people have depended upon alcohol as a means of coping with these anxieties and stresses. As reality becomes increasingly intolerable people turn to behaviors and substances which help to block out confusion and unpleasant feelings. Alcohol seems to have historically served these exact needs. One of the "effects" of our increased awareness of the magnitude of the problem of alcohol addiction has been the development of social agencies and services designed to remedy our present situation. In essence this has amounted to the development of many new alcoholic rehabilitation facilities, alcoholic rehabilitation specialists within the community mental health scene, government funding and support and the development of hundreds of treatment facilities within the military.

Having been a part of this process I have observed a dire need for a text dealing with the global process of alcoholic rehabilitation; it is to this end which this manuscript is directed. Staffing the multiplicity of agencies and facilities now becoming involved in the process of delivering alcoholic rehabilitation services has been difficult. In my experience many of those becoming involved in such agencies are academically prepared at the bachelor's and master's degree level and have very little clinical experience. Hopefully, this text will provide treatment strategies and guidelines for such personnel. It is my feeling that an understanding of the material presented here should provide a basic rationale as to how and why alcohol-addicted individuals get sober. I would hope that the more "seasoned" reader, with regard to both psychotherapeutic treatment in general and alcoholic rehabilitation work specifically, would feel a sense of rejuvenation upon reading this text.

Many have contributed to the completion of this manuscript. Certainly my secretaries and typists, Mrs. Mary Huie, Mrs. Jeannie Moreau, Ms. Isabel Congdon and Mrs. Mary Lou Niebrugge, have been instrumental to the completion of the task. Clinical supervision and sharing with psychiatrists Herb Seymour and Art Knauert has been most helpful, as has debate with Jack Peacock, MSW. My supervision of a number of counselors within two alcoholic rehabilitation facilities has been most meaningful. In this capacity, my work with Jerry Cole and Houston Lirette has been both rewarding and supportive. Finally, the personal growth and experience provided through my work with such patients as Jim B., Ed A., Ken M., Frank S., Bill J., "Stoney," Stella, Jack and Cam W. has provided the understanding essential to my development and ability to create this text.

G.G.F.

CONTENTS

Section One
BACKGROUND INFORMATION AND INITIAL
CLINICAL CONSIDERATIONS

Chapter

Section Two
STRATEGIES OF TREATMENT

THE DIAGNOSIS AND TREATMENT OF ALCOHOLISM

BACKGROUND INFORMATION AND INITIAL CLINICAL CONSIDERATIONS

Chapter 1

WHAT IS AN ALCOHOLIC?

IN spite of a growing recognition that alcohol is the most abused drug in the United States today resulting in alcohol abuse and chronic alcoholism which affects some eleven million individuals, surprisingly little is known of the individual alcoholics comprising this growing segment of society. This general lack of understanding applies to parents, relatives, friends and behavioral scientists, as well as to those actually suffering from alcoholism or problem drinking. Alcoholism per se has been recognized as a chronic disorder involving physiological and psychological variables which render certain individuals incapable of refraining from frequent alcohol ingestion to the point of both continued intoxication and eventual interpersonal and social dysfunction. The WHO Expert Committee on Mental Health defines alcoholics as, ". . . those excessive drinkers whose dependence on alcohol has attained such a degree that it shows in a noticeable mental disturbance or an interference with their bodily and mental health, interpersonal relations and their smooth social and economic functioning."

Extensive review of the literature regarding the definition of alcoholism adds very little to this basic statement. Individuals labeled "alcoholic" manifest four essential characteristics: their drinking is compulsive in nature and as such uncontrollable; their drinking is most typically of long duration, or chronic; their drinking results in intoxication; and their patterns of alcohol ingestion are invariably detrimental to their ability to function interpersonally. Although manifestation of these essential characteristics in no way implies an absolute definition of alcoholism, individuals exhibiting drinking patterns in accord with these characteristics have such similar developmental courses and clinical pictures that they frequently earn the label "alcoholic" or "problem drinker." Although the individual alcoholic or problem drinker consistently manifests these essential characteristics, there are a great many individual differences among any given population of individuals labeled "alcoholic." This applies to both patterns of consumption and lifestyle characteristics. It has been noted that these individual differences are so great one might question whether alcoholic individuals have much in common, aside from their pathological alcohol ingestion.

Perhaps our cultural sterotype of the "alcoholic" is one of the greatest obstacles encountered in attempting to establish who is, in fact, a problem drinker or alcoholic. Within American society the alcoholic has historically been depicted as the skid row bum. Certainly this segment of the alcoholic population is readily visible, yet the skid row alcoholic comprises only 3 to 5 percent of the total alcoholic population in the United States. Social agencies, change agents, significant others and the problem drinker as well have avoided the many issues surrounding alcoholism as a result of this false stereotype. In reality, most alcoholic individuals are in the nation's working and homemaking population. Alcoholism significantly affects and involves persons from every walk and stratum of American life. Individuals recognized as suffering from alcoholism include doctors, lawyers, truck drivers and members of virtually every profession known. Alcoholism transcends race, ethnic group, social class and intelligence. The process of collective identification of the alcoholic as a member of the skid row caste system has probably done more to deter progressive treatment and rehabilitation of the individual alcoholic than any other single variable. This is particularly true of the problem drinker or incipient alcoholic. As part of his denial system the problem drinker or alcoholic must see the "alcoholic" from a skid row perspective. In the process, incipient or actual alcoholics can deny the existence of their own alcohol pathology for as long as twenty or thirty years. Needless to say, social and cultural reinforcement of this false stereotype only serves to enhance the individual alcoholic's pathology. From an educational viewpoint, it is imperative that we break down this false stereotype.

A number of other significant variables interact to make the subject of alcoholism both a difficult subject of study and an area of misunderstanding. Problem drinking and alcoholism have historically been viewed as moral issues within this culture. The father who spends the weekly paycheck on alcohol, the daughter who sexually acts out under the influence of alcohol and the drunk driver are all subject to moral scrutiny. Certainly we evaluate these behaviors, as they incorporate the use of alcohol, as "bad," "evil," "wrong" or perhaps even "crazy." We have tended to evaluate these forms of behavior as socially unacceptable on moral grounds and have all too frequently failed to attempt to understand, empathize and facilitate change. Alcoholism continues to be viewed by Western man as socially unacceptable. In this sense the alcoholic is very much akin to the insane or the lunatic. One is surely destined to social ostracism and rejection within such a context; historically as such, the worst thing an alcoholic person could do was to let neighbors and significant others know he was an alcoholic.

Another related factor facilitating the general lack of understanding surrounding alcoholism has to do with the humor surrounding alcoholism. Indeed, a good deal of the alcoholic's behavior is perceived as funny. The antics of the alcoholic are notoriously good for a laugh. Most of us have encountered problem drinkers and alcoholics who were the "life of the party" and in other ways received a good deal of social reinforcement for their alcoholism. This may apply to the alcoholic who actually causes death or injury as a result of an automobile accident. How often have we heard the tale of the alcoholic involved in an automobile accident which causes serious damage but who was himself uninjured? Frequently this tale is told with a good deal of laughter or humor, suggesting that the proper way to avoid injury in such a situation is to be intoxicated. Automobile accidents involving intoxicated drivers account for some 28,000 lives annually. Is this a laughing matter?

Certainly the lack of innovative treatment and rehabilitation measure directed at the problem of alcoholism can be accounted for in part through the historical attitude of behavioral scientists toward the alcoholic. Hospital personnel long ago learned that alcoholics are, for the most part, repeaters. Within any given medical community, it was well known that medical intervention as a result of alcoholism was to be a recurrent procedure for certain individuals. Once detoxified and treated medically, the alcoholic patient was released only to turn up again in a similar medical state within a short period of time. Needless to say, this process becomes most disconcerting for all involved, particularly when hospitals are pressed to provide services for the multitude of other "sick" individuals. Moreover, intoxicated individuals are not the most pleasant people with which to work. Our middle class values and ethics make it difficult to deal with inarticulate, dirty, disheveled alcoholics. Unfortunately, this is the reality with which behavioral scientists are often presented. Psychiatrists, psychologists and other change agents have been understandably much more responsive to treating private patients for fifty or sixty dollars a session. In essence, alcoholics are simply not an attractive clinical group with which to work (Knox, 1971).

Professional personnel involved in treatment and rehabilitation measures directed at individuals labeled "alcoholic" are confronted with a multiplicity of unknowns. What are the etiological determinants of alcoholism? What is an alcoholic? What are the appropriate treatment modalities for alcoholism? These are but a few of the unanswered questions surrounding problem drinking and alcoholism. Alcohol rehabilitation, although an existing social force for some thirty years, has been, for the most part, a fragmented attempt to reach whatever few individuals possible. It is only during the past ten years that we have consolidated efforts, made more appropriate funding available and received governmental support appropriate to the growing problem of alcoholism. We are only now beginning to find out what rehabilitating the alcoholic or problem drinker really means.

For purposes of definition and identification, four classes or groups of individuals may be identified with reference to drinking patterns:

(1) *Nondrinkers:* Presently it is estimated that 25 to 30 percent of the American adult population are nondrinkers (HEW,

1971).

(2) *Social drinkers:* Individuals classified as social drinkers consume moderately. This typically means two or three drinks on one or two occasions per week and infrequent intoxication. Individuals so classified may from time to time get drunk.

(3) *Problem drinkers:* Although not excessive in their own eyes, these people show excess in the frequency of their becoming intoxicated, or by the medical, social or economic consequences of their level of alcohol consumption. Many of these individuals are cognizant that alcohol is a major problem in their lives; others deny this fact. It should be noted that a sizeable segment of problem drinkers do not progress to the stage of alcoholism.

(4) *Alcoholics:* In addition to the data presented earlier on alcoholism, alcoholics are simply addicted to alcohol. Central to addiction, they are unable to spontaneously give up drinking. Although they may be able to go for varying periods of time without drinking, they inevitably revert to intoxication. Chronic alcoholism is a term usually applied to those individuals whose prolonged life-style of intoxication has resulted in physical abuse of the body. The alcoholic *must* rely on alcohol to enable him to cope with the process of daily living. Estimates of the incidence of alcoholism in the United States currently vary from 6 to 12 percent of the adult population (HEW, 1971).

The following three brief case histories are presented as examples of what it means to be an "alcoholic."

> *Case 1.* Mrs. C., a forty-two-year-old married mother of three has been hospitalized for "alcoholism" five times in the past two years. She states that she first began to drink at age seventeen, but experienced no difficulty with her drinking until seven years ago. At that time she was arrested for driving under the influence. Since that time her drinking has gotten progressively worse, to the extent of including more than one fifth of whiskey per day for the past year. Upon arising she consumes two or three "shots" and continues this behavior throughout the day. Her hospitalizations include psychiatric care in addition to gastrointestinal and other physical complications secondary to prolonged alcohol ingestion. Her al-

cohol consumption has resulted in numerous separations from her husband.

Case 2. A forty-nine-year-old practicing physician was hospitalized four years ago for "alcohol detoxification." He had been consuming increasingly large amounts of vodka since his termination from the Air Force some six years earlier. His alcohol consumption had reached the point of a drink or two in the morning plus barbituates to keep his hands steady enough to operate. Drinking continued throughout the day and into the evening to the point of frequently passing out. Two previous divorces were alcohol related, as were numerous legal involvements.

Case 3. John C., a thirty-six-year-old civil service employee with an alcohol-related job history of twelve years was found "passed out" in a linen closet of a garment factory where he was employed. Fourteen arrests in the past eleven months for public intoxication, drunken driving and similar offenses are part of his case history. The man reportedly consumes two fifths of liquor per day. Approximately three years ago he was involved in a major automobile crash, in which he was both "drinking and driving."

It is imperative that we acknowledge the existence of alcoholism as an entity. Alcoholics or persons experiencing problems related to alcohol consumption can be identified. However, at the same time we must realize that individuals becoming addicted to alcohol consumption can be identified. However, at the same time we must realize that individuals becoming addicted to alcohol are human beings capable of growing and changing. Suffering people have too long been stigmatized. Our social system has a history of identifying and subsequently alienating those select individuals who somehow don't "fit." Alcoholism as a social issue and alcoholics as individuals have felt the brunt of this process. Rather than effectively disengaging these individuals we must seek more effective means of engaging them within the community. As we begin to understand that being an alcoholic or problem drinker has nothing to do with our basic humanness, we can begin to become more effective change agents. Allowing people the freedom to be able to say "I have a problem, I am an alcoholic," is tantamount to the process of beginning to enable individuals to look at themselves realistically and subsequently choosing behavioral alternatives. Being and becoming an alcoholic is not a pleasurable experience. Learning to undo the trap of alcoholic dependency is an extremely difficult and trying process for all involved; however, it may well be the most significant life experience for those who are eventually able to maintain prolonged sobriety.

Chapter 2

DEVELOPMENTAL STAGES
OF ALCOHOLISM

THE study of alcoholism and the person suffering from alcohol addiction is for the most part a study of individual differences. This point is not well understood by those unfamiliar with alcoholism and the treatment of the alcoholic patient. It must be emphasized that each alcoholic has a very personal developmental history. This developmental history includes the sum total of the individual's experiential being. Family relationships, educational experiences, work histories, physical illness and drinking patterns are but a part of this total developmental history. It is well to bear in mind that each individual labeled "alcoholic" is uniquely human.

While realizing the individual nature of any given "alcoholic's" behavior, it has been noted for some time that individuals progressing systematically to the stage of chronic alcoholism have certain similar life experiences with regard to their drinking behavior. These similarities have helped facilitate viewing alcohol addiction from a developmental perspective. One of the most disconcerting or confusing aspects of this perspective has to do with the temporal variability of many individuals' drinking behavior. Behaviors which typically occur early in the process of alcohol addiction may be found late in the case histories of some alcoholics if, indeed, they are ever seen. In our attempt to delineate various developmental stages specific to alcohol addiction and problem drinking this single factor often becomes most confusing. However, the overall developmental model seems to offer an excellent means of evaluating progressive drinking behavior. In choosing to view alcohol addiction from a developmental perspective we must simply recognize that a number of individuals eventually labeled "alcoholic" may not fit our particular series of developmental stages. One may well progress from point A to D without experiencing B and C, whatever they may include. It is felt that as perhaps 85 percent of those eventually reaching the ranks of the "alcoholic" do experience similar drinking stages and alcohol-related patterns of behavior, the developmental approach is quite valuable.

Realizing that it is impossible to delineate a characteristic pattern and sequence of events which occur in the development of alcohol addiction, Jellinek (1962) analyzed more than two thousand case histories in order to produce a basic profile of the developmental stages of alcohol addiction. Rather than systematically presenting the developmental stages depicted by Jellinek, a more generalized developmental model will be considered with reference to Jellinek's stages when appropriate. Again, it should be emphasized that this developmental model should be considered an account of what happens in the majority of severe cases. Many individuals experiencing problem drinking or chronic alcoholism simply will not fit the proposed developmental model.

STAGE 1 — PREPROBLEMATIC STAGE: EXPERIMENTATION AND SOCIAL DRINKING

The rather typical introduction to alcohol within American culture takes place during middle adolescence. It is at this time that most persons experiment and find out the effects of alcohol ingestion. As with all drinking, this experimentation and infrequent use of alcohol is socially motivated. Recently, the experimentation and use of marijuana seems to have taken on many of the historic dynamics surrounding alcohol consumption for this age group.

This initial contact with alcohol is a significantly different experience for the prospective alcoholic than for the "normal" consumer of alcohol. The potential alcoholic experiences a degree of interpersonal and intrapersonal reinforcement from his early drinking that is significantly different from that of the nonalcoholic. The feelings of unlove, unworth, failure and inferiority which many alcoholics manifest from a very early age "set" them up for future alcohol addiction. At this early age, the future alcoholic learns that alcohol helps him feel better. During this era of experimentation, the future alcoholic first learns he can escape persistent feelings of anxiety, depression and the aggregate of other unpleasant effects. Those who later experience the total process of becoming addicted to alcohol are often aware of this initial emotional qualitative and differential response to alcohol. These individuals frequently report that even during their initial contacts with alcohol they seemed to "get higher" and consume more than their peers.

During this stage of experimentation and social drinking there are occasional periods of relief drinking. Moving into late adolescence and adulthood is typically accompanied by "social drinking" in our culture. Social drinking is a poorly defined concept usually applied to any form of social interaction involving the consumption of alcohol. The problem drinker and future alcoholic preconsciously, if not consciously, drink for the explicit purpose of escaping unpleasant feelings at this time. In this respect, the consumption of alcohol is for the explicit purpose of relief. For eventual alcohol addicts, this form of relief drinking becomes increasingly frequent, perhaps becoming a daily occurrence. During this stage intoxication is usually controlled, and socially deviant forms of behavior are for the most part nonexistent. It is well to note that a crucial ingredient in the future alcoholic's behavior at this point is a growing need to increase levels of alcohol consumption in order to produce the desired effect. As is the case with all the developmental stages of alcoholism, this stage may last for several years. For those eventually progressing to the stage of chronic alcoholism, the stage of experimentation and social drinking frequently lasts five to ten years. Fortunately, the vast majority of drinkers never progress past the stage of social drinking.

STAGE II — EXCESSIVE DRINKING

Although differentiation between social drinking and excessive drinking may be initially somewhat hard to establish, there are a number of characteristics which indicate movement in the direction of pathological alcohol consumption. At this point the pattern of alcohol consumption becomes more pervasive. While the basic pattern may remain essentially the same, considerably more time is spent in social drinking. Typically this involves drinking more nights of the week and more hours each night. As this more pervasive pattern of consumption becomes increasingly functional it may require the individual to begin sneaking a few drinks. Realizing that significant others may frown upon extensive drinking behavior, most alcoholics are quite adept at hiding their growing alcohol dependency for an extended period of time. This pattern may well mean drinking round for round with the boys, but it also may mean having a few rounds on the sly. A related strategy is that of beginning to acquire a taste for drinks which have a greater percentage of alcohol. Instead of primarily drinking beer, the individual may at this point begin to drink whiskey or vodka. Another methodology employed to increase the amount of undetected alcohol consumption is barhopping. Instead of drinking at one or two favorite bars during the course of an evening, the individual may begin to frequent five or six locations. In doing so, the acquaintances met in any one given bar will not realize the amount of alcohol the individual may have consumed.

Another significant pattern of social interaction which becomes apparent during this stage is that of change of friendships and peer relationships. As the individual becomes increasingly preoccupied with alcohol and drinking, his interpersonal relationships become increasingly based upon alcohol-related behavior. At this juncture, friendships, social transactions and peer relations may become alcohol based. If one has the choice of playing cards with six different friends, the one most surely to be chosen will be the drinking buddy. A few drinks prior to a social engagement, knowing exactly where the liquor supply is at friends' homes and frequent trips to the kitchen for "ice" readily become a part of this process.

During the stage of excessive drinking the individual drinks for the purpose of escaping from persistent feelings of tension and anxiety. By now the individual has discovered that alcohol ingestion relieves feelings of tension and anxiety. Social interaction, business transactions, dating, dancing and other situations requiring somewhat stressful interpersonal behavior become increasingly dependent upon the presence of alcohol. The housewife learns that she can entertain the husband's boss without anxiety if she has a few drinks before he arrives. The shy and inadequate male learns that he can approach females under the influence of a few drinks; without a few drinks, such approach behavior may be an impossibility for this same person.

Increased alcohol consumption results in an increased tolerance for alcohol. As such the individual must progressively increase his levels of alcohol ingestion to obtain the desired effect. Frequently this process is looked upon with a good deal of positive feeling. The individual characteristically prides himself on his "ability to hold his liquor." He finds that he has become capable of consuming large quantities of liquor while remaining sober. A corresponding change in drinking pattern which takes place during this developmental stage is that of drinking the first three or four drinks as quickly as possible so that the effect may be felt immediately. This global process is indicative of the body's physiological reaction to increasing amounts of alcohol consumption.

Guilt feelings related to patterns of consumption, as well as increasingly ineffective social behaviors, become manifest during this stage. The individual can begin to feel himself being caught in the trap of alcohol dependency. Elaborate explanations and excuses for missing appointments, unfulfilled promises and the like contribute to a growing feeling of personal disdain. Knowing that he is functioning at a level below his capacity, that he is neglecting friends and family and that he is "covering up" can only result in the accumulation of massive feelings of guilt.

The second developmental stage of alcoholism is much akin to the prodromal stage proposed by Jellinek (1962). In addition to the characteristics already discussed, Jellinek posits that the hallmark of the prodromal phase is the experience of "blackouts." A blackout is amnesia for a single event or episode of the previous day. The blackout typically occurs in the absence of extreme intoxication and does not involve loss of consciousness. The individual simply has no recall of a sequel of behaviors carried out under the influence of alcohol. It should be noted that a good deal of controversy surrounds the explanation of the blackout phenomenon (Curlee, 1973; Lisman, 1974; Goodwin, Hill, Powell and Viamontes, 1973). The dissociative nature of such an episode is clearly indicated. The more apparent characteristics of stage two become, the more destined the individual drinker becomes to progress on to stage three. It is the global configuration of alcohol-related behaviors which becomes increasingly important. A few drinking trends may be indicative of growing pathology; a number of such characteristics are prognostic.

STAGE III — ALCOHOL ADDICTION

Once the stage of alcohol addiction has been reached the drinker can no longer decide when and where to drink, let alone how much to drink. At this point the individual has experienced a loss of control over his pattern of drinking behavior. Once he begins to drink, the pattern now includes the inability to stop drinking short of passing out or becoming too sick to consume any more. These drinking bouts may last from a few hours to a few weeks. The drinker is now taking alcohol explicitly for its effect. Needless to say, physical consequences are becoming much more apparent during this developmental stage. The compulsive nature of alcoholism now begins to clearly manifest itself.

It is during this third stage that losses of memory begin to predominate the clinical picture. Upon physical recovery from a drinking bout the alcoholic finds himself unable to recall how he got home, who he was with or what he might have done. Although his behavior may have been generally unexceptional, he will, at this point, begin to frequently question and probe friends regarding the events of the evening or of the episode. While most drinkers cover up their feelings surrounding these losses of memory, a good deal of paranoid ideation frequently surrounds the entire episode. Checking to see if the car has been wrecked or damaged, uneasy feelings at hearing of a hit-and-run accident and similar incidents which may have been related to the drinking bout facilitate paranoia. As this experience of amnesia is usually somewhat traumatic, many individuals are too shocked to admit to themselves, let alone to others, that a time sequel has not been remembered. However, probing will reveal that while many cannot date the first experience of amnesia, nearly all can recall the initial experience. While Jellinek refers to such memory blanks as "blackouts" and dates the origin of such experiences to the prodromal phase, it is during this third developmental stage of addiction that this type of alcohol-related experience becomes rather common. It should be pointed out that although this phenomenon is rather well known, particularly by alcoholics themselves, the term "blackout" is somewhat misunderstood. There is no actual unconsciousness. During this period of amnesia the alcoholic may carry out a number of rather complex motor and social behaviors. The crux of the matter has to do with alcohol-induced physical changes in cortical activity which result in a lack of recall or memory for certain events or for a given period of time.

While many alcoholics will attempt to deny the experience of amnesia, many others will seek help at this point. Attempting to continue to deny that one has an alcohol-related problem may become an overwhelming task. This may dictate seeking relief other than continued intoxication. Medically and psychologically the experience of blackouts or amnesia means that the individual has passed the point of being a moderate or controlled drinker. The drinker is now unquestionably addicted to alcohol and set for a downhill course. Those people unable to seek help or receive some type of significant other-person intervention at this time are headed for increasingly pathological drinking-related behaviors.

During this stage alcohol-induced reduction of interests becomes increasingly more obvious. More time is spent drinking, more energy is devoted to remaining intoxicated. As the drinker continues to devote more time to his alcohol-related activities two crucial areas become affected: family relations and job. Marital discord, aggressive outbursts and behavior problems with the children develop. If the alcoholic spouse happens to be the husband, which is most typical, the wife and children may begin to ally themselves against the often cruel and inconsiderate behavior which he inflicts upon them. At this time the wife must begin to assume a pervasive responsibility for family matters. It is she who pays the bills, organizes, controls and provides for everybody. Resenting the fact that he is becoming progressively irresponsible and less of a father she may begin to confront him with his pathological behavior. Frequently this results in beatings, peace bonds and an entire range of increasingly inappropriate behavior. Separation or divorce may become a reality. Child abuse may enter the picture. Often the husband vacillates between overindulging the children as a means of dealing with his guilt over drinking, and overpunitiveness as a result of the many resentments which his drinking brings out.

A key characteristic of family life at this point is that of social disengagement. The family finds itself becoming increasingly socially isolated. Nondrinking or socially drinking friends and relatives become uncomfortable with the family atmosphere of the alcoholic. Embarrassment on the part of the wife and children facilitates their progressive disengagement from social relationships. The children become afraid to invite peers over to play or watch television. Those closest to the alcoholic can only feel a growing animosity towards him. As he remains continually intoxicated his sexual drive progressively deteriorates. Interpreting this in a stereotyped fashion, he begins to accuse the wife of infidelity. It is she who is involved in an affair with a neighbor or friend, thus she has no need for him sexually. As she has been "turned off" by his drunken behavior for quite some time he interprets this as evidence of her unfaithfulness and coldness towards him. He begins to interpret the most insignificant events as evidence of her infidelity. At this point he has become morbidly jealous, often resulting in episodes of violent acting-out behavior.

As interpersonal relationships continue to deteriorate, so

does job performance. His employer may begin to notice a loss of work efficiency, which may result in reprimands or eventual job loss. Showing up late for work, or job absenteeism may become a standard procedure. Once this pattern becomes evident, it is only a matter of time until the alcoholic shows up for work intoxicated. Keeping a half pint in the desk, going for a few drinks during coffee breaks and drinking over the noon hour can only result in eventual job loss. Again a point of no return has been reached: continued drinking, including consistently being drunk during the daytime.

The alcoholic may now begin to develop delusions of grandeur. In order to compensate for basic inadequacies compounded by his increasingly ineffective lifestyle and guilt, the alcoholic may begin to manifest fantasies which cast him in the role of a highly important person. Business schemes, personal involvement with high-ranking people and the belief that one is capable of omnipotent behavior are part of this clinical picture. Financial extravagance, central to this syndrome, may result in the total depletion of family savings. Indeed, a great many debts of the alcoholic can be related to unrealistic feelings of grandiosity.

As one might predict, these growing patterns of socially inappropriate behavior, precipitated by the process of alcohol addiction, can only facilitate a growing sense of self-hatred. During this third developmental stage, the alcoholic's self-concept begins to consistently show itself in a negative fashion. Self-references such as "I'm no good," "The world would be better off without me" and "I can't ever do anything right" are typical. A self-concept which has historically suffered from a lack of basic good feelings is now totally depleted. This in itself is reinforcement enough to keep many alcoholics in the bottle. A frequent strategy employed by the alcoholic to deal with these feelings of remorse is dwelling on past achievements. Exaggeration, distortion and grandiosity may become a part of this process also. In order to maintain whatever interpersonal ties remain functional, the alcoholic must somehow achieve recognition. Gross lying may become part of the need to compensate for basic feelings of inadequacy and inferiority.

An unfortunate consequence of the accumulating feelings of worthlessness, remorse and despair is that of a suicide attempt by many alcoholics. Although suicidal ideation may have been present during the initial two developmental stages of alcoholism, frank suicidal gestures are rarely part of those stages. During the third stage many alcoholics kill themselves. Suicide attempts are frequent among any given alcoholic population. Such attempts usually take place during a drinking bout and, as a result, are often rather disorganized in character, frequently impulsive and lacking in both motive and plan. Every alcoholic progressing to this stage of addiction has ruminated seriously over the possibility of suicide. Life has become a trap at this point. For many, the only apparent escape from this trap becomes self-destruction.

Progression to the point of alcohol addiction, the third developmental stage of alcoholism, can lead only to a more pathological form of drinking behavior for a large number of those already addicted. This final step in the alcoholic process leads to an active participation in the fourth developmental stage.

STAGE IV — CHRONIC ALCOHOLISM

This final developmental stage is perhaps most clearly physiologically representative of alcoholism as a disease entity. Although physical problems related to prolonged alcohol consumption may have been evident during the preceding developmental stages, they now become floridly manifest. A primary issue related to body physiology is that of nutrition, since the chronic alcoholic typically eats very little. As a result of his total expenditure of time devoted to drinking, the prolonged effect of alcohol upon the stomach and digestive tract and other factors specific to explicit drinking behavior, the chronic alcoholic develops nutritional disorders. Alcoholic cirrhosis is often diagnosed. Other major medical complications related to the lifestyle of the chronic alcoholic include pancreatitis, cardiac complications and various gastrointestinal problems, in addition to neurological impairments. Among the most serious diseases associated with chronic alcoholism are the encephalopathies, Korsakoff's syndrome, Wernicke's syndrome and polyneuropathy. Such neurological impairment is often permanent. Korsakoff's syndrome is characterized by confusion, loss of orientation, generalized impairment of cognitive processes, reality distortion, memory deficit and confabulation. Wernicke's syndrome is distinguished by confusion, memory loss, visual distortion and clouding of consciousness. Wernicke's syndrome responds well to immediate treatment with thiamin. Polyneuropathy is marked by the loss of control of limbs, sensory and motor nerve ending involvement, and sporadic pain and itching. All of these disorders are seen only after years of heavy drinking, when the stage of chronic alcoholism has been reached (Caster, 1978).

As the stage of chronic alcoholism involves continuous drinking from morning to morning, the drinker may remain intoxicated for weeks or months at a time. Many such "benders" are terminated only by hospital admission. Somewhat paradoxically, tolerance often diminishes during this stage. As a result of the years of uninterrupted drinking, the body's tolerance frequently diminishes markedly at this time. When this happens the chronic alcoholic finds that he can no longer consume the vast quantity of alcohol he was formerly capable of consuming. As this process begins to manifest itself, the chronic alcoholic finds his diminished tolerance precipitates feelings of disorganization and helplessness. Feelings of being totally overwhelmed often develop at this point. Many alcoholics realize the physical implications of this sequence of events. The individual may also begin to drink substitutes such as rubbing alcohol, bay rum and after-shave lotion. When these behaviors creep into existence the alcoholic has "hit bottom." The picture of an emotionally disorganized, helpless, overwhelmed child is a realistic characterization of the chronic alcoholic reaching this developmental stage. Continued drinking brings little relief, but not to drink may well bring on all the terrors of the DT's. Delirium Tremens (DT's) involve constant tremor ("shakes"), vivid auditory and visual hallucinations, sensory impairment, marked confusion and a general lack of reality orientation. Chronic alcoholics continue to die annually as a result of the DT's, in spite of medical intervention.

Such an experiential hell motivates many alcoholics to seek help. As he becomes increasingly dysfunctional the alcoholic must become progressively more dependent upon outside support. When he finally reaches the point where significant others want nothing more to do with him, he may seek the help of Alcoholics Anonymous. Medical intervention, frequently required during this developmental stage, becomes another variable which helps engage a number of alcoholics in some form of ongoing treatment. The present emphasis upon alcoholism and rehabilitation efforts directed at the alcoholic patient has opened another avenue of approach to reaching this group of suffering people. Often the chronic alcoholic turns to the church at his turning or crisis point. Individuals who reach this developmental stage of alcoholism and are eventually unsuccessful in the termination of their drinking behavior are confronted with two very real alternatives: death or long-term hospitalization. As those familiar with alcoholism and rehabilitation efforts with this clinical population are aware, this bleak prognosis becomes a functional reality for thousands of chronic alcoholics each year. In this respect the stage of chronic alcoholism is, indeed, the point of no return.

In summary, the process of becoming an alcoholic can be viewed as a developmental sequence. As the experience of biological growth and development can be broken down into a number of primary developmental stages, so too can the process of becoming an alcoholic. The crucial factor has to do with the progressive nature of these developmental stages. Once engaged in the developmental sequence, it is as if certain individuals were "programmed" for the experience of becoming an alcoholic. For these unfortunate people, entry into the stage of experimental drinking leads to the eventual entry into the stage of excessive drinking, until the stage of chronic alcoholism is finally reached. Only now are we beginning to recognize that this pattern can be broken. Rehabilitation efforts continually indicate that the bottom can be raised, that people can change their alcoholic life script.

The concept of developmental stages of alcoholism meshes with the disease model of alcoholism. Both models view alcoholism as an entity which progressively incapacitates the individual. While debate continues over the issue of alcoholism as a disease, it is felt that the reality of the developmental nature of alcoholism is well-accepted. Certainly the stages discussed in this chapter can be demonstrated as clinically valid for those progressing to the point of chronic alcoholism. While many problem drinkers and alcoholics may not experience these developmental stages in the explicit form in which they have been presented, the vast majority have experientially felt the behavioral impact of this process.

Chapter 3

SOCIOLOGICAL AND PHYSIOLOGICAL CONSIDERATIONS RELATED TO ALCOHOLISM

SOCIOLOGICAL CONSIDERATIONS

WHILE alcohol is the most abused drug in the United States today, it must be emphasized that the consumption of alcoholic beverages constitutes typical behavior within this culture, and that most people who drink do not become problem drinkers or alcoholics. The consumption of alcoholic beverages can be traced to prehistoric times. The use of wines and beer is a well-documented part of the archaeological records of the oldest civilizations. It seems apparent that frequent intoxication and alcoholism probably involved only a small segment of these populations as well. Early man seemed to appreciate the mood-changing nature of alcohol, but for the most part he used these fluids with moderation and control. As is the case with American culture, notable exceptions to this general rule stand out. Drunkenness, undoubtedly what we know as alcoholism, was a well-known problem among the ancient Greeks and Jews, as well as the inhabitants of China and India. Governments often made formal and informal attempts to regulate and control drinking within these cultures. Attempts at total prohibition have been historically most unsuccessful. The consumption of alcoholic beverages seems to have enjoyed a rather important place in the development of civilization. Various forms of social interaction, involving a wide variety of group types of behavior, have incorporated the periodic use of alcohol. Religious activities, festive events, such as the Bacchanalia, and medical procedures have relied upon the use of alcoholic beverages. A more circumscribed investigation of interpersonal and social behavior will reveal an almost historic dependence upon the effects of alcohol. Without going into a detailed historical account of sociologically oriented observations which can be made relative to problem drinking and alcoholism, an examination of some of the primary current sociological characteristics related to patterns of alcohol consumption is essential to an understanding of the present problems of alcoholism.

While a good deal of the following sociological and statistical data were gathered and analyzed during the middle sixties, such data have acknowledged as sound.

Cahalan, Cisin and Crossley (1969) in a national survey of drinking behavior report that 68 percent of the adult American population drinks at least once a year. Seventy-seven percent of the adult male population and 60 percent of the female population made up this figure. Fifty-three percent reported drinking once a month or more. These authors report that of the 32 percent who reportedly were abstainers, one-third had previously drunk but had stopped. Of the 12 percent of heavy drinkers reported, one-fifth were male and one-twentieth were female. Similar data have been presented by other authors.

These same authors report that a significantly greater proportion of younger women are choosing to drink. The general trend since WWII has included increased consumption on the part of women, as well as an overall population trend toward more drinking.

A number of sociological variables have been associated with drinking behavior. These variables will be discussed as follows: religious background; socioeconomic level; ethnic group; occupation and education.

Religious Background

It has been found (Cahalan, Cisin and Crossley, 1969; Mulford, 1964) that more than twice as many heavy drinkers (three or more drinks at a time, twice a week or more) report never going to church, compared with those attending weekly. In general, the proportion of heavy drinkers is greater among Catholics than among liberal Protestants. Liberal Protestants drink more than their conservative counterparts. It has been noted that the heavy drinking category for Catholics runs around 20 percent. Protestants other than Methodists and Baptists have the greatest percentage of heavy drinkers. In addition to the Methodist and Baptist groups, the Jewish also rank as the lowest in percentage of heavy drinkers. In contrast to this, the Jewish religion does have one of the highest proportions of drinkers. In spite of the lack of taboos surrounding moderate usage of alcoholic beverages, Jews have a very low incidence of alcoholism. By percentage (Mulford, 1964) 90 percent of the Jewish religion report drinking, 89 percent of the Catholic faith report drinking, and 85 percent of the Lutheran denomination are drinkers. Excluding Methodists and Baptists, other Protestant groups have an average drinking population of approximately 80 percent. Only 48 percent of the Baptist group reports drinking. Personality characteristics also appear to relate to religious background and patterns of consumption (Negrete, 1973).

Socioeconomic Level

It has been found that the highest proportion of drinkers (approximately 90 percent is among young men between the ages of twenty-one to thirty-nine in the highest socioeconomic group (HEW, 1971). The lowest proportion of drinkers (34 percent) is found within the lowest socioeconomic group of females over sixty years of age. Lower socioeconomic groups of both sexes reported less light and moderate drinking than did the higher level socioeconomic groups. It should be noted that the incidence of heavy drinking remains relatively constant for all groups. This report (HEW, 1971) suggests that heavy drinking is somewhat higher within the lower socioeconomic classes. It appears that although middle- and upper-class people tend to report drinking more frequently, they are less prone toward heavy consumption. This finding is somewhat contrary to the belief that it is the lower classes that tend to drink as a means of escaping the reality of a painful existence. As might be predicted, members of the higher socioeconomic groups tend to have their first experiences with alcohol at a later age in life than the lower socioeconomic groups. Moreover, members of the higher socioeconomic levels tend to continue their drinking with increased age.

A related socioeconomic characteristic deals with feelings and perceptions surrounding drinking behavior. People in higher socioeconomic groups tend to perceive alcohol consumption as a rather harmless fom of social behavior and generally feel that such behavior is pleasurable. In contrast to the positive manner in which alcohol consumption is viewed by higher socioeconomic groups, lower groups tend to perceive alcohol-related behavior as potentially more threatening and dangerous and drinking as harmful to both the drinker and his family.

Ethnic Group

Patterns of alcohol consumption are also related to ethnic group membership. Rather than attempting to evaluate and summarize the drinking behaviors of a large number of ethnic groups, only those groups related to American culture will be presented. Thus far we have considered the problem of alcoholism and the multiplicity of factors relating to alcoholism from a general perspective, to include general trends within the United States.

The first ethnic group to be considered is that of the American Negro. It should be noted that very little research has been directed at the drinking behavior of black Americans and that research and literature relative to the black population consistently reports conflicting results. It is relatively well established that the black population does have a high rate of alcoholism, and that drinking is widespread among blacks (Maddox, 1964). Alcohol consumption is both an acceptable form of social behavior among blacks and a frequent cause of problems. Drinking behavior, particularly among the lower black socioeconomic groups, frequently relates to marital, vocational and legal difficulties. Communities with a sizeable black population have experienced social discord related to problem drinking. The rational for higher rates of problem drinking and alcoholism within the black population has historically focused around the psychological need to escape overwhelming feelings of resentment, frustration and unhappiness. Middle and upper socioeconomic level blacks manifest drinking patterns similar to their white class counterparts (HEW, 1971; *Time*, 1974). It should again be emphasized that black patterns of consumption are little understood and presently remain uninvestigated for the most part.

As mentioned earlier, Jewish people as a group tend to drink a great deal. However, as a group Jews experience a very low incidence of alcoholism or problem drinking. A frequent explanation of this phenomena has had to do with the traditional Jewish behavioral introduction to alcohol. The Jewish people have a long tradition of drinking within the home, at celebrations and within their religious ceremonies. It is felt that this early experience with alcohol, plus the integration of drinking behavior within the overall family constellation serves to establish well-controlled patterns of consumption. For the most part the Jewish outlook on drinking is neutral. Drinking is an expected form of social behavior; however, alcoholism and problem drinking are very much disapproved of. Jewish people pride themselves in their sobriety. Those who become alcohol-addicted are looked upon with much disdain. As is the case with black Americans, younger generation Jews manifest drinking patterns similar to other middle-class Americans. It has been suggested that cultural tradition exerts a significant influence toward controlled drinking behavior among the Jewish population. It is felt that alcoholism and problem drinking are related to religious adherence. Those Jews most observant of religious ritual and tradition drink in a most controlled fashion. As orthodoxy diminishes, problem drinking and alcoholism become more prevalent, to the extent of approximating that of the general population (*Time*, 1974).

The French have always been noted for their alcohol consumption, particularly their use of wine. Americans of French descent manifest drinking patterns and behaviors in accord with those of the general U.S. population. However, patterns of alcohol consumption and attitudes toward drinking found among the people of France have been found to vary significantly from American patterns. The vast majority of French drink; in fact, over 90 percent of the adult population drinks. In accord with the projected stereotype of the French drinker, wine is the chosen beverage. Men drink an average of nearly a quart of wine per day. Women consume approximately one fifth of a quart of wine perday. It is of significance to note that over one third of the adult French population drinks more than a quart of wine each day. Many drink more than two quarts per day (Milt, 1969). It has been established that the lower socioeconomic groups in France consume considerably more wine than the middle and upper socioeconomic levels. Laborers and farm workers, who comprise a sizeable segment of the French work force, drink considerably more wine than managerial and white-collar personnel. As is the case with Jewish people, drinking is very much a part of the French cultural tradition.

Historically, alcoholic beverages, such as wine, have been safer to drink on the European continent than water or nonalcoholic beverages. French cultural tradition includes wine consumption with meals. This type of drinking behavior predominates among the higher status French. Farmers, laborers and middle- and lower-class members tend to drink more extensively, even during the working hours. As the French feel that wine is esssential to good health, the working man receives a good deal of positive reinforcement for his drinking behavior. In comparison with other Western countries, France ranks number one with reference to per capita level of consumption of absolute alcohol from all alcoholic beverages. France has the highest rate of alcoholism in the world (*Time*, 1974). In addition to drinking more wine than any other people, the French also get more alcohol from distilled spirits. However, the French have a generally negative attitude toward distilled spirits. Many French consider whiskey or other forms of distilled spirits harmful to the health.

Italian-Americans, although consuming a great deal of alcohol, have relatively few alcoholics and problem drinkers. Research has consistently revealed a significantly reduced rate of alcoholism among Italian-Americans. Italian-Americans are rarely abstinent and drink a wide range of alcoholic beverages. Italy ranks second only to France in level of total alcohol consumption. As is the case with Italian-Americans, the native Italian strongly approves of drinking. Children are initiated into the practice of drinking wine at an early age. Periodic intoxication is accepted, but not condoned. Much like the French, Italians limit their drinking almost exclusively to wine. The drinking of wine is very much a cultural process, beginning early in life and continuing throughout old age. Wine is felt to be essential to good health and it very much a part of "custom." Wine is served with nearly all meals. The Italian constituent of American society drinks significantly less wine than his countrymen, consumes more liquor and subsequently drinks to the point of intoxication more frequently. This movement away from the pattern of wine consumption seems to result in an increase in alcoholism and problem drinking. This applies to first and second generation Italians in America.

In rather marked contrast to the low incidence of alcohol addiction and problem drinking found among Italian-Americans and Jews, the Irish are notorious for their inability to handle alcohol (*Time*, 1974). As an ethnic group the Irish in America have a long history of high rates of alcoholism. Bales (1964) notes that the Irish are at the top of nearly all investigations of the rate of alcoholism among different ethnic groups. This finding is supported, moreover, by such indicators as frequency of arrest for intoxication and drunkenness and police records. McCord and McCord (1960) have reported that a significantly greater proportion of Irish boys mature into alcoholism than do boys from other ethnic groups. While the general position that Irish-Americans do experience a good deal of difficulty related to alcohol consumption seems to be well accepted, very little empirical research has been directed at this group. Perhaps a good deal of the sentiment surrounding Irish drinking behavior is mythical in nature. Patterns of consumption, drinking traditions and similar cultural variables related to alcoholism are areas which have, for the most part, remained uninvestigated. It is known that Ireland ranks low nationally with regard to per capita consumption of alcohol.

The American Indians, have, until recently, been misunderstood with regard to alcohol-related behavior. As is true of the American Irish, the Indian population has been perceived as unable to deal with alcohol (Shore and von-Fumetti, 1972). Movies have traditionally portrayed the Indian as a drunk. The role of "firewater" is an excellent example of this type of Indian characterization. We are only now beginning to realize the sad truth surrounding alcohol addiction, problem drinking and the American Indian. In his first special report to the U.S. Congress on Alcohol and Health, the secretary of HEW (December, 1971) reported the incidence of alcoholism among American Indians is at an "epidemic level." This report indicated the rate of alcoholism and problem drinking among American Indians was at least twice that of the national average. Furthermore, on certain Indian reservations the rate of alcoholism included from 25 to 50 percent of the total population. Those familiar with Indian drinking patterns, the Indian reservation and the life-style characteristics related to this segment of the American population are aware of the magnitude of this problem. The frequency of violent behavior related to drinking among reservation Indians is frightening in itself. Over three quarters of all fines, arrests and legal involvements incurred by American Indians result from drinking.

Occupation

Occupationally, the farmer experiences the least amount of difficulty as a result of drinking. Farm owners have the lowest proportion of drinkers (60 percent of men and 26 percent of women) and heavy drinkers (HEW, 1971). This trend has been clearly evident since the turn of the century in America. In excess of 80 percent of the males comprising the business and professional occupations are drinkers. Businessmen seem to experience more significant problems with alcohol, as nearly 30 percent fall within the heavy drinking category. Only 18 percent of the professional group fall within the heavy drinking category. Of all the occupational groups of men, the semiprofessional group has the highest proportion of heavy drinkers.

Thirty-eight percent of this group reported heavy drinking patterns. Of the female drinking population, service workers report the greatest percentage of heavy drinkers. Seventeen percent of this group fall within the heavy drinking category. Mulford (1964) reports that among those who earn $10,000 a year or more, seven out of eight are drinkers. In the group earning $3,000 a year or less, only one out of two are drinkers.

Education

With regard to education, Mulford (1964) reports that only 46 percent of those without a high school diploma drink. In contrast to this, 80 percent of those who have gone to college drink. It is apparent that the well-to-do, better educated and higher ranking professional people consistently drink more than the poor, uneducated and lower status vocational members. This educational trend is even more apparent for women (*Time*, 1974). Although female college graduates are much more likely than other women to be drinkers, they are much less likely to be heavy drinkers. The vast majority of all college graduates tend to be light or moderate drinkers. Those most likely to be heavy drinkers are males who have completed high school or males with some college education but who did not graduate from college.

A number of other interesting trends and variables relating to patterns of consumption have been found. For instance, the highest proportion of both drinkers and heavy drinkers is to be found in the New England, Middle Atlantic, Pacific and East North Central geographical regions. The South, East South Central States and the Mountain States have the lowest proportion of drinkers. On the average only some 50 percent of the population in the latter areas drink, as opposed to over 80 percent of the former (Milt, 1969).

Large cities also have the highest proportion of drinkers. Rural populations have the smallest percentages of both drinkers and heavy drinkers. As might be expected, the highest rate of heavy drinkers is to be found among residents of the largest inner cities. This trend also applies to the other variables used as indices of general social pathology.

Some of the known statistics surrounding drinking behavior clearly indicate that alcoholism is a major problematic social issue in the United States: alcohol is presently the most abused drug in the United States, encompassing an estimated 7 percent of the adult population. This figure includes known alcoholics and problem drinkers and currently numbers about eleven million men and women; it has been estimated that 5 percent of the nation's work force is alcoholic, in addition to 5 percent classified as problem drinkers; alcohol is involved in over 50 percent of the annual highway fatalities reported in the United States, and resulted in 28,000 deaths in one recent year. Sixty percent of the auto fatalities include young people aged sixteen to twenty-four; alcoholism and alcohol-related forms of pathological behavior cost the economy an estimated fifteen billion dollars per year. This includes ten million lost via missed work in business, the military and industry; two billion incurred for health and welfare services rendered to alcoholic persons and their families; and three billion invested in property damage, medical expense and general overhead; legally, one third of all arrests reported annually are for public intoxication. This figure does not take into account such offenses as driving under the influence and disorderly conduct. It has been estimated that 40 to 50 percent of all arrests would be alcohol related if these offenses were included.

These figures are taken directly from the 1971 HEW report to the U.S. Congress on Alcohol and Health and should provide the reader with a basic understanding of the current magnitude of the alcohol problem.

PHYSIOLOGICAL CONSIDERATIONS

Prolonged alcohol ingestion precipitates or is in other ways related to physiological and biological changes in the human body. Rather than attempting an in-depth investigation of these changes, a cursory evaluation of the effects of alcohol upon different body systems will be presented. The following body systems will be discussed as they relate to alcoholism or prolonged alcohol ingestion: cardiac, gastrointestinal, neurological and muscle and nutrition.

Cardiac

Heart problems have long been related to excessive alcohol consumption. A nutritional factor was formerly felt to be of major importance in alcoholics or excessive drinkers who later manifested signs of heart disease. Today alcoholic cardiomyopathy is perceived as a syndrome occurring in persons who have led a prolonged lifestyle of alcohol abuse (Burch and Giles, 1971; Louhija, 1972). The clinical characteristics of this disorder include either a slow or sudden onset of left- and right-sided congestive heart failure. In addition, the heart is enlarged, neck veins are distended, there is a narrow pulse pressure, diastolic blood pressure is elevated and peripheral edema is present. It should be noted that gross and microscopic findings are not specific for this syndrome. The heart is usually large and flabby, with focal myocardial fibrosis and endocardial thickening. Pathological, biochemical and clinical data do support the position that alcoholic cardiomyopathy is a distinct syndrome (Burch and DePasquale, 1969; Pader, 1973).

Many specifics of this syndrome remain unknown. Individuals suffering from alcoholic cardiomyopathy are treated with measures appropriate to congestive heart failure. Needless to say, total abstinence is a prerequisite to successful treatment. Some patients do have irreversible heart disease by the time they avail themselves of treatment. Alcohol consumption results in the increase of resting cardiac output, heart rate and myocardial oxygen consumption. This form of prolonged stress simply helps "wear out" the various cardiac apparatus. Such a process might well be akin to driving a car for a prolonged period of time at 90 miles per hour instead of 60 miles per hour. It is unknown whether this process results in the development of alcoholic heart disease, or whether ethanol directly affects the heart cells, or whether a possible metabolic interaction precipitates the basic clinical picture. Most patients who receive proper treatment will recover if they terminate their alcohol consumption.

Gastrointestinal

Prolonged patterns of heavy alcohol consumption result in a number of gastrointestinal problems. The liver is most often seriously affected by long-term alcohol abuse. Striking imbalances in liver function are a product of alcohol metabolism, of alcohol-precipitated increases of fat in the liver and of the development of extensive fatty liver. An inflammatory liver disorder, alcoholic hepatitis, may supervene. This is a form of cellular degeneration. A variety of liver disorders often progress to cirrhosis. Cirrhosis, characterized by extensive scarring of the liver, is estimated to involve at least 10 percent of the known alcoholic population. Medical statistics show an increase in the incidence of alcoholic cirrhosis (Kramer, Kuller and Fisher, 1968). In New York City cirrhosis of the liver is ranked as the third leading cause of death between the ages of twenty-five and sixty-five (HEW, 1971). A significant number of individuals continue to drink in spite of an awareness that they have cirrhosis. Many individuals with alcoholic cirrhosis die as a result of hemorrhage from portal hypertension or from hepatic failure. Other disorders include scarring of the small veins in the liver and hypertension of the veins feeding the liver (Lieber, 1973).

The specific determinants of cirrhosis remain unclear. Alcoholic cirrhosis is typically seen only after fifteen to twenty years of heavy drinking (Wooddell, 1978).

While the effects of alcohol on other organs of the gastrointestinal tract have received less attention than the liver, it has been established that chronic alcoholism or prolonged heavy drinking results in a variety of gastrointestinal complications (Winawer, Bejar, McCray and Zamcheck, 1971). The stomach is affected by heavy drinking in a number of possible ways. The overproduction of stomach acid, delayed emptying of the stomach and damage to the gastric mucosal barrier are all related to heavy drinking. Gastritis and achlorhydria are common chronic conditions seen among any given alcoholic population. Gastric ulcers are common in alcoholic persons. Problems of the small intestine have also been related to prolonged periods of heavy drinking. Alcoholism has been associated with pancreatitis and pancreatic insufficiency (Dreiling, Richman and Franklin, 1952). In the case of both intestinal and pancreatic pathology, a reversal of symptomatology is usually rapidly initiated upon the termination of alcohol ingestion (Mezey, Jow, Slavin and Tobon, 1970). Again, the specific process of alcohol-facilitated cellular and structural damage is not understood. Prolonged alcohol ingestion is related to these various gastrointestinal complications.

Neurological

The various neurological syndromes associated with chronic alcoholism were mentioned in Chapter 2. The encephalopathies include Korsakoff's syndrome, Wernicke's syndrome and polyneuropathy. Niacin deficiency (Jolliffe's) encephalopathy and Marchiafava's disease are also forms of neurologic disorder attributed to long-term alcoholism (HEW, 1971). All these disorders are the result of fifteen or more years of heavy drinking. Once this stage of alcoholism has been reached, many of the symptoms are irreversible (Kissin and Begleiter, 1972). This is particularly true in the case of Korsakoff's syndrome, which is marked by confusion, disorientation, impairment of cognitive processes and a generalized reality disturbance. Memory failure and confabulation are also central to the syndrome. Upon hospitalization it is frequently found that patients who do not recover within a few weeks continue to manifest these symptoms on an indefinite basis. This clinical syndrome is seen most frequently among state hospital and institutionalized alcoholics (Knanert, 1977).

Wernicke's syndrome is characterized by memory loss, confusion, clouding of consciousness and visual distortion involving paralysis of the eye nerves. This condition is associated with an acute severe deficiency of Vitamin B and usually responds well to thiamin treatment. Polyneuropathy, or peripheral neuropathy is marked by loss of control of limbs, sensory and motor nerve ending involvement and sporadic pain and itching. Niacin deficiency results in a general clouding of consciousness, cogwheel rigidities of the arms and legs and uncontrollable sucking and grasping reflexes. This condition is caused by an acute total deficiency of niacin and responds well to vitamin B complex therapy. Marchiafava's disease involves the specific degeneration of the corpus callosum and causes severe mental dysfunction. This disease is extremely rare, the diagnosis almost always based upon medical autopsy. The list of psychiatric conditions and diagnoses secondary to alcohol addiction or problem drinking is virtually unending. Psychotic episodes precipitated by alcohol withdrawal are classic. Anxiety reactions, depressive reactions, sociopathic states and psychoneurotic disorders are all common features seen within any population of alcoholics.

Muscles and Nutrition

Muscle weakness has long been attributed to chronic alcoholism (Fahlgren, Hed and Lundmark, 1957; Myerson and Lafaire, 1970). This syndrome, known as alcoholic myopathy, may manifest itself in either an acute or chronic form (Perkoff, 1971). Acute alcoholic myopathy is a condition in which the patient experiences sudden cramps. These cramps usually last for only a day or so. The condition is associated with severe myoglobinuria, the presence of muscle pigment in the urine. Following a prolonged period of intoxication the person experiences severe pain and swelling of the muscles, accompanied by marked weakness. This syndrome usually follows years of prolonged intoxication, and primarily involves the arms and legs; recovery is totally contingent upon the cessation of alcohol ingestion. The chronic form of alcoholic myopathy involves muscle weakness and atrophy affecting almost any muscle in the body. This condition is essentially independent of nutritional factors.

Malnutrition is almost genetic to the problem of long-term alcohol addiction. As alcohol provides a significant source of calories, the alcoholic experiences a diminished need to eat and fails to meet basic bodily requirements of protein, vitamins, etc. Economic factors also reinforce malnutrition. Heavy alcohol ingestion alone significantly interferes with the normal process of food digestion, contributing to the problem of malnutrition. A multiplicity of diseases is related to defective nutrition in alcoholic persons. A number of these have already been discussed. Nutritional disorders are but one aspect of the medical processes which operate to reduce the alcoholic's life span by as much as ten to twelve years (Lieber and Rubin, 1969).

In summary, chronic alcohol addiction can result in any number of medical complications. These complications involve a range of disorders including heart function, the gastrointestinal tract, neurologic and psychiatric disorders, muscle conditions and nutrition. These are only the more recognized areas of complication. While the issue of cause and effect remains clouded, causative relationships continue to become clearer. Prolonged ingestion of heavy amounts of alcohol results in a number of predictable medical outcomes. The reality of this medical and behavioral paradigm can no longer be denied and distorted on the grounds of a lack of adequate research and clinical evidence.

In this chapter we have discussed some of the fundamental sociological and medical considerations essential to an understanding of alcoholism and problem drinking. Many of the issues surrounding these areas remain controversial. It is only through a growing awareness and understanding of this basic information that we can begin to initiate more successful methods directed at the rehabilitation of individuals addicted to alcohol.

Chapter 4

PERSONALITY CHARACTERISTICS
OF THE ALCOHOLIC

PERSONALITY is a rather difficult term to define. Characteristically we think of one's personality as a reflection of observable behavior. Viewed in this manner, John may be described by friends and family as "happy-go-lucky," "serious minded" or "nervous." At any rate, we all tend to be perceived by significant others in rather consistent, stereotyped ways. However, variation also enters the picture. While John may basically be perceived by significant others as a happy-go-lucky fellow, he may periodically act depressed. While this depression may be a part of John's basic personality structure, he will in all probability be perceived as something apart from his "old self." If John appears as an outgoing, jovial chap 90 percent of the time, his 10 percent experience of depression will surely be viewed as atypical. Seen in a depressed state, friends and relatives will directly assert that John is "not himself," that his personality has changed. Hopefully this example will serve the purpose of helping elucidate how personality, as a construct, both changes and remains static. Long-term familiarity with many people seems to reveal that in certain respects they change very little. Others seem to change drastically. This brings up the issue of inner beliefs, attitudes and feelings. These aspects of personality are certainly more difficult to quantify, evaluate and interpret than manifest behaviors. The subjective nature of personality surely contributes to this complexity (Knanert, 1978).

Personality, as used in this chapter, may be viewed as the rather consistent self-system presented in the process of daily living. This includes both the consistent perceptions of others and the multiplicity of inner feelings. For the most part covert operations, or the inner affective state, become overtly manifest in the process of daily interpersonal relations. If one is trained in the participant-observer role of human relations, he hopefully has the ability to make accurate evaluation of inner feelings based upon observable or manifest behaviors. The essential point is that personality, although a hypothetical construct, can be observed, described and quantified behaviorally. This applies both to the individual and groups of individuals, such as alcoholics. At this point, personality assessment becomes more than intuitive.

Many people have the misconception that alcoholics manifest a single personality type or configuration. The fact that there is no single alcoholic personality needs to be emphasized. Just as alcoholic individuals come from every ethnic group, every socioeconomic level and every known vocational specialty, so do alcoholic people manifest a wide range of personality characteristics or traits. In spite of this diversity of personality characteristics within a given group of individuals labeled "alcoholic," it has been found that certain personality features are consistently a part of the behavior and life-style of those labeled "alcoholic" or "problem drinker." It is these frequently recognized personality characteristics which we shall discuss in this chapter. These characteristics have been identified and observed for the most part among alcoholic persons engaged in psychiatric or psychological methods of changing their alcoholic behavior. This group of people is certainly in the minority. We must remember that the vast majority of alcoholics and problem drinkers are never evaluated by the behavioral scientist. Therefore, we cannot be sure that these personality characteristics are truly representative of the alcoholic.

DENIAL

The more traditional psychological and psychiatric meaning of denial has to do with the unconscious or preconscious blocking from reality those aspects of the self which might precipitate anxiety feelings capable of overwhelming or disorganizing the total self-system. Denial has been viewed as one of the basic defense mechanisms. Alcoholic denial is very much related to this general paradigm, yet different in certain basic respects. Neurotic and psychotic forms of denial are aimed at a multiplicity of feelings and thoughts disturbing to the individual. Alcoholic denial is usually focused around the specific reality that alcohol has assumed complete control of one's life. The fact that inner feelings, overt behavior and interpersonal relations are controlled to a large extent by alcohol is a potent reality. This single factor, denial that one is alcohol addicted, is perhaps the most significant barrier to be overcome in the process of attaining sobriety. Overcoming denial is certainly a prerequisite to seeking treatment. Experience with an alcoholic population suggests that certain individuals will deny to the point of dying. Certain people will seemingly die before admitting that they are in fact alcoholic. We can all appreciate the fact that denial is a rather basic human quality. All of us find it difficult to admit that certain of our behaviors are beyond our conscious control. A large part of the alcoholic's system of denial has to do with the fantasy of being able to quit drinking on his own.

Aside from denying that one has a problem with alcohol and that one may, in fact, be controlled by alcohol, denial becomes related to an aggregate of other painful reality operations for the addicted person. Denying that one is at fault in the marital relationship, denying that one has long been an academic failure, that one is an inadequate father, etc., become a part of the process of alcoholic denial. A great deal of denial precedes actual involvement with alcohol. Those individuals who eventually become addicted to alcohol have experienced chronic feedback which has facilitated their need to deny certain things about themselves. At the point of becoming dependent upon alcohol one begins to use alcohol for the explicit purpose of denying those emotionally painful aspects of the self and the environment.

Denial has been used to explain a good deal of the alcoholic's pathology. Often the concept of denial has been employed in obscure and inappropriate ways which have not served to clarify our understanding of alcoholism. Some have postulated that an individual's alcoholism cannot be dealt with effectively until the issue of denial has been resolved. Aside from these issues, the fact remains that denial, as a behavioral process and personality trait, is a central issue in the development and maintenance of most alcoholic's pathological addiction. Very often denial becomes a nonverbal process. While verbally admitting to being alcohol addicted, as well as admitting to various other aspects of the self which have been pathologically denied, the alcoholic may continue to behaviorally deny his alcoholism by continuing to remain intoxicated. Suffice it to say that the alcoholic relies extensively on the mechanism of denial (Forrest, 1978).

ANXIETY

Anxiety is a cornerstone in psychiatric and psychological literature dealing with pathological or ineffective human behavior. In fact, anxiety as a construct has been central to nearly all the theories of personality. The definitions of anxiety are numerous. Typically, anxiety is defined as an affective state involving various levels of psychological discomfort. Essential to this feeling of discomfort or apprehension is the fact that the source of such feelings is for the most part unknown. People suffering from anxiety states frequently report that although they are extremely upset and "nervous," they do not know or cannot explain why they feel this way. This clinical picture best describes "free-floating" types of anxiety feelings. Anxiety states are known to approximate fear reactions, both physiologically and psychologically. However, in fear reactions the source of threat is usually apparent. This has been used to differentiate between anxiety and fear.

Anxiety features are essential to the drinking behavior of most problem drinkers and alcoholics. It is felt that feelings of marked anxiety have a long developmental history in the lives of the majority of alcohol-addicted individuals. Childhood was an experience of persistent anxiety and insecurity for many who eventually become alcohol addicted. In the middle teens those who have experienced the unpleasant pangs of anxiety for extended periods of time often find that alcohol helps relieve these feelings. In this sense, learning is very much a part of the process of becoming alcohol addicted. Through experience these particular individuals learn that they can escape feelings of anxiety by drinking. Drinking at this point becomes functional. It may serve the explicit purpose of blocking these unpleasant feelings. However, as the individual progresses into the more dysfunctional stages of alcohol addiction, the very behavior that once served to help extinguish the feelings of anxiety — drinking — now becomes a major source of anxiety. This paradox is not easily understood by most alcoholics. What once worked so well no longer helps; in fact, what once worked now has turned into a major source of anxiety. As such, what helped precipitate drinking-anxiety-may at a much later stage become that which helps extinguish drinking behavior. Anxiety associated with drinking often results in seeking help.

Most alcoholics describe their anxiety as "bad nerves" or nervousness. Restlessness, poorly controlled hyperactivity and poor attention span form the manifest behaviors of anxiety for these individuals. Clinical experience with a number of different types of alcoholics indicates that tranquilizers such as Valium® and Librium® are often quite ineffective in reducing experiential anxiety levels. By contrast, a few beers or other forms of alcoholic beverages quickly extinguish feelings of anxiety and tension. These particular cases represent the example par excellence of the paradoxical good-bad nature of alcohol. Research has also consistently indicated anxiety as a crucial ingredient in the pathology of alcoholism.

DEPRESSION

Perhaps the most important single affective state contributing to general drinking behavior is depression. In our culture a standard recommendation for the moderately depressed individual is to have a few drinks or perhaps get drunk. This procedure appears to "work" for many. In the process of attempting to escape persistent feelings of depression one may fall into the trap of alcohol dependency. Many problem drinkers and alcoholics have turned to alcohol as a means of coping with their chronic or acute depressive trends. Depression is generally described as an affective state in which the depressed person feels worthless, is often unable to eat or sleep, is slowed down motorically and has an overall "dampened" emotional outlook on life. Preoccupation with ideas of self-destruction is rather common. Some persons manifest different behaviors as a result of depression; for example, rather than being unable to eat and/or sleep certain individuals will begin to eat constantly and/or remain in bed for fifteen to twenty hours a day. For the most part depressive trends result in feelings of inadequacy, worthlessness and similar negatively oriented self and worldly referrents.

While controlled drinking may help the "normal" drinker deal with periodic depressive feelings, increased alcohol consumption for the purpose of dealing with these same depressive types of feelings can only contribute to the problem drinker's or alcoholic's depression. Added marital conflict precipitated by drinking, legal confrontation and poor job performance are just a few of the interpersonal transactions which add fuel to the depression. The more the problem drinker depends upon alcohol to relieve his feelings of depression the more dysfunctional drinking becomes in this respect. Seen from this perspective one realizes how inappropriate it is to suggest any form of further drinking behavior for the problem drinker or alcoholic. Drinking is simply not the treatment of choice for depression among persons with prior dependency problems!

Many conceive of depression as a turning inward of feelings of anger and resentment. This seems to be particularly true for individuals becoming alcohol addicted. Marked depressive behavior may shift in the direction of anger with prolonged sobriety. It seems as though the alcoholic, while drinking, must continue to remain depressed. Upon achieving sobriety the alcoholic can begin to understand and deal more effectively with the aggregate of variables which initially precipitated and subsequently maintained his depressive feelings. The alcoholic is an angry person. While angry behavior may not be apparent, depressive appearances may serve to mask a raging lion. It is imperative that depressive and aggressive feelings be explored when the alcoholic is sober.

ANGER

One of the fundamental characteristics of man and human interaction is that of aggression. We all feel angry from time to time and have a need to express these feelings. The alcoholic or problem drinker is a chronically angry person. This is often the case in spite of outward appearances. Outwardly most alcoholics are not angry, hostile individuals. Inwardly these same people are often seething with rage. The source of these feelings of anger and resentment is hard to determine. A life-style of unending frustration may account for a good deal of the anger and hostility. Most problem drinkers and alcoholics are frustrated as a result of not measuring up, of failure and so on. Moreover, American culture places rather stringent controls upon the expression of aggression and hostility. We must all seek culturally appropriate channels for our feelings of anger and hostility.

We are familiar with the tale of the drinker who was an "easy going" nonviolent man when not drinking. However, this same person allegedly turned into a violent "madman" after a few drinks. While this may have been true in this particular case, it is not the norm. Alcoholics are angry people; however, they are not as a group the violent, combative type of individual they are often made out to be. Wife beating and child abuse are expressions of anger and hostility which are a part of the personality structure of some alcoholics. Fortunately, the violent nature of these types of behaviors involves only a limited segment of the alcoholic population.

A more typical method of channeling these feelings of anger and hostility has to do with self-defeating or self-destructive behavior. The alcoholic seems to have a pervasive need to punish himself. This process basically involves turning feelings of anger and aggression back on the self. The frequency of auto accidents, arrests and jailings, suicide and self-inflicted medical complications based upon alcohol consumption attests to the reality of this process of channeling anger and hostility against the self. Rather than directing feelings of anger and aggression toward an external object, the alcoholic often channels these destructive feelings inward. While this process may remain at an unconscious or preconscious level for most problem drinkers and alcoholics, once sober for a prolonged period of time these same individuals begin to understand this process very well. Statements such as "The only person I was really mad at was myself" and "The only person I really wanted to hurt was me" are typical examples of becoming able to understand and emotionally integrate the fact that one has embarked upon a journey of self-punishment. The paradoxical nature of alcoholism is again apparent with regard to feelings of anger. Rather than directing feelings of anger and hostility toward the environment, the alcoholic very frequently turns these same feelings back upon himself. The alcoholic drinks to preserve himself and maintain whatever level of interpersonal functionality he has been able to achieve. In accord with the self-destructive anger of alcoholism, he may kill himself in the process.

IMMATURITY

Immaturity is a concept used to describe a number of behaviors which seem to indicate that a person has not reached a state of emotional development congruent with his chronological age. Age- and role-appropriate behaviors are essential to the mature personality. Some general indicators of immaturity include excessive needs for approval and acceptance, the inability to detach oneself from home and family ties, self-centeredness and a preoccupation with the past.

A primary dynamic seen in many alcoholic personality configurations has to do with relationships within the family, particularly with the mother. This is even more so with male alcoholics. Many male problem drinkers and alcoholics have experienced an overly close relationship with their mothers. Childhood experiences built on intense and prolonged ties with mother continue on into adolescence, adulthood and even old age. This dynamic often manifests itself in dating and courtship behavior. The result may be the selection of a mother substitute for a spouse. Those who are unsuccessful in this quest for a mother substitute may choose never to marry. Instead, family ties, and specifically the relationship with the mother, are maintained at an age and role level appropriate to early adolescence.

The emotionally immature personality often demands excessive amounts of attention and approval. This is certainly a part of the drunk who is consistently the "life of the party." Very often a good deal of the behavioral process of becoming alcohol addicted can be viewed as a means of gaining attention and approval. Self-centeredness or narcissism are similarly central to immaturity. The alcoholic progressively becomes the focal point of the family. In many respects this amounts to being the perpetual "bad boy." Nonetheless, the alcoholic becomes the center of attraction.

Dwelling on past achievements frequently takes on a similar flavor. Those events and behaviors of the past which form the basis for today's conversations and interpersonal transactions are in fact attention-getting events. These pathological manifestations of immaturity are age and role inappropriate. Having to be the drunken clown of the party, relating to a family or mother as one did at the age of twelve instead of twenty and dwelling on events of the past all share the common denominator of being age and role inappropriate. Needless to say, these are not the only mechanisms by which alcoholic immaturity is identified. The alcoholic personality is often pervasively immature. While this aspect of the alcoholic self may be well hidden and masked, it is central to the alcoholic personality.

DEPENDENCY

Strong dependency needs are central to the alcoholic personality. As is true of the earlier discussed personality characteristics, dependency needs manifest and express themselves in a number of possible ways. We are all dependent. Aside from biologic dependence, psychological dependence is evident from the earliest stages of life. Infants deprived of human contact have actually been shown to die. Such is the case in spite of adequate food, clothing, medical attention and other essentials of life. Becoming addicted to alcohol is a singularly excellent example of dependency. Many alcoholics are openly dependent. Perhaps the most readily observed example of the dependency needs of the alcoholic pertains to the marriage relationship. Wives who pay the bills, manage the household and in numerous other ways accept the responsibility for family life are meeting the alcoholic husband's inordinate dependency needs. As the alcoholic progressively becomes addicted he or she simultaneously becomes more dependent upon the spouse and significant others. This dependency may involve virtually every aspect of human interaction. Some individuals have always had a strong need to be taken care of and have openly expressed this need. Openly dependent males tend to function well in highly structured environments such as the military. Rules and limits are set, material necessities are provided and the demands for independence and initiative are virtually nonexistent. In this respect the military symbolizes an essentially good mother.

In marked contrast to the openly dependent alcoholic is the addicted person who has led an extended life-style of apparently complete independence. This type of alcoholic seems to have always avoided relationships involving clearly dependent behavior. Alcoholics of this personality type have been called counterdependent. Very often the counterdependent alcoholic is an outgoing, well-liked type of individual. Frequently athletic abilities, leadership qualities, vocational success and dangerous sporting endeavors, such as racing cars, are characteristic of this type of alcoholic personality. Very early in life this type of person learns to repress or deny feelings of dependency while establishing and developing socially acceptable behaviors which appear independent. As might be expected the counterdependent alcoholic is often a highly defensive person. As long as his masculinity and overall pattern of adjustment can be maintained, the probability of his changing drinking behaviors is extremely low.

A sizeable segment of any alcoholic population will vacillate between these two forms of dependent behavior. Openly dependent one day and aggressive the next, these individuals often prove extremely difficult to relate to. People close to these individuals never know what to expect in regard to dependency-independency behavior. As is true in the case of other forms of dependent behavior, the individual who fluctuates from one extreme to the other is attempting to resolve his personal conflicts surrounding the issue of independence-dependence.

A frequently observed dynamic of the dependent personality is that of switching dependencies. Alcohol-addicted persons are notorious for their potential to switch to drug dependency. Hospitalization for the effects of prolonged alcohol dependency frequently presents an excellent opportunity to become dependent upon such medications as Librium, Valium and Mellaril.® Switching dependencies is a significant problem in the therapeutic management of perhaps 20 percent of the overall alcohol-addicted population.

SEXUALITY

A sizeable segment of the problem drinking and alcoholic population manifests significant sexual pathology. Realizing sexual deviation to be a topic of extensive debate and generally defined within wide perimeters, it is nonetheless clearly evident that sexual problems are often a part of the alcoholic personality.

Alcohol consumption is very much a part of the American masculine identity. Indeed, certain ethnic groups and various socioeconomic levels are oriented toward drinking as a measure of masculinity. This type of atmosphere strongly reinforces drinking behavior. Hard work and hard drinking become the measure of one's manhood. Those individuals able to consume large quantities of liquor without passing out or becoming dysfunctional in other ways are looked upon with great favor. Many children and adolescents are taught to look upon this type of individual as a role model. A good deal of drinking behavior within the military and college environments has to do with this type of identification.

Perhaps the most common form of sexual difficulty encountered by alcoholics and problem drinkers is that of promiscuity. Prior existing needs for love, acceptance and attention are exacerbated by alcohol ingestion. Controls break down, barriers become weakened and the intoxicated person begins a long history of sexual acting-out. Frequently this results in illegitimate births, unwanted pregnancies and divorce. Proving one's masculinity or femininity is often genetic to this process.

Many male alcoholics and problem drinkers find it extremely difficult to relate to women. Such individuals feel most uncomfortable just being around women. However, under the influence of a few drinks these same individuals may become capable of talking, dancing and perhaps even initiating sexual behaviors with members of the opposite sex. A part of this type of difficulty may be related to patterns of latent homosexuality. Various authors have pointed out the latent and overt homosexual component of drinking behavior. This is more clearly the case with male alcoholics and problem drinkers. Typically drinking takes place in a basically male environment, particular males tend to drink together, etc. Accounts of heterosexual men who have awakened following a night's debauch to find themselves in bed with another man are not atypical. Freudian interpretations of the orality of drinking and the nature of oral preoccupations among alcoholics further supports this position. In this sense oral dependency is viewed as genitally related.

A major issue with many married male alcoholics is that of impotence. While this type of difficulty may be in part related to nutritional factors, lack of sleep and other physiologically oriented variables, it remains for the most part a psychological problem. Ejaculato praecox is another form of male impotence frequently encountered. Often these aspects of the alcoholic personality are most threatening to both husband and wife. Sobriety is the first step in process of resolving these conflicts.

Primary sexual deviation, either the choice of a love object of the same sex or primary sexual behavior other than intercourse, is an infrequent aspect of the alcoholic personality. Homosexuality, frank sadomasochism, voyeurism and fetishism are not typically encountered. Marital relationships characterized by a good deal of sadomasochistic behavior on the part of both husband and wife are seen. The mutual confrontations, verbal and physical, typically deviate from the true sadomasochistic pattern. In short, the entire gamut of sexual difficulties may be a part of the personality structure of the alcoholic.

INFERIORITY

Inferiority has enjoyed a long history of importance and relevance to the field of alcohol addiction. Aside from the professional emphasis upon inferiority as an essential mechanism in the alcoholic personality, members of Alcoholics Anonymous and the general public have been aware of the role of inferiority feelings in the development of problem drinking. We have all experienced the "little man" who becomes a big man after a few drinks. The concept of inferiority implies a rather consistent devaluation of the self. Individuals who manifest rather global feelings of inferiority tend to feel that they are really no good at anything. This generalized feeling about the self may apply to academic abilities, physical attractiveness, athletic abilities and general self-worth. While most of us are aware of our individual inadequacies and weak points, we nonetheless tend to capitalize upon our assets and generally perceive ourselves as equal to the majority of those around us. This is frequently not true with regard to the alcoholic personality.

For a large portion of the alcoholic and problem drinking population the genesis of such feelings of inferiority is rather easily understood. Those coming from broken homes, who are ill-equipped to deal with academic and interpersonal demands, experience a world which chronically conveys to them that they do not measure up. Constant and prolonged feedback to the effect that one is inferior and inadequate can only produce a self-concept devoid of basic positive self-esteem. Many alcoholics and problem drinkers have led a life-style of this sort. These people learn early that a few drinks help make the feelings of inferiority less threatening. It is also well to bear in mind that our culture is comparative oriented. Those who are unable to keep up with the Joneses are often looked down upon in a very similar manner. In reality lower status individuals are often perceived and treated as if they are inferior.

Even those problem drinkers and alcoholics who have apparently grown up in the most adequate of families and who have been quite successful in academic and vocational endeavors manifest this basic feeling of inferiority. They too have never been able to measure up to crucial internal and external measures of adequacy and success.

Often the grandiose side of the alcoholic personality represents a defensive mask for an underlying morass of feelings of inadequacy and inferiority. This aspect of the alcoholic personality configuration has remained poorly understood. While some problem drinkers and alcoholics seem to have manifested a long-term character structure characterized by grandiosity, others only periodically evidence this type of worldy outlook and behavior. In order to compensate for deep feelings of inadequacy and inferiority, many alcoholics learn that by behaving in a manner juxtaposed to these basic feelings they can avoid the painful reality of inadequacy. Such behavior can often mask underlying feelings of inferiority for given periods of time, particularily with people only superficially acquainted with the alcoholic. However, significant others can know and feel the unreality of this grandiosity in a rather short period of time. In addition to other factors, alcoholics often choose to relate basically to other alcoholics because of their mutual acceptance of such unreality.

Feeling inadequate and inferior is a tremendously painful experience. It is just this type of emotional pain that helps "set up" given individuals for the pathology of alcohol addiction. Feelings of inferiority help account for the alcoholic's apparent shyness and timidness, his social withdrawal and disengagement and even the oft-noted simple inability to establish and maintain eye contact.

INTERPERSONAL RELATIONS

Individual and group patterns of interpersonal behavior are contingent upon the previously discussed personality characteristics, as well as numerous other personality dynamisms and interacting variables. Gross patterns of interpersonal behavior are a significant part of the behavior of all people, certainly including the alcohol-addicted individual. In this section one particular such pattern or personality trait will be discussed, the "loner" syndrome.

Many alcoholics and problem drinkers are simply uncomfortable around other people. Frequently they describe themselves as "loners." Personal acquaintance with this type of drinker will establish a historic life-style of aloofness and relative social isolation. This may be the case in spite of marriage and family. Although many are unable to establish the interpersonal closeness demanded by marriage and family, others experience this same isolation within the confines of the family constellation. Spouse and children report these individuals to be emotionally detached, removed from many of the person- and family-oriented transactions specific to their household. This type of alcoholic often perceives his role as that of physical and material provider. Interest in the children's school behavior, social get-togethers and similar occasions calling for interpersonal involvement and interaction are simply shunned. These people often tend to choose vocational careers such as the military, where they are separated from family and children a great deal of the time. Within such a milieu one moves from place to place and is not subject to the demands of establishing prolonged, functional interpersonal relationships.

Drinking may help break down the anxiety surrounding interpersonal relations for such individuals. The shy, inadequate, non-person-oriented individual may become capable of apparently normal interpersonal relations after a few drinks. By the same token, many such individuals retreat even further into their interpersonal isolation when intoxicated. Remaining intoxicated for weeks at a time in a cheap motel room is frequently a part of this picture.

In essence, the "loner" who becomes alcohol addicted is simply unable to tolerate close interpersonal relationships. A part of becoming alcohol addicted may be central to this prolonged inability to relate to significant others. The alcoholic learns early that feelings of inadequacy, social inferiority and similar affective states facilitating interpersonal anxiety can be rendered less potent and threatening by the consumption of alcohol.

PSYCHOLOGICAL ASSESSMENT AND THE ALCOHOLIC PERSONALITY

As many alcoholics and problem drinkers seek psychiatric and psychological help and are evaluated with reference to personality characteristics, a brief discussion of the most commonly found results of such evaluations is appropriate. Perhaps the most widely researched and accepted psychological test designed to evaluate personality is the Minnesota Multiphasic Personality Inventory (MMPI) (Dahlstrom and Welsh, 1960). This instrument has been used extensively in the evaluation of the alcoholic personality for more than twenty years.

Gilberstadt and Duker (1965) report a particular MMPI profile type, the 2-7-4, which results in the diagnosis of alcoholism. The 2-7-4 personality configuration represents a combination of personality characteristics. Central to this configuration are depression, obsessive-compulsive and sociopathic features. These authors report the following primary traits: anxiety, marital discord, financial problems, insomnia, tension and depression. It is reported that the incidence of heavy drinking is 96 percent for this profile. Elevation of the MMPI Psychopathic Deviate scale (PD or 4) has been reported as the most significant personality feature of the addicted individual by a number of authors (Pennington, 1954; Olson, 1946; Gilbert and Lombardi, 1967; Astin, 1959; Hill, Haertzen and Davis, 1972; Sutker, 1971; Forrest, 1973). Cardinal features of the 4 or PD personality (MMPI) type include the following: irresponsibility, immaturity, impulsiveness, egocentricity and a good deal of sexual acting-out. This type of personality has often experienced an overprotective mother. Suicidal attempts, aggressive outbursts toward wives and alcoholism are the most frequent causes of hospital admission.

The alcoholic personality, as stated initially in this chapter, is a nonexistent entity. Those who become alcohol-addicted manifest individual patterns of behavior, as well as individual personality traits. Certainly the personality characteristics considered in this chapter do not exist as separate entities. These personality characteristics exist together, as a part of a particular personality configuration or pattern. The significantly greater potential for self-destruction among alcoholics may be related to depressive trends within this population. Oral needs have been related to both depression and dependency. Anger has been related to both homicide and suicide, as well as depression. Attempting to identify the multifaceted interaction of these personality constructs as they relate to the individual alcoholic or problem drinker is a most difficult task. However, we can say that the personality characteristics or traits discussed in this chapter do have a particular relevance to the alcohol-addicted individual. Years of clinical experience with alcoholic persons has indicated that these personality characteristics are seen within this population of people far more frequently and more intensely than with other clinical populations. It should also be emphasized that the personality characteristics we have discussed can be expressed in various ways. The evaluation of alcoholic behavior, from a group perspective, is much simpler than the assessment of the personality make-up of the individual addicted to alcohol.

Chapter 5

THE RELEVANCE OF DIAGNOSIS IN THE TREATMENT OF ALCOHOLISM

THE relevance of diagnosis to the global field of behavioral science has long been an issue of heated debate among various professionals and paraprofessionals. This controversy was historically initiated as a result of a progressive movement away from the more traditional medical model of therapy and treatment. Certainly an accepted and fundamental cornerstone of medicine per se has been and continues to be diagnosis. While the profession of psychiatry quite early in its development recognized the many deficiencies and inadequacies inherent in the process of psychiatric diagnosis, it has continued to emphasize the role of diagnosis in the treatment and management of psychiatric patients. Recently a sizeable segment of the psychiatrically trained behavioral scientists have, for all practical purposes, completely rejected the validity of diagnostic procedures relative to the process of psychiatric treatment. As the field of behavior science has come to encompass psychologists, sociologists, social workers, guidance personnel, rehabilitation counselors and others currently grouped within this general rubric, the role of diagnosis has become even more controversial. I suspect that the "secondary citizen" status allowed such newer professions has helped facilitate the recent criticism and outright rejection of the relevance of diagnosis to the treatment and management of people experiencing emotional difficulty of various types and degrees. Certainly the Rogerian, humanistic and existential "schools" have been actively involved in the education and training of behavioral scientists who are less than enthusiastic about the role of diagnosis in the helping professions. To a lesser extent this same general attitude prevails among the behavior therapists, the advocates of behavior modification and other approaches to the treatment of emotional disorder presently in vogue. Reality Therapy, Transactional Analysis and Primal Therapy are but a few of the more recent treatment innovations nondiagnostically oriented in general philosophic basis as well as treatment approach. Clearly the behaviorally oriented helping professions have relied less and less upon the fundamental medical model of treatment, which has historically leaned heavily on the role of diagnosis. As therapists continue to emerge from the ranks of professions other than medical, the importance and relevance of the process of diagnosis appears to continue to decline. Regardless of treatment context, be it a state hospital, private clinic, community mental health or Veterans Administration, today the vast majority of patients seen for counseling and psychotherapy are treated by other than medically trained therapists. Treatment of a psychotherapeutic nature seems to be increasingly the role of paraprofessionals and often marginally prepared "counselors." Needless to say, diagnostic expertise and relevance often transcend such counselor's academic preparation and training, let alone their clinical skills. This exact situation is floridly manifest within the current alcoholic and drug addict rehabilitation scene.

Realizing the current, as well as historic, controversy and dissonance surrounding the relevance of diagnosis to the treatment of emotional disorder, I want to now discuss some of my feelings and observations relative to the role of diagnosis in the treatment of individuals experiencing significant difficulty as a result of their drinking behavior.

I would like to initially explore some of the ramifications of psychological and psychiatric "labeling." While diagnosis theoretically entails both a purpose and process far beyond mere classification and categorization, all too frequently within psychiatric settings and in dealing with emotional disorders of a wide variety of types, diagnosis has unfortunately resulted in an individual being labeled for life. This has certainly been the case with regard to such labels as "schizophrenic" or "alcoholic." It appears as if such labels ending in "ic" and based upon diagnosis frequently become indelible stamps which persist for life. What has been most unfortunate with regard to such labeling is the process of social disengagement which these labels both facilitate and maintain. The felon who becomes incarcerated as a result of his criminal behavior continues to be a "con man" upon release from prison. This may well be the case in spite of successful rehabilitation. We are all well aware of the negative effects of this process. Finding a job, social acceptance and similar essentials to effective interpersonal relations often become significantly more difficult as a result of one's label. Behavioral scientists are currently embarked upon a program of education designed to modify this social and interpersonal reality. Needless to say, this exact situation persists with regard to the problem of alcoholism. While a select few individuals learn to transcend the stigma associated with the "ic" label, countless others give up or use the label as a means of validating their lack of personal responsibility. In this respect being labeled an alcoholic, a schizophrenic or whatever amounts to a license to continue the inappropriate or "crazy" behaviors which happen to be associated with the particular label. It is my feeling that professional and paraprofessional personnel involved in the treatment of individuals experiencing emotional difficulty of such diagnostic "ic" types must continually come to grips with issues such as these as they perform roles relative to diagnosis. These issues are germane to the growing movement within the mental health-oriented services away from diagnosis.

It is apparent that the process of diagnosis relative to the treatment of emotional disorder is essentially paradoxical in nature. This is very much the case with regard to the treatment of the alcohol-addicted patient. As a professionally trained psychologist employed in a large alcoholic rehabilitation center, my foremost concern continues to be treatment per se. In this respect I have come to view diagnosis as an essential ingredient in the actual treatment or rehabilitation of alcohol-addicted individuals. I make this statement only in regard to those individuals suffering from alcohol addiction. In my experience the role of diagnosis specific to drinking behavior manifestly facilitates the total process of rehabilitation. It is this relationship between the diagnosis of the alcoholic patient and subsequent rehabilitation and treatment strategies which I now wish to discuss.

Let me begin by acknowledging the difficulty inherent in the process of diagnosis relative to drinking behavior (National Council on Alcoholism, Criteria Committee, 1972; Schuckit, 1973). While a number of psychological instruments have been designed for the explicit purpose of alcoholism diagnosis, it is my feeling that these procedures leave much to be desired. Historically the diagnosis of alcoholism was totally based upon medical evaluation and opinion. Definitive criteria on which to base a diagnosis of alcoholism or problem drinking simply do not exist. This situation applies to medical, psychological and psychiatric criteria, as well as the other essentials of the clinical evaluation process. Tissue damage as well as behavioral symptoms is extremely difficult to relate to alcoholism in a causative or one-to-one fashion. Nevertheless, data of this type can provide an adequate basis for diagnostic formulations. For practical purposes I have found it useful to differentiate between two gross diagnostic categories with regard to drinking behavior. Again, these categories have proved personally beneficial from the treatment perspective.

The diagnosis of alcoholism or chronic alcoholism is most appropriate in those cases involving long medical histories (from a few months duration to any number of years) relative to the consumption of alcohol. Individuals so diagnosed very frequently manifest organic or tissue damage of the cirrhosis, gastrointestinal and neurologic types. High blood pressure, diabetes, and a variety of psychiatric symptoms (Crowley, Chesluk, Dilts and Hart, 1974) are clearly a part of the overall clinical picture with individuals falling in this diagnostic category. It would seem that viewing alcoholism as a disease process would be highly congruous with the physical and behavioral status of individuals falling within this diagnostic category. Behaviorally the diagnosis of alcoholism or chronic alcoholism frequently includes marital discord and possible divorce, chronic work adjustment difficulties, extended legal complications, interpersonal and general social difficulties, identity and role conflict, and parental inadequacy. In short, this amounts to an almost total life-style constructed around drinking behavior. The hallmark of this life-style is general inadequacy and ineffectiveness. The global and all-encompassing obsessive-compulsive nature of alcohol addiction is most apparent in this diagnosis. Individuals so diagnosed have typically been very heavy drinkers for at least five years, with a medical history relative to the effects of prolonged alcohol ingestion. Dissociative phenomenon (blackouts, memory deficit, etc.) are an essential dimension of this diagnosis.

Just as all behavior, be it of the self-actualizing or most pathological forms, exists on some form of continuum, so does individual or collective drinking behavior. This reality contributes significantly to the difficulty of diagnosis relative to drinking behavior.

The second gross diagnostic category which I have found useful to employ is that of problem drinker. Obviously such a classification falls on the drinking continuum somewhere short of the initial diagnostic category discussed. While it is for all practical purposes impossible to delineate exactly where these points on the diagnostic continuum overlap, I do feel there are a number of relatively clear-cut differences between the two categories. The diagnosis of problem drinker entails a life-style in which major accidents, difficulties and traumas have been alcohol facilitated. For the most part individuals falling in this category are younger and do not manifest the physiological tissue damage specific to the diagnosis of chronic alcoholism.

Behaviorally, individuals diagnosed as problem drinkers display a pattern of consumption which is markedly less obsessive-compulsive in nature. While such individuals may from time to time engage in the prolonged daily drinking ritual, this pattern usually only persists for a matter of days or, at most, weeks. Indeed the problem drinker may well abstain for three or four months, if not longer, between drinking bouts. Essential to this diagnosis are the actual behavior problems which arise upon the individuals initiating drinking. It is at this time that a variety of acting-out behaviors, both socially and interpersonally unacceptable, become apparent. For the problem drinker, automobile accidents, sexual affairs, job absenteeism, aggressive outbursts and similar unacceptable behaviors become manifest with the initiation of drinking. It is not at all uncommon to find that the problem drinker functions quite well in the absence of drinking; however, initiating drinking seems almost without exception to precipitate specific, if not global, difficulty. It is not uncommon to find individuals who abstain for weeks or months, who almost without exception initiate wife beating or wreck the car upon reverting to drink. Such specific behaviors become a predictable outcome of drinking for many problem drinkers. Limited memory and recall may be a part of the overall clinical picture of many individuals diagnosed as problem drinkers.

All too frequently those individuals meeting the criteria of the problem drinker diagnosis progress to the diagnosis of chronic alcoholism. I suspect that perhaps 70 percent of the individuals initially qualifying for the problem drinker diagnosis progress to the later diagnostic category. Again, there are both qualitative and quantitative dimensions which differentiate between the diagnosis of problem drinker and alcoholic.

These two primary diagnostic categories are essentially in accord with the material presented in Chapters 1 and 2 relative to the classification and developmental stages of drinking behavior. Although many behavioral scientists or change agents might question the validity of a bona fide diagnosis of alcoholism or problem drinker, I personally have found these categories to be surprisingly "pure" with regard to patterns of styles of drinking behavior. Various professionals have asserted the "alcoholic" or problem drinker to be diagnostically a character behavior disorder, a sociopathic personality or a passive-aggressive personality at core. Others have theorized the addictive behavior to be a defense mechanism against schizoid or more regressive phenomena. While there is a good deal of clinical validity to such theoretical positions, it is my impression that the addiction per se is the focal point to be dealt with therapeutically. Dealing with the addictive drinking behavior preempts the therapeutic management of manipulative, acting-out, impulsive and other characterological dynamisms. Clinically I have found such characterological features to be at least significantly more controlled in the absence of intoxication. Attempting to therapeutically deal with any of the behavioral symptoms of the alcoholic or problem drinker while he or she is intoxicated or partially intoxicated is a virtual waste of time, in my opinion. While the ingestion of alcohol loosens inhibitions and facilitates a wide variety of acting-out behaviors for nearly all drinkers, this situation becomes one characterized by an almost total lack of control for the pathological drinker. Automobile accidents, physical confrontations and aggressive outbursts, sexual escapades and similar socially unacceptable patterns of interpersonal behavior for the most part terminate when the individual simply quits drinking. Once the patient has achieved initial sobriety the therapeutic alliance or program of rehabilitation can begin to focus upon the life-style and daily living problems which have served to both facilitate and maintain the addiction process. Neurotic patterns of adjustment or less than optimal interpersonal life-style behaviors may be the outcome of extended programs of rehabilitation for many alcoholics or problem drinkers. Pragmatically this may be the ultimate goal or desired outcome of treatment or rehabilitation. Certainly the criteria for successful rehabilitation remain an area of debate. In my experience the diagnosis and subsequent treatment of the actual addictive behavior, be it diagnostic alcoholism or problem drinking, must be the initial focal point of the rehabilitation process. Anxiety, depression, marital conflict, acting-out and similar behaviors reflect symptoms which must be dealt with secondarily to the process of initiating sobriety.

A problem related to the diagnosis of alcoholism, problem drinker or whatever other label one might happen to attach to individuals experiencing difficulty as a result of their drinking behavior, is that of inaccurately assessing the relationship between actual alcohol ingestion and psychopathology. More simply, the problem of misdiagnosis potentially means labeling individuals "alcoholic," "problem drinker" or such when their essential pathology rests in some area other than the addiction or drinking behavior per se. In reality I have found this to be an issue of minor importance; particularly with regard to community, state and military alcoholic rehabilitation agencies. Regardless of referral source, roughly 95 percent of the individuals reaching such treatment facilities qualify for the diagnosis of alcoholism or problem drinking as delineated earlier. Quite often mental health personnel unfamiliar with the dynamics surrounding work with alcohol-addicted individuals fail to accurately understand just how much alcohol-facilitated "crazy" behavior these individuals often engage in prior to contact with an actual treatment center. This applies to both the frequency and duration of such behaviors. When individuals do "show up" for treatment who rather obviously do not manifest the symptoms earlier discussed, in my experience they frequently do so as a result of either another agency's or some other third party's simple lack of knowledge of what to do with the individual in question. Usually such individuals do manifest social or interpersonal behaviors which are a bit removed from that of the "average" citizen and as such they attract attention and are often subsequently referred to psychiatrically oriented agencies. In such cases the fact that the referral is inappropriate should readily be made known to both the individual in question and the referring party. If treatment of a psychiatric, medical or other identifiable nature appears to be appropriate, referral by the alcoholic rehabilitation agency is indicated. Determination that an individual does not have significant alcohol-related behavior problems can best be documented through the clinical interview, case history data and contact with immediate family members and significant others relative to the individual in question. As a result of the manifest denial problem central to the alcoholic and problem drinker I have found it most efficacious to structure my relationship with individuals diagnostically in question in such a manner as to observe them over an extended period of time — one month being the minimum period of contact and observation. This situation can be handled quite well on a weekly outpatient basis. When we err diagnostically, it is most typically in the direction of accepting the denial and manipulation of the patient and hence, all too frequently, we may become a source of secondary reinforcement to continue drinking behavior. A notable exception to this situation is sometimes found within alcoholic treatment facilities staffed almost exclusively with "recovered" alcoholics. Viewing any drinking behavior as indicative of alcoholism or potential alcoholism and other problems may serve to facilitate the development of an atmosphere which in itself may be psychonoxious in this respect. As a means of enhancing accurate evaluations and diagnostic procedures I strongly advocate staffing alcoholic rehabilitation facilities with no more than 40 percent "recovered alcoholics." A staff made up of both formerly addicted individuals and professionally trained personnel who have not experienced significant drinking pathology tends to balance out the trend toward being "conned" on the one hand and seeing alcoholism in all drinkers on the other.

An initial diagnosis of problem drinker quite frequently amounts to an essential prerequisite for a later diagnosis of alcoholism or chronic alcoholism. In the absence of therapeutic intervention of an ongoing nature, be it involvement with Alcoholics Anonymous, individual therapy or rehabilitation strategies of a more comprehensive nature, perhaps as high as 70 percent of those initially diagnosed as problem drinkers will eventually qualify for the diagnosis of alcoholism. This movement from being diagnosed as a problem drinker to an alcoholic amounts to a developmental process. Eventual qualification for the diagnosis of alcoholic usually encompasses a time frame of some five to ten years, but frequently this progression may take place in a matter of months. It is apparent that the progressive nature of the process of alcohol addiction is inherent in the delineation of these two essential diagnostic categories. It is my feeling that while many question the disease model of alcohol addiction, particularly from the strict medical standpoint, we have overlooked the disease orientation as it applies to the progressive development of behavior pathology relative to the addiction. Certainly behavioral patterns, perhaps most clearly the obsessive-compulsive dynamism, progressively become more manifest and all-encompassing in the process of moving from the diagnosis of problem drinker to chronic alcoholic. We have tended to underevaluate this behavioral progression; it is my firm opinion that this developmental process can be accurately assessed from a behavioral perspective.

Throughout the course of this chapter I have stressed the relevance of diagnosis to the treatment process for both the problem drinker and the alcoholic. It is this relationship between diagnosis and the treatment of the alcoholic and problem drinker which I now want to discuss.

Traditionally, diagnosis has served as an essential prerequisite to the determination of a particular treatment process. As mentioned earlier, this has been particularly true with regard to medically oriented treatment strategies. My position relative to the role of diagnosis and subsequent alcoholic rehabilitation measures, while sharing a number of the essential aspects of a more medically oriented approach, may be viewed as somewhat "radical" by various members of the rehabilitation team, regardless of training or philosophical orientation. It is my contention that upon completion of a patient evaluation for drinking pathology, the results of this evaluation should be explicitly conveyed to the patient — while he or she is in a sober state. In essence this amounts to informing the individual of the diagnostic formulation, be it alcoholism, problem drinker or the lack of alcohol-based psychopathology. I realize the many implications inherent in such a procedure. Perhaps certain individuals might respond to such a procedure by "fleeing" from treatment. Others may feel stigmatized and act out various resistances as a result.

In spite of these potential negative aspects of informing the individual of his or her diagnostic status, I am firmly convinced of the overall therapeutic gain offered by such a methodology. From a strictly therapeutic juncture, the primary source of gain offered by this approach seems to me to lie in the realm of breaking down the alcoholic or problem drinker's system of massive denial. This particular defense mechanism, while in part culturally determined and reinforced, represents a pathological core dynamism in the practicing alcoholic's *modus vivendi*. When we fail to openly inform the individual of our clinical evaluation of his or her drinking behavior we may become a very integral part of this system of denial, thereby only serving to reinforce the addictive behavior. There are many additional sources of gain to be derived from such an approach. As is true with the behavioral and contractual approaches to treatment, such a method initiates a process whereby specific maladaptive behaviors can be identified by both therapist and patient. Mutual agreement as to treatment goals and objectives, as well as other specifics relative to the treatment process can be based upon such an initial diagnostic procedure. Providing feedback relative to an individual's drinking pathology via clinical diagnosis amounts to a potentially significant reality input. Although individuals diagnosed as either alcoholic or problem drinker may manifest a variety of other more diffuse symptoms, focusing upon drinking behavior specifically as a target symptom provides all parties involved in the actual treatment or rehabilitation process with a concrete behavioral baseline with which to view subsequent behavior.

It is apparent from the discussion thus far that I am not advocating a specific diagnostically based treatment regimen. Such a model would be essentially congruous with the medical role of diagnosis. Treatment of the alcoholic or problem drinker, while diagnostically based in certain respects, must remain for the most part an individual matter. Clinical decision making relative to the treatment process must take into account individual psychodynamics, marital status, medical variables and a multiplicity of other such issues. The diagnosis of alcoholic may result in an Antabuse® maintenance program for individual X, while a similar procedure may be contraindicated for individual Y, also manifesting the criteria essential to the diagnosis of alcoholic.

Another somewhat radical aspect of this approach has to do with the dimension of simply telling another human being that he or she is an alcoholic or problem drinker. We have been led to believe that this is the explicit domain of the medically trained expert. It is my feeling that the diagnosis of alcoholism or problem drinker is essentially no more valid when made by medically trained experts than when made by other adequately trained alcoholic rehabilitation personnel. Moreover, the myth that only the alcoholic or problem drinker can determine the extent of his or her pathological addiction must be acknowledged as fallacious. Frequently I have observed trained alcoholic rehabilitation personnel falling into the trap of accepting this position, which in many cases serves to reinforce the denial mechanism, thus facilitating drinking behavior on the part of the individual questioning the reality of his or her substance dependency. Drinking behavior can be quantitatively and qualitatively assessed. It is the responsiblity of alcoholic rehabilitation personnel to convey this message to both addicted individuals as well as society at large. While our diagnostic evaluations of drinking behavior may appear crude and less precise than desirable, we nonetheless possess the pragmatic ability to discriminate between such gross categories as alcoholic, problem drinker and nondrinker. It is my vehement conviction that education, training and experience less than the medical degree or the doctorate can be adequate preparation for discriminating between these diagnostic categories.

A significant source of gain to be found in this approach to diagnosis is more related to therapist focus than patient benefit. Quite frequently we are confronted with individuals who resist to various degrees our rehabilitation or treatment efforts. The process of providing direct feedback to individuals relative to their drinking behavior and subsequent staff diagnostic evaluation of this specific behavior typically elicits a good deal of defensive behavior upon the part of the individual receiving such diagnostically oriented feedback. Such behavior provides the therapist with a good deal of insight relative to various treatment dimensions. For certain therapists this process may provide input of such a nature as to facilitate the decision not to attempt treatment with a particular patient or type of patient. Referral decisions may be based in part upon such data. At the other end of the continuum we frequently observe individuals who respond to such diagnostically oriented feedback with apparent relief. Both consciously and preconsciously such individuals have been cognizant of their drinking pathology for extended periods of time and have in all probability been asking for help in various ways. In such cases engagement in the rehabilitation process can be a most welcome event.

In short, such a diagnostic procedure more clearly defines the role of the therapist and the rehabilitation program relative to the addiction or pathology of the individual patient. It is considerations such as these which convince me of the overall clinical worth and therapeutic gain offered by such a diagnostic methodology. Certainly such a procedure is not without pitfalls. However, it is my opinion that this particular diagnostic model provides a framework in which to begin effective treatment of the alcoholic and problem drinker. In this respect many may choose to view this general model of diagnosis as essentially medically based. While advocating the diagnostic process to be an essential ingredient in the global rehabilitation effort, which is medical in orientation, I hope that I have clearly conveyed to the reader those points of divergence from the more medically oriented model which I feel to be germane to the specific treatment of the alcoholic and problem drinker.

CONCLUDING REMARKS

The role and relevance of the diagnostic process are historically steeped in medical tradition. Within the spectrum of services provided by behavioral scientists we have witnessed a progressive rejection of both the diagnostic process and the general medical model of treatment and rehabilitation. All too frequently diagnosis seems to result in labeling an individual as a deviant or social outcast. Certainly the purpose of diagnosis is totally antithetical to this unfortunate and frequent manipulation of the diagnostic process.

Throughout the course of this chapter I have strongly advocated the role and relevance of diagnosis in the treatment of alcoholism and problem drinking. Two explicit diagnostic categories relative to drinking behavior and pathological patterns of consumption have been outlined in this chapter. These diagnostic categories are alcoholism or chronic alcoholism and problem drinking. The diagnosis of alcoholism or chronic alcoholism entails an extended history of pathological drinking behavior, typically including alcohol-related medical complications. Tissue involvement most frequently includes the gastrointestinal tract, liver, heart and central nervous system. The disease model of alcoholism would appear to be most appropriate in cases qualifying for this diagnosis.

Behaviorally the diagnosis of alcoholism or chronic alcoholism encompasses a florid manifestation of the obsessive-compulsive dynamism. Loss of control is an essential ingredient in this diagnosis. Marital problems, vocational difficulty, legal involvement and identity conflict are but a few of the other behavioral manifestations of this diagnostic category. Individuals so diagnosed have reached a point in their addiction where the actual drinking process encompasses the total life-style. It should be noted that a significant number of individuals diagnosed as alcoholic do not manifest observable tissue pathology specific to their addiction. Anxiety, depression and other affective components are also central to this diagnosis. Dissociative phenomena are central to virtually every diagnosis of alcoholism.

Differential diagnosis is not without its caveats within the realm of alcohol addiction. Determining a diagnosis of problem drinker rather than alcoholism may be both tenuous and difficult to do in many cases. Certainly these gross categories exist somewhere on a continuum. The diagnosis of problem drinker is most appropriate in those cases in which major conflicts and traumas have stemmed from pathological drinking behavior. While this certainly applies to the diagnosis of chronic alcoholism, there are a number of significant temporally oriented considerations which serve to differentiate the categories. The problem drinker, perhaps as a result of extended abstinence, may encounter such alcohol-facilitated complications yearly or at other extended intervals. Actual consumption is markedly less obsessive-compulsive in nature, the problem drinker rarely manifests tissue damage specific to prolonged alcohol ingestion, and generally these individuals are younger and tend to appear to be socially and interpersonally more functional than the alcoholic. Clinical experience indicates that perhaps 70 percent of those individuals initially diagnosed as problem drinkers will eventually progress in their addiction to the diagnosis of chronic alcoholic. Diagnostic errors in my experience tend to be in the direction of false positives. However, alcoholic rehabilitation personnel do sometimes fail to recognize their trend toward a generalized scotoma relating to viewing any drinking behavior as pathological. Individuals found not to be diagnostically an alcoholic or problem drinker should be made aware of this fact and referred for other services when appropriate. We must recognize that the consumption of alcohol is both good and bad; it is only for this reason that alcohol ingestion has remained such an integral part of the social and interpersonal historicity of mankind.

Before concluding this chapter I think it is important to mention that there is a small group, perhaps 5 to 8 percent of the population of individuals diagnosed as alcoholic or chronic alcoholic, who more accurately should be diagnosed "reactive alcoholic." These individuals are very often tissue addicted and evidence the various other clinical characteristics of the alcoholic diagnostic group. However, in contrast to the alcoholic diagnostic group the "reactive alcoholic" diagnosis almost always can be associated with a traumatic object loss, and the addiction pattern of an individual so diagnosed is typically of a shorter duration than that of the chronic alcoholic. Reactive alcoholism is often manifested later in life. In these few cases the addicted person begins to drink alcoholically following the death of a spouse, family member or loved one. The reactive alcoholic is relatively easy to treat and rehabilitate once referred to the psychotherapist or a rehabilitation program. Certainly this clinical distinction, again a problem of differential diagnosis, can be both extremely important in some cases and rather inconsequential in others.

The foremost source of therapeutic gain to be derived from the diagnostic approach advocated in this chapter lies perhaps in the realm of dealing with the problem of denial. In this respect I have very strongly advocated that alcoholic rehabilitation personnel provide explicit feedback to patients relative to their diagnosis. If an individual is diagnosed as an alcoholic or problem drinker, it is my opinion that he or she should be made aware of this evaluation in no uncertain terms. This amounts to direct feedback and input relative to the specific drinking behavior of the patient. This type of confrontation is reality oriented and as such a potentially significant source for breaking down the denial mechanism. Providing such feedback also forms the basis for future behavioral evaluation of drinking, as well as enabling the therapist to ferret out other patient resistances and dynamics. It is my feeling that adequately trained alcoholic rehabilitation personnel, very definitely those with less than medical or doctoral training, are capable of making accurate diagnostic evaluations according to the criteria delineated in this chapter. In addition to undergraduate academic work in the behavioral sciences, one or two years of clinical experience in the alcoholic rehabilitation field should hopefully prove adequate to the development of such diagnostic abilities.

I should also point out that there are many more esoteric sources of rehabilitation gain to be derived from the diagnostic process. Diagnosis (literally "knowing through") incorporates the magic of words. In many respects patients seem to pay money to hear seemingly magic words. This is certainly apart from the negative aspect of "alcoholic" as a stigma. Naming the problem, alcoholic or problem drinker, is tantamount to the therapist's saying, "Your problem is known and has causes — we can do something to effect a change." Rollo May (1973) and others have pointed out the relief offered to patients by such a procedure.

SECTION TWO

STRATEGIES OF TREATMENT

Chapter 6

TREATMENT I
INDIVIDUAL PSYCHOTHERAPY

THE area of individual psychotherapy with alcohol-addicted patients has received relatively little professional attention. Extensive review of the literature pertinent to the problem of alcohol addiction indicates a marked dearth of process-outcome types of psychotherapy research. Behavioral scientists have long attempted to evaluate the effects of individual and group psychotherapy upon various clinical populations, to include a wide range of psychoneurotic and psychotic disorders. This is simply not the case with alcohol addiction. Those few investigations dealing with the effects of individual psychotherapy upon alcohol-addicted individuals notoriously suffer from poor design and marginal research methodology. Avoiding the general controversy surrounding the effects of counseling and psychotherapy, it is felt that the global strategies of treatment presented in this chapter are effective in producing behavioral change upon the part of many alcohol-addicted persons. Meltzoff and Kornreich (1970) recently concluded after extensive review that: "Far more often than not, psychotherapy of a wide variety of types and with a broad range of disorders has been demonstrated under controlled conditions to be accompanied by positive changes in adjustment that significantly exceed those that can be accounted for by the passage of time alone." Most professionals working in the area of alcoholic rehabilitation have long manifested a similar consensus of opinion.

In this chapter the reader will be presented with an interpersonal model of psychotherapy found to be effective in the modification of alcoholic behavior. This model or basic therapeutic approach is effective in dealing with perhaps 85 percent of the overall alcoholic population. The model is based upon extended clinical practice, as well as a practical and theoretical knowledge of a number of theories of counseling and psychotherapy. Considerable time will be devoted to practical issues found to be important in the effective therapeutic enterprise with alcoholic patients. Particular therapeutic strategies will be discussed. It is hoped that this approach to the individual psychotherapeutic treatment of the alcoholic patient will provide the reader with ample guidelines and understanding to appreciate the nature and worth of this enterprise.

INITIAL CONSIDERATIONS

Psychotherapy and counseling have been defined according to a number of rather consistent criteria for quite some time. In the present context, many of these essential historic criteria are acknowledged as central to the process of psychotherapy. For our present purposes, the terms psychotherapy and counseling are used interchangeably, to explain a particular form of human interactional process. In essence this interactional process involves at least two individuals, one of whom is experiencing significant difficulty in the process of daily living, and another who, by virtue of both professional training and select life experiences, is potentially capable of helping facilitate positive behavioral growth or change on the part of the person experiencing difficulty.

People seek psychotherapeutic treatment for a wide range of reasons. While one might suspect that the alcoholic or problem drinker typically enters a counseling or therapeutic relationship in order to terminate drinking behavior, this aspect of the rationale for seeking treatment is often secondary or tangential. Many alcoholics enter treatment in order to "get the wife off my back," to retain a job or appease the employer, etc. Experience indicates that the majority of alcoholic and problem drinkers entering treatment do so with a great deal of ambivalence. While alcohol has helped facilitate a good deal of interpersonal pain in the addicted person's life space, it must be remembered that alcohol has also helped extinguish a good deal of pain. Selective recall tends to focus upon the more pleasurable aspects of drinking, thus blocking out the unhappy consequences of alcohol ingestion. This being the case, most alcoholics are rather apprehensive about the possibility of giving up their drinking behavior. This is the case with self-referred patients who are verbally desirous of terminating their drinking behavior, as well as with more openly resistive patients who have been "forced" into treatment. A part of many alcoholics' desire to return to the ranks of the controlled drinker is related to this ambivalence. Particularly during the early stages of treatment, many alcoholics express the goal of becoming a "normal" drinker. Very few alcoholics and problem drinkers actually want to give up their addiction. One quickly learns to disregard verbage to the effect of "I'll never touch the stuff again." The desire to continue drinking may consciously be present in spite of five or ten years of total sobriety. Individuals who have attained prolonged sobriety and possess self-insight are very much aware of their ambivalent feelings regarding alcohol consumption. Such individuals frequently make it known that they would initiate drinking again were it not for the consequences they would suffer as a result of further drinking. Time and again I have found it of the utmost importance to remember that alcohol addiction is but a neurotic defense mechanism which has essentially "worked" for an extended portion of the addicted person's life space. Although economically inefficient, from the defense mechanism perspective of neurotic or maladjustive behavior, the alcoholism or problem drinking behavior has helped enable the addicted individual to function interpersonally. In this sense alcohol addiction is viewed as symptomatic. Alcoholism or problem drinking is but the target symptom of other underlying personality conflicts. In the face of increasingly ineffective modes of interpersonal adjustment, the addicted individual must progressively turn to alcohol as a means of coping. Once engaged in this vicious circle it becomes next to impossible to get at the basic issues involved in the individual's drinking pathology. This is most certainly the case as long as the person continues to drink. As such, the initial prerequisite for any form of treatment with alcohol-addicted individuals is that of sobriety. This is most certainly a paradoxical situation.

TOWARD AN INDIVIDUAL PSYCHOTHERAPY WITH ALCOHOL-ADDICTED PERSONS

Let me reiterate that the proposed therapy model has proved extremely successful with 75 to 85 percent of the alcohol-addicted individuals who have been treated according to the basic guidelines of the model. Patients found to respond well to this treatment approach were within the thirty-five to fifty age range, were from the upper-lower through middle socioeconomic income levels, functioned within the "normal" range of measured intelligence, were married and single, had drinking histories of fifteen to twenty years including numerous medical hospitalizations for "alcoholism," were vocationally functional and were not psychotic. Extended legal complications were a part of the behavioral profile of many of the successfully treated individuals. The two extremes of the alcoholic population have not been a part of the clinical population upon which this model has been constructed. The skid-row alcoholic and the extremely affluent alcoholic simply have not been a part of the clinical experience upon which this model is based.

Early investigation of the effects of psychotherapy produced considerable variation regarding improvement rates. Matz (1929) reported an improvement rate of 41 percent. Maas (1955) indicated an improvement rate of 42 percent. In contrast to these indications of relatively little success, Irgens (1936) reported improvement rates as high as 91 precent; Ross (1936) reported an improvement rate of 77 percent. Levitt (1957) reported an average improvement rate of 67 percent, which approximates the recent extensive research of therapeutic outcome by Eysenck (1960, 1965, 1967). Both clinicians and research psychotherapists have long been aware of the inadequacies of such studies of therapeutic outcome. In an attempt to account for such outcome disparities an effort was directed at the assessment or evaluation of therapist characteristics which might serve to either enhance or impede therapeutic outcomes. Whitehorn and Betz (1954) provided initial research in this area suggesting that successful as opposed to unsuccessful therapists could be differentiated in terms of attitudinal approach to psychotherapy. These authors reported that more successful therapists appeared to be more understanding and accepting of the patient in a very personal, immediate way, whereas less successful therapists tended to emphasize psychopathology and generally related in a less personal manner. This research resulted in the Whitehorn and Betz A-B therapist model or paradigm. Since the advent of this type of research, including such similar models as the Fiedler studies (1950, 1951), considerable evidence has been amassed to the effect that certain variables are essential to effective psychotherapy. Regardless of therapy orientation, the medium of the therapist-patient transaction remains the point of behavioral change and growth. In the absence of a meaningful relationship, psychotherapy as a process simply cannot take place. While all therapists are dependent upon the patient-therapist dyad, what actually takes place within this encounter is in part determined by the theoretical orientation and training of the therapist. While research has indicated that the theoretical orientations of the therapist tend to dissipate with experience, research has also rather clearly indicated that certain types of therapist behavior are consistently related to patient growth and personality reorganization. This seems to be the case regardless of patient diagnosis or pathology. Rogers (1952) was one of the pioneers in relationship-oriented therapy, and through his client-centered approach to psychotherapy the systematic investigation of therapist qualities was initiated. The sixties provided a wealth of research knowledge in this realm. Truax and Carkhuff (1967) in a rather convincing summary of this research identify three essential therapist ingredients in the effective psychotherapeutic enterprise; accurate empathic understanding of the patient, nonpossessive warmth and therapist genuineness or authenticity. Therapists who consistently respond to their patients with high levels of these facilitative conditions tend to help effect significant positive behavioral change upon the part of their patients. Therapists unable to provide adequate levels of these facilitative conditions have been shown to consistently produce minimal or even negative therapeutic results.

With regard to these essential ingredients of successful therapy, therapist genuineness or authenticity is felt to be most fundamental. Genuineness has been defined as the therapist's ability to be open to his own experience within the therapeutic encounter and to honestly express these feelings to the patient. More simply, the therapist is a real person; he wears no facade, expresses feelings and experiences to the patient within the therapeutic encounter, and makes every attempt to relate in a personally relevant manner within this context (Truax and Wargo, 1966).

A second variable in the therapeutic triad is therapist communication of nonpossessive warmth for the patient. Basically this concept relates to the therapist's warm acceptance of the patient (both experiences and feelings) without any conditions. The therapist accepts what *is,* rather than being concerned with what *should be.* The failures and depressions of the patient, as well as his successes, are shared by the therapist. It has been asserted in the literature that warmth is a precondition for the therapist to accurately perceive the inner feelings and experiences of the patient, as well as a precondition for the patient's trust and self-exploration (Truax and Carkhuff, 1967).

A third ingredient within the successful psychotherapeutic encounter is that of accurate empathic understanding. Accurate empathy refers to the ability of the therapist to be both affectively and cognitively attuned to what the patient is currently feeling and experiencing and to communicate to the patient an understanding of these feelings. Furthermore, the therapist who is accurately empathic explores the more latent cues expressed by voice, posture and content (Truax and Carkhuff, 1967).

One of the most potent findings of this research has had to do with the generalizability of findings to diverse clinical populations. Hospitalized chronic schizophrenics, depressives, college underachievers, juvenile delinquents, etc., have been included as research populations in studies made by Truax and Carkhuff (1967) and others (Truax and Lister, 1971; Shapiro and Gust, 1974). It is felt that these essential therapist ingredients have a very cogent bearing upon the therapeutic enterprise with alcoholic patients. Indeed, a primary prerequisite to the therapeutic process with alcohol-addicted individuals is the presence of a therapist who can offer consistently high levels of these facilitative conditions within the therapeutic context. This is particularly the case with the alcoholic patient found to repond well to the therapy model presented in this chapter. Addicted individuals have led a life-style devoid of feelings of warmth and concern. They have felt the prolonged pangs of unworth and unlove. For the most part their lives have been spent with feelings of loneliness and despair. Self-punitive and punitive behavior by significant others has been very much a part of their interpersonal mode. A therapist who consistently relates and communicates to the alcoholic a sense of basic self-worth and human concern becomes the instrument by which the alcoholic can begin to feel differently about himself. Once this process is initiated, it becomes the addicted person himself who becomes responsible for behavioral change. Only when the alcoholic can begin to feel good about himself and the process of being sober can he attain prolonged sobriety. Initially these therapist-offered facilitative conditions enable the alcoholic to love the therapist to the extent that he is willing to remain sober for him. It is just this type of interpersonal relationship that the alcoholic has been seeking for perhaps all of his life. As the alcoholic remains sober he progressively develops the ability to maintain his sobriety for himself rather than for the therapist or significant others. This becomes a powerful source of positive reinforcement.

Being able to consistently relate to the alcohol-addicted individual in a facilitative manner is often difficult. The therapist and other personnel involved in the actual treatment process are often faced with a patient who appears hostile, noncooperative and generally disinterested in the process of behavioral modification. At times, alcoholic patients prove extremely trying for all involved in the rehabilitation effort. They frequently miss appointments, engage in intermittent drinking sprees and other such forms of alcoholic behavior while involved in the rehabilitation program, and in numerous other ways exhibit the classic characteristics of "resistance." In spite of these seeming obstacles, therapists and staff who maintain a relationship with the alcoholic which conveys feelings of basic human dignity and worth will eventually be able to mutually experience the reward of interpersonal growth and behavioral change. Experiential learning is very much a part of this process. A therapist and an environment which consistently provide psychological input to the simple effect of "You are a human being, and *we* are concerned with you and the process of life" provide the alcoholic an excellent opportunity for healthy identification and modeling.

While this aspect of the therapeutic relationship with the alcoholic and problem drinker is essentially Rogerian in theoretical orientation, experience indicates that certain basic Rogerian strategies are inappropriate to the therapeutic encounter with this clinical population. Psychotherapy and counseling with alcohol-addicted individuals must include a behaviorally activist therapist. The mere reflection of feelings, clarification and other nondirective aspects of Rogerian therapy are not well suited to the majority of alcohol-addicted individuals entering treatment. To begin with, many alcoholics are incapable of dealing with this type of interpersonal environment upon entering a treatment program. Frequently one or two individual therapy sessions characterized by little therapist activity, to include the essentially nondirective behaviors of the Rogerian therapist, will result in the alcoholic's fleeing from treatment. At this point the alcoholic sorely needs to feel human. Therapist behaviors which communicate a sense of willingness to actively participate in the patient's living problems are essential. This may well involve direct participation in vocational, marital and legal aspects of the patient's present life situation. Initially the therapist must be willing to become involved in the patient's day-to-day problems. Needless to say, as the patient begins to progress in the ability to deal more effectively with his global life process, the therapist becomes increasingly less involved in the direct support and control of the patient's life. What must remain essentially Rogerian is the attitude of humanism toward the patient; what must be changed in working with the alcoholic and problem drinker is technique.

The paramount issue with regard to technique is that of therapist involvement and activity. Involvement is often equated with directiveness. In this sense involvement and activity are beyond the simplicity of directiveness. Therapist activity must include an experiential commitment to "being" involved in the totality of the patient's life space. It is through this type of relationship that the patient develops the capacity of trust another significant human being and in this process to both love that significant other as well as himself. In the absence of a meaningful relationship with at least one other human being, one is unable to experience the feeling of being loved, and in turn, one is unable to love. This has been the alcoholic's unfortunate dilemma in life. In the absence of such a relationship the alcoholic has only one alternative; to remain intoxicated.

Once the therapeutic groundwork of establishing a meaningful relationship of the type already characterized has been developed, the nature of the therapy process must become the focal point in treatment. Within this context the principles of Reality Therapy (Glasser, 1965) are extremely well suited to the ongoing process of psychotherapy with alcoholic and problem drinking individuals. This approach to the interactional process of individual psychotherapy emphasizes dealing with reality issues, responsibilities, failure and behavioral alternatives. That reality has been an unpleasant and painful experience for the alcohol-addicted individual is an elementary issue. Interpersonal relationships, educational experiences, socioeconomic status, etc. have almost invariably helped produce an experience with oneself and the world which is unpleasant at best. A learned method of escaping the reality of this form of experiential being has become that of alcohol addiction. This is, in itself, a most unreal adjustment to the process of daily living. Simply being sober is the first step in the process of daily living. Simply being sober is the first step in the process of beginning to deal with reality. One can begin to appreciate how significant an issue this seemingly inconsequential step is if the patient has been consistently intoxicated for fifteen or twenty years. In essence, this amounts to fifteen or twenty years of living a grossly non-reality-oriented life-style.

Within the therapeutic context the addicted individual and the therapist must deal with those issues and feelings which have contributed to the patient's inability to tolerate the reality of his experiential being. Learning and reeducation may well be an important part of the therapeutic enterprise at this juncture. Figuring out just what it is that has historically, as well as presently, helped to contribute to the inability to deal with reality issues constitutes a significant learning experience about oneself. More basic educational matters, such as the physiologically harmful nature of alcohol addiction, may also be important. Many of the myths and misconceptions of alcohol addiction have tangentially served the purpose of maintaining certain individuals' addiction. Elementary education about alcohol and support may be enough to significantly change the drinking behaviors of a small segment of the alcohol-addicted population seeking or otherwise entering treatment. The more involved learning about self which is inherent in more traditional forms of individuals psychotherapy often has to do with basic identity issues for the long-term alcohol addict.

Indeed, basic identity conflict is often genetic to the problem of alcohol addiction. Focusing on those interpersonal processes which originally helped facilitate negative or confused perceptions and feelings about the self is a frequent aspect of the therapeutic encounter with addicted individuals. Social inadequacy, inferiority and similar aspects of simply not measuring up are often core issues related to basic self-dislike. Interpersonal transactions which conveyed these feelings to the individual early in life have often been perpetually reinforced by subsequent experience in the interpersonal realm. A major issue is often that of integrating the fact that one is an alcoholic. When one has reached the point of entering treatment for alcohol addiction, this aspect of his experiential being has probably been essential to his identity for quite some time. Simply being able to incorporate "I am an alcoholic" into the self-system is of paramount importance to the addicted individual's ability to establish his identity with regard to alcohol. Understanding this aspect of the self means, in effect, understanding or at least realizing some of the consequences of continued intoxication. Once this stage of the therapeutic relationship has been reached the alcoholic is confronted with the future responsibility of drinking or not drinking. While this may seem to be a secondary issue, it is nonetheless of major significance. Prior drinking behaviors have revolved around the denial that one has a problem with alcohol or is an alcoholic. Once a part of the addicted individual's basic identity incorporates the reality of his addiction, it is he who must begin to assume responsibility for the addictive aspects of his drinking behavior. While many alcoholics may continue to drink after reaching this issue within the therapy relationship, it is my feeling that once this groundwork has been dealt with therapeutically a permanent wedge has been established in the individual's drinking behavior. I suspect that a sizeable segment of those who do continue to imbibe after dealing with this material therapeutically do so with a great deal of guilt or other powerful feelings of uncomfortableness. This is certainly the case if they attempt to continue to drink while in treatment.

Another reality issue, which is best dealt with early in the treatment process, is that of the self-destructive nature of the addicted individual's drinking behavior. I have found that most alcoholics, in spite of their massive denial systems, are aware of the reality of this aspect of their pathological behavior. Frequently this awareness of the self-destructive nature of their addiction amounts to a glib verbal affirmation such as "I'm killing myself." In-depth exploration of this type of dialogue, within the framework of the patient-therapist relationship, helps establish the actual reality of this process of self-destruction for the alcoholic. Rather than merely giving lip service to this process, the alcoholic can begin to meaningfully understand the reality of this aspect of his alcoholic behavior.

Particularly during the initial stages of therapy, as well as for the duration of treatment, the therapist must stress the existence of behavioral alternatives. As the alcoholic and problem drinker have learned a rather concrete behavioral set to the experience of unpleasant feelings, i.e. drinking, it becomes imperative that they be made aware of the simple fact that they are capable of learning new behaviors within these stress situations which have previously been related to their patterns of pathological drinking. The message "when you feel uptight or depressed, you don't have to get drunk" is potent. The point is that the alcohol-addicted individual must learn to respond to stress and unpleasant feelings by some manner other than drinking. When patients begin to actively engage in some of these alternative behaviors, the fact should be acknowledged and positively reinforced within the therapeutic context, as well as on a more general level if possible. Choosing behavioral alternatives other than drinking means, in essence, accepting responsibility for one's behavior. A major source of the unhappiness in many alcoholic lives has been lack of responsibility. When the addicted person begins to behave in a more responsible fashion he must be reinforced. That the patient has not led a life-style of responsibility should be pointed out early in therapy. One of the therapeutic goals to be initially established is that of increased patient responsibility. The failure to pay bills, work absenteeism, marital infidelities, etc., are all attributes of the patient's irresponsibility and should be pointed out in the early stages of treatment. In so doing, the therapist and patient establish behavioral goals and limits which are essential to later evaluations of patient progress and growth. The therapist must consistently and unfalteringly expect the patient to change in the direction of increased responsibility. Lapses of drinking, i.e. nonresponsible behavior, are to be expected. However, when these relapses do occur they must be fully explored within the therapeutic context. Such relapses must be interpreted as lapses in responsibility. It must be pointed out to the patient that once he reaches the stage of being able to effectively deal with the responsibility issues pertinent to his own being, he will no longer be dependent upon alcohol as a means of dealing with irresponsibility.

Interpersonally, the interrelationship of a number of these issues is clearly evident. Experiences compounded to form a basic failure identity precipitate difficulties in dealing with reality issues relative to the process of daily living. The addicted individual learns quite early that he can escape this painful reality by drinking. At this point the individual enters a progressive cycle of irresponsible behavior, which must of necessity become increasingly more pathological. In accord with this overall process, behavioral alternatives become increasingly defunct. At some juncture the addicted person becomes the proverbial "man in the trap."

The psychotherapeutic process with alcohol-addicted individuals must deal extensively with the here-and-now. While the first three or four sessions may focus rather explicitly upon the patient's early life, traumatic factors and other past-oriented material, the ongoing crux of the therapeutic process must deal with the present-oriented experiential being of the patient. Exploring current feelings, present interpersonal relationships and present vocational status are all a part of the here-and-now orientation. Within the patient-therapist encounter virtually every aspect of the patient's current experiential being becomes material for exploration. Within this context, stressing behavior per se becomes increasingly important. As the therapist interacts with the patient he has the continued opportunity to be a part of or in contact with the patient's various behaviors. He knows and emotionally shares in the patient's episodes of intoxication. He becomes aware of the patient's marital conflicts, his legal difficulties, etc. Dealing with those concrete behaviors which the patient has previously and is presently engaging in which result in ineffective or pathological patterns of interpersonal behavior is imperative. Coming to grips with these issues, i.e. confrontation is the *sine qua non* of this process. Needless to say, confrontation dictates a good deal of therapist activity. Being able to openly communicate to another human being that one is engaging in inappropriate or bizarre behavior may be elementary. Effective psychotherapy and counseling with alcohol-addicted individuals requires therapist behavior apart from the more detached participant-observer role. Confrontation includes being able to say "bullshit." It may include direct feedback to the effect that certain behaviors are "crazy." It may well also include direct communications to the effect of "I like you" or "I love you." Regardless of the verbal content of the confrontation, the underlying message must always be one of caring and involvement on the part of the therapist. The message must also include the belief in the patient's ability to change and grow; it must always incorporate an exploration of possible alternative behaviors for the future. Generally speaking, confronting people about their behaviors which are interpersonally noxious is a difficult undertaking. In working with alcohol-addicted individuals therapeutically this must be a constant process. In this fashion the patient is able to learn what it is about his behavior that "turns others off." Therapists must be capable of confronting patients; secondly, confrontation must be carried out in a nondestructive fashion. The facilitative conditions discussed earlier (Truax and Carkhuff, 1967) are always central to interpersonal process which are essentially confrontation oriented. It is felt that the consistent exploration of these noxious or inappropriate behaviors within the therapeutic dyad is auspicious for successful psychotherapy with alcohol-addicted individuals.

It was indicated earlier that failure has long been a potent variable in the development of most alcoholics' self-system. In contrast to earlier educational experiences, interpersonal relationships and the processes of daily living which have historically seemed to build a basic failure identity for most alcoholics, the therapist-patient encounter must be a success-oriented endeavor. In this sense it is imperative that "slips" or periods of uncontrolled intoxication while in treatment are not interpreted as *ipso facto* proof of the patient's inability to change. The therapist must strongly reinforce indicators of positive growth and change, no matter how small or seemingly inconsequential they may seem to others. Communication to the effect that the patient has failed again, in the face of a "slip" is tantamount to therapeutic impasse. Such situations dictate an exploration into the dynamics surrounding the drinking episode, further exploration of alternatives open at the point of choosing to become intoxicated, including the responsibility issue, and finally pointing out the indicators of gain prior to the drinking episode with a firm conviction that the patient will continue to be progressively more successful in the future. The self-fulfilling prophecy of failure as it relates to alcoholism is well known. The therapist must clearly communicate to the patient that he does not expect the patient to remain intoxicated, that the patient can change in spite of what he might believe, and wherever possible he must point out positive gain made by the patient. Pervasive failure in the process of daily living perpetuates expectancies based upon future failure. Only success can terminate such a life-style. Indeed, failure has been a red thread in the lifestyles of most alcohol-addicted individuals. The establishment of a functional interpersonal relationship built upon mutual concern and respect and not involving alcohol is a major success in itself. Through this medium initiated within the therapeutic relationship, generalization of success becomes possible.

GENERAL CONSIDERATIONS

Convincing evidence has been massed to the effect that very little change has in reality taken place within the broad rubric of "psychotherapy" since the advent of psychoanalytic treatment (Strupp, 1973). Indeed it is strongly suggested that psychotherapists, regardless of training and theoretical orientation, seem to rely upon certain predictable and consistent interpersonal processes as a means of changing or modifying patient behaviors (Arbuckle, 1974). Aside from these essential similarities, relative differences in therapeutic technique and therapeutic strategies have been delineated within the various schools of therapy. In this regard it has been suggested that the more analytic therapies are particularly inappropriate for the general alcoholic population. Candidates for psychoanalytic psychotherapy allegedly must possess a good deal of ego-strength, in addition to being capable of delaying gratification, psychologically minded, vocationally functional, relatively intelligent and successful in the process of daily living. Such individuals are clearly neurotics, who for the most part function relatively well. Those at all familiar with the "typical" alcoholic patient (if there is such a thing as a typical alcoholic) seen within the outpatient rehabilitation facility setting are aware that this population of patients simply does not meet the criteria for analytic treatment. The alcoholic seen within this setting generally is impulsive and immature, has a history of marginal vocational performance and has a developmental life script of "loser." The ability to relate interpersonally is very often not a part of the alcoholic's behavioral repertoire. This single factor would serve to eliminate analytic treatment for most alcoholics.

Historically a good deal of the psychotherapy conducted with alcoholic patients has been along the lines of "supportive" or relationship-oriented therapy. This approach is less concerned with the unconscious determinants of behavior. Personality reorganization is not a basic goal of this form of therapy. Supportive psychotherapy with alcoholic patients has generally been directed at the immediate relief of target symptoms and the overall reduction of anxiety specific to these symptoms. Needless to say, the primary target symptom dealt with is that of alcohol consumption. Therapist behaviors include a good deal of sympathetic understanding and emotional support. This form of therapist behavior often initially precipitates a relationship built on patient dependency. Because the patient is frequently dysfunctional at the point of entering treatment, rather than choosing to allow the patient to remain in this incapacitated state, the therapist chooses to become actively involved in the patient's process of daily living. As the patient progressively regains control of his behavior and interpersonal being, the therapist correspondingly becomes less involved in the direct support and control of the patient's life.

The fundamental medium of behavioral change and growth remains that of the patient-therapist relationship. It is felt that such change is not possible in the absence of a transference relationship. The alcoholic, more than anything else, needs to establish a meaningful interpersonal relationship with a significant other human being. The nature of the patient-therapist dyad lends this relationship the potential for becoming one of the most significant events in the totality of the patients's life space. Dealing with authority, simply relating to another human being, being able to disclose all the inadequacies and feelings which have been denied for so long, are all a part of the healing nature of the psychotherapeutic encounter with alcohol-addicted individuals. I seriously doubt that psychotherapy has anything special to offer addicted individuals other than being a deeply meaningful human relationship. While therapy does help facilitate change, no one is "cured" in the sense of being restored to a *status quo ante.* I suspect that we all become recipients of psychotherapy, i.e. interpersonal engagement with significant others, at those particular points in our own lives when we become depressed or otherwise psychologically upset.

Basic trust is a central issue in the therapeutic enterprise with alcohol-addicted individuals. Experience quickly indicates that most alcoholics have learned not to trust others. A significant characteristic of the therapeutic relationship is the opportunity provided for the alcoholic to learn that another human being can be trusted. Being able to share feelings without being hurt in return and knowing that the therapist is a concerned helper in the struggle of life is very much a part of this process. Another crucial issue relating to the matter of trust is the development of self-trust upon the part of the alcoholic. A significant part of the experiential self-system of most alcoholics has to do with basic feelings of self-distrust. This is particularly the case with regard to drinking per se. The alcoholic has learned that he cannot trust himself when it comes to the temptation to drink. Once engaged in the therapeutic process, the patient learns that he can control his drinking, as well as other responsibility-oriented issues. In this sense, trust becomes a developmental offspring of the therapy relationship.

Insight is also very much an aspect of the successful therapeutic enterprise with alcohol-addicted individuals. While it is often difficult to ferret out exactly what is meant by insight as applied to the particular type of learning relative to the process of psychotherapy, it is felt that alcoholic patients benefited by therapeutic treatment do develop a more realistic and meaningful understanding of their interpersonal behaviors. Frequently insight may take the form of developing some understanding of rather concrete cause-and-effect relationship. At other levels, insight may involve the development of some meaningful appreciation for the various dynamics of the "corrective emotional experience." One is often surprised how quickly certain alcoholic patients develop an understanding of the parataxic nature of their interpersonal behaviors. I am firmly convinced of the reality of psychotherapy as a form of educational experience. Learning about oneself, the external world and, more importantly, developing a more functional understanding of how one behaves interpersonally certainly constitutes an educational process par excellence. Much of what psychotherapy is all about has to do with relearning. In this sense therapy can be viewed as a unique educational experience in which the therapist (teacher) attempts to reeducate the patient (student) through the medium of the interpersonal relationship of psychotherapy. What must be relearned by the patient are feeling and behavioral responses more conducive to effective interpersonal functioning. Needless to say, value systems, modeling and more esoteric matters may be a part of this educational process.

CONCLUDING REMARKS

Individual counseling and psychotherapy with alcohol-addicted individuals require therapist skills apart from the more traditional psychoanalytic and client-centered approaches. The general outline presented in this chapter is proposed as a specific quasi-model for individual counseling and psychotherapy with alcohol-addicted individuals. Hopefully the model might prove heuristic. A good deal of this chapter has focused upon therapist ingredients or behaviors. This in essence relates to the issue of therapist technique. While much of what occurs in the process of psychotherapy currently defies evaluation and quantification, considerable clinical experience as well as research evidence supports the general effectiveness of the proposed model. Certainly the area of therapist skills and behaviors has become the touchstone of recent psychotherapy research. Ubiquitous as the process of psychotherapy is, it must be accepted that significant potential for growth and behavior change lies within the patient-therapist dyad. Working with the alcoholic and problem drinker in a therapeutic fashion demands a relationship characterized by high-level facilitative conditions (Truax and Carkhuff, 1967). It is felt that this is the initial and perhaps foremost essential to the successful treatment of this patient group. Beyond this, the parameters of effective treatment become less apparent. The present model stresses the importance of dealing with responsibility and the identification and exploration of behavioral alternatives, in addition to incorporating the concept of failure as a cogent determining force in the development of any individual's alcohol addiction. A good deal of this approach stems from the work of Glasser (1965). Moreover, it is felt that the psychotherapeutic enterprise with alcohol-addicted individuals must be basically present oriented. Dealing with present feeling, current life problems and other material oriented to the here-and-now is indicated with alcohol-addicted patients. This therapeutic approach consistently advocates an activist therapist role. Therapist involvement and commitment are felt to be essential. The role of a mere observer, one who basically reflects and interprets behavior and feelings, is rejected. The therapist must risk involvement. He must have a deep and genuine commitment to the patient and a pervasive dedication to help (Forrest, 1977).

A tremendously potent source of gain within the therapeutic encounter is patient modeling of therapist behaviors. A part of this emulation and modeling with alcohol-addicted individuals has to do with the therapist's commitment to a basically chemical-free lifestyle. A major aspect in all successful psychotherapies is learning. Psychotherapy is a process of reeducation.

These strategies have proved most effective in the process of individual psychotherapy with alcohol-addicted patients. However, it must be acknowledged that this approach is highly tentative and should remain subject to modification and change as need be. Hopefully this outline of a therapeutic approach with the alcoholic and problem drinker might stimulate further research. The question of duration and frequency of therapeutic sessions remains highly tentative. For patients not concomitantly involved in Alcoholics Anonymous or group psychotherapy, I have found that biweekly, one-hour sessions of at least six months duration are essential to continued sobriety. For patients involved in the totality of an alcoholic rehabilitation program, weekly, one-hour sessions for a period of some four months seem adequate to establish long-term sobriety for most. This is a highly individual matter, depending upon such clinical issues as drinking pattern, prior adjustment, marital situation, vocational status, etc. Until quite recently very little research effort was directed at the psychotherapeutic enterprise with alcohol-addicted patients. As behavioral scientists we must continue to question and evaluate our own techniques and approaches. Freud (1953) summed up this attitude well: "As you know, we have never prided ourselves on the completeness and finality of our knowledge and capacity. We are just as ready now as we were earlier to admit the imperfections of our understanding, to learn new things and to alter our methods in any way that can improve them."

Chapter 7

TREATMENT II
GROUP PSYCHOTHERAPY

GROUP psychotherapy has attained widespread acclaim in the treatment of alcoholic and problem-drinking individuals. Indeed, group psychotherapy is the primary treatment *modus operandi* within many alcoholic rehabilitation settings. As is true with the evaluation of the effects of individual counseling and psychotherapy in general, considerable question regarding the efficacy of group treatment methods had been directed at the particular population of individuals labeled "alcoholic." Recently, group psychotherapy has been found to be a generally successful treatment modality for alcoholism and problem drinking (McGinnis, 1963; Killings and Wells, 1967; Hoff, 1968; and Forrest, 1973). Other researchers have been unable to demonstrate positive outcomes as a result of group treatment procedures with alcohol-addicted individuals (Hill and Blane, 1967; Wolff, 1967, 1968; and Hoy, 1969).

It is my opinion that group treatment approaches are presently perhaps the most promising treatment modality specific to the problem of alcoholism. This opinion has a strong clinical experience basis, as well as a research basis. At this point it would seem appropriate to provide the reader with an operational definition of group psychotherapy (used interchangeably with group treatment in the present context). Group psychotherapy is essentially an interpersonal transaction involving a group leader, who by virtue of a particular type of educational training and life experience, can potentially help facilitate behavioral growth and change on the part of the other group members, who in this particular context share the common problem of alcohol addiction. A group may be composed of two individuals or twenty. Beyond two, the number of group members is inconsequential as long as effective interpersonal communication remains the group mode. While the role of a group leader is stressed, it is understood that group members other than the leader are inherently involved in the causation of growth and personality change potentially by all group members. Members who eventually resolve their addiction through the experience of the group medium are not infrequently found to be effective leaders within similarly constructed groups.

In this chapter we shall discuss the entire gamut of issues relative to group psychotherapy with alcohol-addicted individuals. The matter of technique will be considered at length. Theoretical issues will be discussed. Clinical impressions and observations will be explored.

Group psychotherapy evolved as a developmental offspring of individual psychotherapy for a number of very real and practical reasons. The beginning of psychoanalytic therapy prompted people to actively seek help for their emotional problems and interpersonal anxieties on an ever-growing scale. Prior to this time people obviously managed to procure "therapy" from whatever means available. I suspect that therapeutic individuals within any community have always been existent and have correspondingly been sought out for their advice and support. The church has a long history of active ministry to those experiencing emotional difficulty. With the advent of formalized psychiatry, psychology and eventually social work, a type of helping profession was established which dealt explicitly with emotional problems. As mankind has always had to struggle with its interpersonal and collective insecurities, anxieties and other emotional presses, it is to be expected that individuals and professions claiming to be capable of resolving these problems should be actively sought out. This is a very real aspect of the developmental history of the behavioral sciences in general, and the field of psychotherapy in particular. While many behavioral scientists engaging in various forms of therapeutic practice initially perceived group treatment methods to be somewhat antithetical to individual treatment methods, practicality in many respects demanded movement toward the group-oriented treatment approaches. Individuals, institutional facilities and, in essence, society itself suddenly began to demand "treatment" of a hopelessly large dose. Practitioners were simply unable to deliver therapeutic services on an individual basis. In fact, we continue to be plagued with an overwhelming number of people who both want and need psychotherapeutic treatment. It was from the midst of this dilemma that group psychotherapy developed. It can scarcely be argued that the *Zeitgeist* was right for the growth of group-oriented treatment strategies.

It is somewhat paradoxical that a number of the original stimuli for movement in the direction of group treatment procedures have proved the very touchstones of the effectiveness of this overall treatment modality. This has been the case despite a good deal of skepticism, doubt and frequently outright criticism.

It is my feeling that the significance of working with a group of people experiencing interpersonal difficulties, rather than attempting to work with the conflicts of an individual patient, is a tremendously crucial source of potential therapeutic gain. Aside from the economy of being able to treat eight or ten patients simultaneously, the group procedure simply offers a multiplicity of sources of therapeutic gain which the dyadic therapeutic encounter fails to provide. While this is the case with many clinical populations and within diverse treatment settings, I feel this is particularly true with alcohol-addicted patients seen within the context of an alcoholic rehabilitation setting. The interpersonal relatedness provided by group therapy is precisely what most alcohol-addicted individuals need most. Case histories of the alcoholic and problem drinker readily attest to the reality of these individuals' inability to relate to other people. Within the confines of the group experience such individuals are provided with an atmosphere in which they can begin to explore some of the causative factors of their inability to relate to significant others. Simply being able to relate to other group members is a paramount issue for many alcoholics. Needless to say, sharing feelings and the multiplicity of other affective components of the group therapy experience are also powerful determinants of behavior change.

The support offered by fellow alcoholics and problem drinkers within the group is another tremendously important source of gain. For many the group setting proves less threatening than individual treatment. Being able to share experiences which have often been most threatening, often antisocial and perhaps even bizarre with others who have a personal history which includes these same behaviors and feelings enables the alcoholic to perceive himself as something other than a social outcast and deviant. This is particularly the case if a number of the group members have been sober for extended periods of time and have been able to once again become responsible and functional individuals.

Part of the process of breaking down the initial resistance to admitting one is an alcoholic or problem drinker lies in the ability to emotionally understand that alcoholics are people, not some kind of subhuman species which exists on skid row. Unfortunately most actual alcoholics and problem drinkers maintain this stereotype, as does the general public. The group setting in this sense allows the addicted person the opportunity to look at himself, his behaviors and subsequently the freedom to say "I have a problem with alcohol." Within the group, the alcoholic or problem drinker constantly sees a part of himself within every other group member. This aspect of the social reality of the group experience cannot be underestimated as a potential source of growth and change. Group psychotherapy with the alcoholic population demands group members who have been sober for at least six months or more. This poses an initial problem with beginning groups; nonetheless it is my opinion that this is a crucial ingredient in successful group work with alcohol-addicted individuals. While it is difficult to explicitly determine how many group members need to meet this requirement, it is my feeling that the modeling effect of having individuals within the group who have been sober for extended periods of time is one of the most potent sources of strength for other group members. I suspect that for a group of ten, at least two of the members should meet this requirement of prolonged sobriety.

In this milieu the alcoholic is confronted with other human beings who have been through the same experiential hell, but have resolved their addiction. Seeing the positive changes in these sober individuals lives constantly reminds the struggling alcoholic that he too can change and experience the benefits of sobriety. He also learns that a good deal of his difficulty has to do with basic problems in living. Group members who have been sober for long intervals quickly make it known that, while things are much better with sobriety, the world does not change overnight. Living with the constant strains and anxieties of everyday life is a taxing effort, and many of these struggles will continue in the presence of sobriety. As many alcoholics expect their problems to dissipate with termination of their drinking, it is imperative that they be prepared to accept the fact that they must begin to come to grips with other interpersonal issues.

While the group experience offers a good deal of emotional support, an opportunity to learn to express and deal more effectively with the affective dimensions of behavior and the additional benefit of a social reality which includes fellow "drunks" who have been successful in the termination of their drinking behavior, it also provides an emotional climate in which individuals can be confronted with the pathological aspects of their behavior in a way which is conducive to both personal awareness and change. While most alcoholics and problem drinkers have believed themselves expert in the "art of deception," they quickly learn that the group readily sees through their manipulation and lack of honesty. Confrontation by fellow group members is often a means of letting the patient know that others care. Confrontation may also be an uncomfortable emotional experience. The issue of when to confront and to what degree is a very sensitive area and demands a good deal of therapist skill. Premature or overdoses of confrontative behavior can result in the patient fleeing from treatment. Effective confrontation with alcoholic patients in group therapy must be a constructive endeavor geared at enabling the patient to more realistically evaluate his own behavior. An essential ingredient of the process of confrontation must be the message that fellow group members have engaged in the same parataxic behaviors, that these behaviors were a part of their alcoholism and that the rationale for pointing out these distortions has to do with the fact that the group members are concerned and care about the individual they are confronting. Dealing with excuses for "slips" and general drinking behavior within the group is an excellent area for confrontation. The rationalizations, denial and distortion surrounding "slips" proves excellent grist for group confrontation. The group typically confronts members who regress to old patterns of drinking with the reality of their excuses for such regression.

Being made aware of group feelings toward individual members is another potent form of confrontation. This is the case regardless of the drinking issue. Letting people know how we feel about them, how we perceive them and that we are concerned about what happens to them constitutes a powerful affective confrontation. Alcoholics and problem drinkers are notoriously poor at handling these aspects of human behavior and interaction. The group experience provides an excellent interpersonal framework in which to learn these aspects of our own experiential being. In a related fashion, the group provides extensive reinforcement of specific as well as global patterns of social interaction and behavior. Positive feedback for continued sobriety, negative feedback for intoxication and similar patterns of reinforcement are but a part of the reinforcement paradigm inherent in the group psychotherapy process. It is imperative that the group leader or therapist be an active part of the process of group reinforcement of select behaviors. In this process value orientations and existential issues become an integral part of the group identity.

People who have had little experience with alcohol-addicted individuals often fail to appreciate the profound significance of a group of alcoholics simply getting together and relating on a sober basis. It is my feeling that any form of social interaction of a group nature which is non-drinking-oriented is extremely beneficial to the alcoholic's process of learning not to drink. The long-term problem drinker and alcoholic has played cards, fished, danced and engaged in other forms of group-oriented behavior under the influence of alcohol for twenty or thirty years. To be able to engage in these same social transactions while sober constitutes a potentially significant learning experience. It is my opinion that agencies attempting to provide rehabilitation services for the alcoholic and problem drinker must aside from providing traditional forms of therapy also provide ample opportunity for simple, group-oriented types of interaction such as cook-outs and fishing trips. Life is certainly not lived in a therapeutic vacuum! The group-oriented social nature of Alcoholics Anonymous is, in all probability, as much a part of this organization's success as any of the other aspects of the organization.

Earlier I noted that group size was relatively unimportant. This is related to my feeling that the alcoholic and problem drinker must learn more effective group-related behaviors which cannot take place in the absence of people. Group psychotherapy with alcohol-addicted individuals can be effectively conducted in groups as large as twenty or twenty-five. With larger groups it must be stressed that communication be directed at the group *in toto,* rather than small group side conversations. In working with larger groups the therapist or leader must establish this ground rule during the initial sessions and must continue to reinforce this rule as new members join the group or as necessary.

As is the case with individual therapy with alcohol-addicted individuals, group treatment should emphasize the here-and-now. Personnel involved in group therapy with alcoholic patients are cognizant of the tendency for sessions to move in the direction of "drink-a-logs" in which a good deal of the group focus becomes past-oriented accounts of drinking escapades. The therapist must actively structure the group therapy experience along the lines of present-oriented feelings and behavior. This by no means excludes dealing with past experience. The ongoing group therapy process must be oriented toward present material. In many respects a weekly group therapy experience becomes a mirror of the significant behaviors and interpersonal transactions of the individual group members for that week. It is also well to structure the group experience around the drinking issue. This usually proves to be the case without undue therapist intervention. However, groups comprised of a number of individuals who manifest a good deal of resistance toward the termination of their pathological drinking behaviors frequently avoid content related to their drinking behavior. Within such group settings the therapist must frequently assume a direct approach. Pointing out avoidance behaviors, interpretation and confrontation prove effective therapist techniques for handling such resistance. Dealing with the destructive nature of general drinking behavior often works well as a method of overcoming such resistance. Most alcoholics and problem drinkers understand that their addiction is a destructive process. The frequency of automobile accidents, bodily trauma and depressive episodes related to drinking behavior for this population is such a reality that most patients readily involve and relate themselves to these issues.

The group setting also proves conducive to the exploration of problem-solving behaviors. Within the group, members often share and work out solutions to practical problems which they are confronted with in the process of daily living. Many of these issues are far from recondite. Evaluating alternatives, the consequences of different choices of action and personal feelings regarding many aspects of decision making are all grist for the group process. Engaging in such behavior in a rational, sober fashion is an important step. In the past, most alcohol-addicted individuals have made major decisions regarding vocation, the family and other crucial matters while intoxicated or while under the influence of alcohol. In fact, a good deal of their lives have lacked planning and have generally been conducted on a haphazard basis. Being able to experience the benefits of adequate decision making helps reinforce the value and meaning of sobriety.

A good deal of the previously discussed approaches to group psychotherapy with alcohol-addicted individuals are contingent upon therapist or group leader behaviors. While therapist training and experience may be a function of any number of "schools" or orientations, it is essential that the therapist be able to help create a nonthreatening, emotionally warm climate, in which "therapy" can take place. I suspect this may be a significant barrier for select therapists, as a sizeable segment of the alcoholic population is openly antagonistic toward "shrinks" or behavioral scientists. The therapist must both be able to handle these initial and sometimes persistent feelings, as well as to eventually help resolve a significant amount of this resistance. The therapist in many respects is the example par excellence of an authority figure, and it is this very area in which many alcoholics and problem drinkers have experienced prolonged difficulty. The therapist or group leader must become a benevolent father who is trusted and loved. He must be able to support, confront and like his patients as well. At times the leader must be as much a part of the group as any other member; at other times he must assume the role of leader and expert. Being able to function in this manner demands a great deal. Therapists who are personally uncomfortable with alcoholic patients, therapists who basically dislike these individuals and therapists who function in a perfunctory manner are doomed to failure in their attempt to work with this clinical population. I personally suspect that a good deal of our overall avoidance as behavioral scientists or our dislike for treating alcoholics in the past has been related to feelings of discomfort and dislike for alcoholics. An additional factor may stem from our own borderline drinking patterns. At any rate, working with this population therapeutically demands a good deal from the therapist. It is unrealistic to expect all or the majority of personnel trained in group work to possess the necessary skills to work effectively with alcohol-addicted patients.

I have consistently found successful group therapy with alcohol-addicted individuals to be theme oriented. While themes may vary from session to session, and indeed some sessions may seem to be totally nontheme oriented, the ongoing successful group therapy process seems to revolve around three or four major themes. Foremost is the honesty theme. Initially through leader reinforcement and eventually by group members themselves, honesty within the group becomes a fundamental ground rule. It is openly acknowledged within the group that in the past a good deal of the individual patient's life revolved around manipulation and "con" games. Lying and deceitful behaviors are openly recognized as the alcoholic *modus operandi*. Being honest with oneself, as well as with significant others, becomes a goal toward which the alcoholic begins to strive within the group. Self-disclosure is very much a part of the process of learning to become basically honest.

Another theme of major importance has to do with getting sober for oneself. Every alcoholic and problem drinking has tried to "get sober" hundreds of times for the wife, kids or to salvage a job. Somehow this never works. Within a week, or at best within a matter of a few months, the individual finds himself drunk again. Having repeatedly experienced this process, group members strongly reinforce the idea of getting sober for oneself. After all, if the alcohol-addicted individual himself gains nothing from being sober, sobriety will be of short-lived duration. The group effectively teaches new members that they are responsible for their sobriety and that the only way to achieve prolonged sobriety is to get sober for themselves. I know many alcoholics who have been sober from three to fifteen years who will quickly let others know that their sobriety means more to them than anything else "on the face of this earth," including wife, children and significant others. "Until we can get sober for ourselves" is a major theme in group work with alcohol-addicted individuals.

Another theme has to do with "looking at ourselves." The case history of most alcoholics and problem drinkers includes a good deal of projection. Job losses, divorce and missed promotions have always been the result of someone else or extenuating circumstances rather than self-oriented. Within the group therapy experience patients learn to look at themselves. Most recognize that alcohol has been a part of their need to blame others. Themes dealing with self-destruction and the consequences of further intoxication are very much a part of ongoing group psychotherapy with alcohol-addicted patients. Reality operations are another matter dealt with extensively within the group context. The fact that group members are both sober themselves and concerned about the sobriety of other group members must be a consistent theme. This basic message includes love, human concern and a shared group identity. While these fundamental themes in no way exhaust the issue, it is felt that they are crucial ingredients within the context of the successful group psychotherapy enterprise with alcohol-addicted individuals.

Theoretical consideration of the group psychotherapy process usually includes the issue of open-closed group membership. As a matter of practicality most groups conducted within the confines of an alcoholic rehabilitation setting will be open ended. As new patients enter the rehabilitation facility they will be included in the ongoing group therapy program. Particular rehabilitation centers or given group therapists may choose the closed group model; however, for practical reasons, most therapy programs for alcohol-addicted individuals are of the open-ended variety. While a particular group may be open-ended, I would recommend limiting the percentage of new patients to 50 percent at most. As I noted earlier, the nucleus of the group should also include a number of patient models who have themselves been sober for extended periods of time (six months to a number of years of total sobriety).

This brings us to the issue of duration of group treatment. Certainly the debate over length of treatment, be it individual, group or any other treatment modality, has never been satisfactorily resolved. Freud (1951) initiated this question in his work "Analysis Terminable and Interminable," and it remains an issue of heated controversy today. Based upon clinical experience with alcohol-addicted patients in group treatment, it is my feeling that a minimum of six months of weekly group psychotherapy (one and one-half-hour sessions) is essential for the establishment of long-term sobriety. It is extremely difficult to make a statement such as this, realizing the tremendous diversity in patterns of consumption, personality and behavioral dynamics and other variables of significant differentiation within any given group of alcoholic individuals. Nonetheless, it is my experience that involvement less than this frequently proves inadequate in terms of maintaining the individual's sobriety, let alone initiating behavioral gain in other significant areas of the patient's process of daily living.

There does appear to be a small segment of the treatment population reaching the rehabilitation setting (perhaps 10%) which is capable of long-term sobriety with only minimal support and treatment. Four or five group sessions, in addition to periodic individual sessions, may be enough to keep such individuals totally sober. At the other end of the continuum, one is confronted with individuals who seem only to be able to remain sober through continued group attendance or A.A. involvement. This is particularly the case with certain active A.A. members who have perhaps attended meetings virtually every night of the week for as long as ten or fifteen years. Such is a rather florid example of switching compulsions. However, few would argue the comparative benefit of this change in compulsion. It should also be noted that a number of alcoholics who do achieve their sobriety through experience in group psychotherapy and A.A. of six months to a year do develop sufficient interpersonal skills to become effective change agents within the group context with other alcoholics. As a result of our lack of trained personnel in the area of alcoholic rehabilitation as well as other delimiting factors, I feel we should view the prolonged experience of group therapy as a potential training experience for select individuals. This form of training could potentially represent a significant future source of change agents relative to the problem of alcoholism and pathological drinking. Granted, such a training model would of necessity demand close supervision, evaluation and selection, and would in all probability involve a good deal of controversy.

Optimal behavior gain for the alcoholic patient is often a function of the inclusion of a separate group therapy program for the spouse. Although some of the spouses of alcohol-addicted patients are reluctant to enter a therapy group, usually as a result of feeling that the problem is not "theirs," many are eager to engage in this type of experience. This is especially the case in marriages which have not reached the crucial stages of becoming dysfunctional. Often the nonalcoholic spouse will readily become involved in the group therapy program as a means of keeping the marriage together. Indeed, many spouses are ready to attempt anything in order to keep the marriage intact. While this attitude may include a good deal of pathology, particularly in the realm of dependency needs, it is generally a favorable prognostic sign. Within the group therapy experience the nonalcoholic spouse can initially ventilate and explore feelings of frustration, depression and hostility. Frequently this initial "unloading" or catharsis proves extremely therapeutic, as the nonalcoholic spouse has been attempting to deal with these unresolved negative affects in a relatively unsuccessful manner for extended periods of time, perhaps as long as ten or twenty years.

As the spouse progressively becomes involved in the group therapy process she or he can begin to learn new ways of relating to the alcoholic which help foster sobriety. Learning how the nonalcoholic spouse has actually contributed to the patient's alcoholism is very much a part of the group therapy program. Needless to say, changing these patterns of marital interaction which have maintained or fostered the dependence upon alcohol becomes material for the process of group psychotherapy. Problems with self, the children and indeed the sum total of one's interpersonal experience may well be related to the development of pathological drinking. It is just this material which the nonalcoholic spouse can explore and learn to deal more effectively with by virtue of the group therapy experience.

In my experience most of these nondrinking spouses' groups are also tremendously supportive. This too may well become nontherapeutic at certain points. Again, as is the case in group psychotherapy with the alcoholic and problem drinker, therapist training and skills specific to the successful resolution of these parataxic distortions are essential. The nonalcoholic spouse who rejects the group therapy program may do so for a variety of reasons. It should be emphasized that successful treatment of the alcoholic patient does not dictate the involvement of the spouse in treatment. In marriages which have become dysfunctional, perhaps the best solution is divorce. This must be determined and worked through by both the therapist and patient within the confines of the therapy process. Marriages in which both parties are problem drinkers or alcohol addicted are not atypical. Moreover, blatant cases of the nonalcoholic spouse "arranging" for the husband or wife to remain intoxicated are not infrequently observed. These issues will be considered in subsequent chapters; however, these are often crucial issues which must be dealt with therapeutically. In accord with the rationale discussed earlier, these matters are often best handled within the context of group psychotherapy.

Another group-oriented treatment strategy found to be highly effective in rehabilitation work with the alcoholic and problem drinker is that of placing both the patient and spouse in an explicitly marital couples' group. While drinking behavior per se accounts for a good deal of the alcoholic's marital conflict, clinical experience indicates that significant marital adjustment problems of a more diffuse and pervasive nature underlie the fundamental marital relationship. This applies to both spouses. Involvement in the marital couples' group enables both patient and spouse the opportunity to begin to communicate and relate to one another more effectively. The alcoholic marriage appears to be predicated on both a lack of interpersonal communciation as well as distorted or essentially parataxic patterns of communication. It is not at all surprising to find couples who have lived together for as long as twenty years in the absence of effective relating and communicating. Within the couples' group, patient and spouse can begin to learn to relate upon a more healthy feeling level. Both parties can begin to recognize their particular patterns of interaction and relating which have served to maintain and reinforce the drinking, as well as other less than optimal marital behaviors. The essential sources of gain discussed earlier with regard to group therapy in general apply to the marital couples' group. Disclosing, sharing, dealing with the affective components of behavior and more effective decision making are but a few sources of gain. Support, social and interpersonal reality input, and realizing that other couples have experienced the same difficulties and have learned to deal with them in a more effective manner are but a few of the other potent sources of gain offered via the marital couples' group experience. Perhaps the most significant or crucial therapeutic contribution provided by the couples' group experience rests in the area of dealing with dependency needs, role-appropriate behavior and identity conflict. Both the alcoholic and spouse share a pathological dependency relationship which is at core based upon marked identity confusion. This situation becomes manifest via role reversal and general conflict regarding perceived role-appropriate behaviors. As was the case with general group psychotherapy and for basically the same reasons, I strongly advocate the inclusion of one or two couples in the marital couples' group who have for the most part been able to successfully resolve conflicts of this nature. I have found it advisable to limit the number of couples comprising such a group to ten at most. One and one-half to two-hour weekly sessions over a six-month period of time seems to provide excellent therapeutic gain. The marital couples' group functions most effectively when conducted on a closed basis — contracting with six to ten couples for the earlier noted time frame works quite well. The Al-Anon group approach is recommended for those spouses unwilling or for whatever other reasons unable to attend the marital couples' group. In fact, experience indicates that involvement in both of these group procedures simultaneously tends to accentuate and accelerate behavior change and growth. A cogent aspect of every "recovery" is that of involvement and commitment of a group nature (Forrest, 1976).

CONCLUDING REMARKS

Group psychotherapy is perhaps the single most effective treatment modality currently available for alcohol-addicted individuals. In this chapter we have discussed a number of the primary issues specific to this form of treatment. It was pointed out that the relearning of more appropriate social and interpersonal behaviors, support, confrontation and the human relatedness of the group therapy experience are central to the process of behavioral growth and change upon the part of the alcoholic or problem drinker. As many alcohol-addicted individuals have led an extended life-style devoid of satisfactory interpersonal relationships, it is felt the group experience provides an excellent environment in which to learn these badly needed skills. Learning to effectively relate to significant others demands the presence of people. The reality orientation of the group experience is of particular importance in working with alcohol-addicted individuals. Dealing with present-oriented behaviors and feelings is recommended. The problem-solving potential of the group experience was noted. A number of the primary themes felt to be central to successful group therapy experiences with alcohol-addicted individuals were explored. Finally, the beneficial nature of a group therapy program for the nonaddicted spouse was emphasized. This point will be strongly supported by those who view alcoholism as a family-oriented pathology.

Marital couples' therapy provides an excellent source of gain for both the alcoholic and spouse. Many of the facilitative conditions characteristic of group therapy in general apply to the marital couples' group experience. It is suggested that the marital couples' group be conducted on a closed basis. Learning more effective communication and relating behaviors, as well as dealing with inordinate dependency needs and identity conflict are suggested as focal points for the marital couples' group process.

Based upon clinical experience, a number of practical strategies were offered the reader as a means of enhancing the probability of maximizing therapeutic gain relative to the group psychotherapy program. The importance of including patient role models who have been sober for extended periods of time was pointed out. Successful group work with alcohol-addicted patients usually requires an ongoing experience of at least six months duration. The clinical experience of this author suggests that approximately 75 percent of a random group of individuals labeled "alcoholic" or problem drinkers can be expected to be successful in the resolution of their addiction with six months of one and one-half hour weekly group psychotherapeutic treatment. Therapist or group leader skills were also briefly considered. Perhaps the most crucial role of the group leader is that of helping provide a therapeutic atmosphere consistently characterized by high level facilitative conditions (Traux and Carkhuff, 1967).

This chapter includes a truncated consideration of many of the crucial issues relative to group psychotherapy with alcohol-addicted individuals. However, it is hoped the material provided in this chapter will provide the reader with sufficient parameters to begin to appreciate and more fully understand the process of group psychotherapy with this particular clinical population. Group therapy with people experiencing difficulty as a result of their drinking behavior can be a stimulating and challenging endeavor. It is also an often arduous and demanding task for all involved in the therapeutic process, yet group psychotherapy represents one of the very real methods by which select individuals can begin to function more effectively.

Chapter 8

TREATMENT III
ALCOHOLICS ANONYMOUS

ALCOHOLICS Anonymous has long ministered to the problem drinker and alcohol-addicted individual. In fact, many believe Alcoholics Anonymous to be the only means of achieving and maintaining prolonged sobriety for those experiencing marked difficulty as a result of their drinking behavior. This organization originated in Akron, Ohio, in 1935. A New York stockbroker and an Akron physician were responsible for the initiation of Alcoholics Anonymous. The late Dr. William D. Silkworth, a New York specialist in alcoholism, is also regarded as a paramount figure in the development of Alcoholics Anonymous. Following the Akron model a second group was formed in New York, followed with a third group in Cleveland during 1937. As the membership of A.A. continued to grow so did the number of members who were able to achieve substantial sobriety. By 1939 the membership had grown to approximately 100 men and women. With the publication of the book, *Alcoholics Anonymous,* in 1939, this previously nameless group began to be recognized as an organization of significant merit. It was at this point that the society was officially called Alcoholics Anonymous. During the early forties the clergy and political figures began to publicly acknowledge the existence and worth of A.A. Needless to say, Alcoholics Anonymous soon mushroomed into a national institution. By 1950 the impact of this organization had become so widely felt that a first International Conference was held at Cleveland. As of 1971 there were over 16,000 A.A. groups in over ninety countries with an estimated membership of more than 500,000. A fellowship-wide survey in June, 1968 indicated that 25 percent of the A.A. members in the U.S. and Canada were female. A.A. membership is increasing at the rate of approximately 7 percent a year.

Once embarked upon this process of growth and development, Alcoholics Anonymous discovered the principles by which the individual alcoholic could live. Principles by which A.A. groups and the entirety of A.A. could survive and function effectively were developed. Examples of these principles include the following: no alcoholic man or woman could be excluded from A.A.; leaders might serve but never govern; each group was to be autonomous and there was to be no professional therapy; there were to be no fees or dues; all members ought to be anonymous at the level of press, radio, TV and films; and under no circumstances should members give endorsements, make alliances or enter public controversy.

It is the sentiment of A.A. that much of the organization's success can be attributed to two reasons: the large numbers of recoveries and reunited homes. Reportedly 50 percent of the alcoholics who came to A.A. and made a concerted effort got sober at once and were able to retain their sobriety. Another 25 percent attained sobriety after a few relapses, and among the remainder, those who remained active with A.A. showed improvement. Alcoholics Anonymous does acknowledge that many who initially attend the program decide not to continue; however, two out of three eventually return to A.A. Certainly Alcoholics Anonymous has received continued support from the medical profession, the clergy, the press and a variety of other groups.

In order to provide the reader with a basic understanding of both the operation and structure of Alcoholics Anonymous, as well as a framework within which to appreciate the therapeutic nature of this organization, a good deal of material will be presented from the chapter on "How It Works" in the basic text for Alcoholics Anonymous.

HOW IT WORKS

Rarely have we seen a person fail who has thoroughly followed our path. Those who do not are people who cannot or will not completely give themselves to this simple program, usually men and women who are constitutionally incapable of being honest with themselves. There are such unfortunates. They are not at fault; they seem to have been born that way. They are naturally incapable of grasping and developing a manner of living which demands rigorous honesty. Their chances are less than average. There are those, too, who suffer from grave emotional and mental disorders, but many of them do recover if they have the capacity to be honest.

Our stories disclose in a general way what we used to be like, what happened and what we are like now. If you have decided you want what we have and are willing to go to any length to get it — then you are ready to take certain steps.

At some of these we balked. We thought we could find an easier, softer way. But we could not. With all the earnestness at our command, we beg of you to be fearless and thorough from the very start. Some of us have tried to hold on to our old ideas and the result was nil until we let go absolutely.

Remember that we deal with alcohol-cunning, baffling and powerful! Without help it is too much for us. But there is One who has all power — that One is God. May you find Him now.

Half measures availed us nothing. We stood at the turning point. We asked His protection and care with complete abandon.

Here are the steps we took which are *suggested as a program of recovery*. We:

(1) Admitted we were powerless over alcohol — that our lives had become unmanageable.

(2) Came to believe that a Power greater than ourselves could restore us to sanity.

(3) Made a decision to turn our will and our lives over to the care of God *as we understood Him.*

(4) Made a searching and fearless moral inventory of ourselves.

(5) Admitted to God, to ourselves and to another human being the exact nature of our wrongs.

(6) Were entirely ready to have God remove all these defects of character.

(7) Humbly asked Him to remove our shortcomings.

(8) Made a list of all persons we had harmed and became willing to make amends to them all.

(9) Made direct amends to such people wherever possible,

except when to do so would injure them or others.

(10) Continued to take personal inventory and when we were wrong promptly admitted it.

(11) Sought through prayer and meditation to improve our conscious contact with *God as we understood Him,* praying only for knowledge of His will for us and the power to carry that out.

(12) Having had a spiritual awakening as the result of these steps, we tried to carry this message to alcoholics and to practice it in all our affairs.

Many of us exclaimed, "What an order! I can't go through with it." Do not be discouraged. No one among us has been able to maintain anything like perfect adherence to these principles. We are not saints. The point is that we are willing to grow along spiritual lines. The principles we have set down are guides to progress. We claim spiritual progress rather than spiritual perfection.

Our description of the alcoholic, the chapter to the agnostic and our personal adventures before and after make clear three pertinent ideas:

(a) That we were alcoholic and could not manage our own lives.

(b) That probably no human power could have relieved our alcoholism.

(c) That God could and would if He were sought. (*Alcoholics Anonymous,* 1939)

As was noted earlier, these **TWELVE STEPS** constitute the suggested program of recovery. Indeed, these steps are the cornerstone of A.A. and in many respects the basis of the therapeutic nature of the organization. Upon joining A.A. the individual is confronted with a good deal of the reality he may have been attempting to deny for twenty or thirty years. Admitting that one is in fact an alcoholic (powerless over alcohol) is prerequisite to membership in A.A. Acknowledging that one's life has become unmanageable, that one's sanity is in question and turning to a higher power for help are all very much a part of beginning to deal with the reality of the individual alcoholic's experiential being. I suspect that the majority of those who are initially "turned off" by A.A. are those who experience difficulty accepting the religious flavor of the program. However, this aspect of the A.A. program also allows for a great deal of individuality, which may eventually provide the alcoholic with his first meaningful religious involvement. The realization that "God as we understand him" can include virtually limitless types and forms of religious involvement may be an extremely meaningful personal revelation for someone who has never "known" God. In accord with A.A. sentiment, this degree of religious flexibility in many respects actually negates the need for individual acceptance of any form of formal or structured religion.

A major source of therapeutic gain provided by A.A. is the identification of and continued struggle with certain character defects felt to be of particular significance to the alcoholic personality. These character defects include resentment, dishonesty, self-pity, jealousy, criticism, intolerance, fear and anger. In order that the reader may more clearly understand the meaning of these character defects, I will discuss a few of the defects as they appear in the A.A. publication, *The Little Red Book* (1957).

Resentment

Resentment is common to all alcoholics. We are never safe from it and as intangible as it may seem, it does pay off in material ways with destructive force and energy. Resentment is dynamite to the alcoholic.

In studying the book, *Alcoholics Anonymous*, we are reminded that "resentment is the Number One Offender." It destroys more alcoholics than anything else. From it stem all forms of spiritual disease, for we have not only been mentally and physically ill, we have been spiritually sick. Resentment is pure mental drunkenness. We must treat it mentally and spiritually to remain physically dry.

In dealing with resentments we set them on paper. We list people, institutions and principles with whom we were angry. We ask ourselves why we were angry. In most cases we found that our self-esteem, our pocketbooks, our relationships (including sex), our ambitions were hurt or threatened. So we were sore; we were burnt up.

Make up your grudge list; see whom you are enclosing in your circle of hatred; determine why you hold them there.

Has your life been any happier because of this resentment? Were they really the offenders?

The founders of Alcoholics Anonymous answer the question with the definite statement: "It is plain that a life which includes deep resentment leads only to futility and unhappiness. To the precise extent that we permit these, do we squander the hours that might have been worthwhile."

They explain that resentment dwarfs the maintenance and growth of spiritual experience which is the only hope of the alcoholic and that "without the sunlight of this experience the insanity of alcoholism returns and we drink again" (*The Little Red Book*, 1957).

Dishonesty

Those who do not recover through the help of our program are usually men and women who will not give themselves to the program and who are constitutionally incapable of being honest with themselves.

Dishonesty requires little further comment. It has no place in our program. It must be eliminated if we are to succeed at all.

Honesty with yourself, God and your fellow man is the keystone in the A.A. bridge that spans the alcoholic chasm to permanent, happy sobriety.

Without honesty the A.A. program would become an inconsistent, hypocritical way of life. It would become negative and antagonistic to recovery. The practice of dishonesty in any form helps to tear down the alcoholic's defense against that first drink which he will eventually find himself taking, if he cannot be honest with himself (*The Little Red Book*, 1957).

Fear

The tendency of alcoholics to discount fear as contributing to alcoholism often causes newcomers to underrate its importance to their inventories. They erroneously associate fear with cowardice and want no part of it. Yet fear had much to do with their drinking and full knowledge of it is essential to their recovery.

It is an emotion that has a definite place in the lives of all human beings. Primitive man could not have survived without it. Experience made him afraid of dangerous or destructive things against which he was powerless and fear then supplied the extra energy needed to avoid or escape them.

When used for actual purposes of self-preservation, fear gives us the caution and the discretion necessary to the requirements of everyday living. Fear prompts us to take safe procedures and to protect our families against poverty and disease. Under its impulse we gain energy to build houses, to work, to face reality and to assume responsibility.

As alcoholics we have used a few of fear's positive qualities but utilized mostly the negative ones, specializing to a great extent on anxiety, dread, worry, uncertainty and apprehension of harm or evil that always seemed just around the corner. Urged by fear of hangovers and alcoholic insomnia we hid liquor all over our homes. Fear of truth filled us with dread and uncertainty. Anxiety constantly beset our effort to conceal addiction, to uphold our lies, to dodge our creditors. Fear of domination, public opinion, loss of home and finances allowed no peace of mind.

The negative elements of fear belong in our inventories. Reference to paragraph 24, Chapter 5, of the A.A. book will give examples of fear in our lives and outline a way of classification. Part of our personality change centers around our understanding and treatment of this emotion.

The A.A. program is not founded upon fear. It is a spiritual "Way of Life" based on Power other than our own, on faith in a Power greater than ourselves to overcome fear and other defects of our alcoholic personalities. We have seen members try to find contented sobriety basing their attempt on self-education motivated by the fear of alcohol. They do not stay sober long. We have known them to try to protect themselves from drinking by total absence from bars and night clubs under the assumption that they would be sorely tempted by such environment. From their experience we believe that such abnormal worry indicates a half-hearted attempt at the program and is in reality an unacknowledged desire to drink again.

Our book, *Alcoholics Anonymous* states, "In our belief any scheme of combating alcoholism which proposes to shield the sick man from temptation is doomed to failure. If the alcoholic tries to shield himself, he may succeed for a time, but usually winds up with a bigger explosion than ever. We have tried these methods. These attempts to do the impossible have failed. So our rule is not to avoid a place where there is drinking if *we have a legitimate reason for being there.* Go or stay away, whatever seems best. But be sure you are on solid spiritual ground before you start and that your motive in going is thoroughly good.''

Being on spiritual ground is the important thing but we must not overlook the fact that we have a definite part to play. God can help us only if we are willing and trying to get well. Realization that temptation will always be present and that we never have successfully avoided it before should bring us close to God for help. We have no knowledge of how or when the urge to drink will come. We know that it will, however, and that we cannot wait until it is upon us. We must prepare ourselves with faith and prayer for our hours of need.

- Steps one and two suggest that we come to an understanding of all our alcoholic problems. We are never to forget our powerlessness over alcohol and the insane behavior and unmanageable living it brings. Nature backs up this theory with drunken dreams. Dreams that are so realistic they fill us with genuine remorse and further our determination to gain contented sobriety.

We must admit that we are alcoholic, it is good for us to do so. All members should strive to cultivate an honest realistic evaluation of what alcohol does to them as partial insurance against a possible return to drinking. This does not imply the use of fear but rather of intelligence to avoid further alcohol addiction. We are not afraid of alcohol. Alcohol can be all around us without harmful effect if our "spiritual ground" is right and we are on a twenty-four-hour practice of our philosophy. We should, however, be afraid to drink it, just as afraid of it as any other poison.

Thus we fortify our minds with prayer and with the mental resources God has given us. Intelligent use of mental portraits, based on knowledge of our alcoholic status, is invaluable to our recovery from alcoholism. We do not rebel against the fact we cannot drink or use poisons generally. Contented sobriety will come easier when we have learned to take alcohol out of the beverage classification and place it where it rightfully belongs for us — among the poisons.

Members who are unable to overcome their fear by practice of the A.A. program should consult their doctor or psychiatrist who will probably be able to help them. Such aid plus help from our program usually straightens them out and makes contented sobriety possible.

Fear that does not constitute an obsession can be corrected by the philosophy provided in our A.A. program. Fear is nothing more or less than a distorted faith in the negative things of life and the evils that might beset us.

A.A. philosophy does not concern itself with anxiety or fear. As alcoholics we were once unstable because of problems and anxieties that seemed impossible to remedy. The spiritual concepts of this program have removed them and have replaced them with peace of mind. We no longer worry; we have received a spiritual reprieve. This reprieve is extended from day to day by God in recognition of our appreciation of His help and the unselfish service we render to others.

Our antedote for fear is faith, not the distorted faith in fear, but rehabilitating all our faith in God as we understand Him. We have found this to be an effective measure in overcoming all fears the alcoholic is subjected to (*The Little Red Book*, 1957).

Dealing with the issues relative to these and the other A.A. character defects in effect means establishing a radically different lifestyle. Those familiar with the total A.A. program are aware of the global impact of this organization upon members who become abstinent and dedicated to the A.A. "Way of Life." Once actively engaged in the A.A. life-style, the individual continually looks at himself. Character defects are actively and vigorously explored, with an ever-present press to change. The A.A. member eventually finds himself unable to become intoxicated. Living the A.A. program is an experience so antithetical to the life-style of the "practicing" alcoholic that it becomes virtually impossible to drink while actively engaged in the program. Those who prematurely disengage themselves from the A.A. program eventually wind up intoxicated. Some feel that A.A. must be a lifelong experience. Usually these individuals are the ones who have on a number of occasions terminated their affiliation with A.A. only to find themselves drunk again. This is certainly an area of controversy. When is A.A. no longer needed? Can an alcoholic "recover," or return to the ranks of the so-called normal drinker? These issues will be discussed at length in the chapter on recovery. At this point they are mentioned in order that the reader might gain some insight into the complexity of many of the issues surrounding the totality of the problem of alcohol addiction.

THE FELLOWSHIP OF ALCOHOLICS ANONYMOUS

It is my clinical opinion that within A.A. the single most potent variable effecting behavior change along the lines of sobriety is that of human relatedness. The hallmark of the alcoholic is interpersonal anxiety. Becoming a chronic alcoholic means the termination of meaningful interpersonal relationships. This problem is a people-oriented problem. Alcoholics Anonymous provide an interpersonal environment in which the alcoholic can learn and relearn more effective patterns of interpersonal behavior. The emotional climate of A.A. is essentially one of total acceptance. Once the addicted individual has decided that he is an alcoholic and wants to actively do something about his alcoholism, he is accepted into the fellowship of A.A. Alcoholics Anonymous is a tremendously supportive organization. This acceptance and support means being treated as an equal. This in itself is of major significance as most alcoholics have a long developmental history of feelings of inferiority and inadequacy which have served to facilitate movement away from people and into the bottle. It is just the A.A. milieu which helps facilitate movement toward other people. Perhaps for the first time in years, if not the first time in his life, the alcoholic finds he has some friends. Once friendships and meaningful relationships with others begin to be established, the alcoholic or problem drinker finds himself learning and developing an entirely new range of social behaviors. Simple social behaviors such as fishing, playing cards and cook-outs with others take on increased meaning. Engaging in these as well as other social behaviors while sober constitutes a new learning experience for the long-term, alcohol-addicted patient. It is this type of sober experience which helps to reinforce more generalized, effective social and interpersonal behaviors. I have observed time and again the healing nature of this process of social engagement. Once the alcoholic begins to develop friendships within A.A. based upon a more healthy identity, to include sobriety, rather drastic personality changes become clearly evident. The seemingly sarcastic, unhappy, socially isolated individual may, within a period of two or three months, become a people-oriented, cheerful, helping type of person. Once this process begins to unfold, even those tangentially related to the alcoholic are readily cognizant of such change.

Alcoholics Anonymous is more than an organization. It is my feeling that the fellowship of A.A. includes a basic philosophical orientation which relates to the total life-style of the individual. Success in the resolution of one's alcohol addiction requires a total commitment to the A.A. program. The life-style inherent in "working" the A.A. program is antithetical to the many dynamisms which serve to maintain the process of alcohol addiction. Once embarked upon the A.A. program of daily living, the individual finds himself or herself experiencing a type of strength and serenity heretofore unknown. The development of personal esteem and positive feelings about the self begins to open new doors and broaden one's horizons to the point that the individual becomes capable of many behaviors which earlier constituted insurmountable tasks. In my experience with A.A. a significant degree of this form of personal growth has to do with an ever-increasing ability to help others. Indeed, this process has been central to the ongoing growth and success of Alcoholics Anonymous. As individuals become increasingly successful in the resolution of their own alcohol addiction and daily living problems, they often feel a need to assist others in whatever way they can. As a good part of this increased interpersonal effectiveness is directly related to the A.A. experience, it is only reasonable to expect that the "recovered" or "recovering" alcoholic should want to spread the message to others. In this respect helping other alcoholics may become an ongoing source of therapy for the formerly addicted person. This form of ongoing involvement within A.A. itself is extremely beneficial for many A.A. members who have been sober for as long as ten or twenty years. While some A.A. members may tend to "evangelize" in this regard, most tend to be much less outspoken. They are most definitely not out to "sober up the world" or in other ways preach the gospel of A.A. However, they are very quick to make it known that they do care about others caught in the trap of alcoholic dependency and that they will correspondingly do whatever is within their power to help those suffering individuals. This is exemplified by "Twelve-stepping." Those who sincerely want help are only a phone call away from an A.A. helper. Such calls lead to the eventual sobriety of thousands of people each year.

As an organization, the impact of Alcoholics Anonymous is felt upon the total family constellation rather than merely the addicted member of the family. This is in large part due to the Al-Anon and Alateen programs which are an active and integral part of the overall Alcoholics Anonymous organization. Al-Anon is a program for the spouse of the alcoholic. Within the Al-Anon group he or she receives a good deal of factual information and education about alcohol and alcoholism, finds an opportunity to ventilate and explore feelings within a context of support and understanding, and perhaps even more importantly is taught ways of relating to an alcoholic spouse which help to both resolve alcohol-related marital discord and extinguish his or her alcohol addiction. The social reengagement which Al-Anon offers the spouse of the alcoholic is tremendously important. As the spouse has become progressively addicted most spouses have disengaged themselves from meaningful interpersonal relationships. Feelings of guilt, embarrassment and social rejection frequently effect such social withdrawal. Most, if not all spouses of alcoholics become increasingly emotionally disturbed as they attempt to cope with the process of living with an alcoholic. Involvement with Al-Anon helps break up this growing circle of pathology.

The Alateen program is designed for the teenage children of

the alcoholic. While the younger children of the alcoholic may not cognitively understand (emotionally they do understand) the pathological patterns of alcohol-related family interaction, the teenager has reached the point of understanding the meaning of alcohol within the family. Adolescence for the boy or girl with an alcoholic parent often accentuates the normal process of rebellion, independence, resentment and other developmental changes apparent at this time. By this time feelings of hate and total lack of concern and respect may well predominate the teenager's attitude toward the alcoholic parent. I suspect that these very affective components may help initiate pathological drinking trends for many of the children of alcoholic parents who eventually become addicted themselves. At any rate, Alateen provides another means of helping reestablish more healthy patterns of family interaction. I also suspect that Alateen has some measure of preventive effect. Active and prolonged exposure to Alateen might eventually prove an effective change modality in the resolution of the "like father, like son" syndrome relative to problem drinking and chronic alcoholism.

It is apparent that total involvement with Alcoholics Anonymous can amount to a form of family treatment for alcoholism. I believe this to be the case. This form of treatment does work well for many alcoholics and the families of alcohol-addicted individuals. While heated debate may focus on the "treatment" nature of Alcoholics Anonymous, little question can be made of the fact that such "treatment" works and has worked for thousands of alcoholics and their families. Were this not the case, Alcoholics Anonymous would have become defunct long ago. It is imperative that comprehensive alcoholic rehabilitation programs include A.A. within their overall treatment milieu. Outpatient facilities should include community referral to local A.A. chapters. While many patients seen within such treatment-oriented facilities are initially reluctant to become involved with A.A., eventually most become aware of the potential gain which this organization has to offer. Indeed, many of those who initially resist engagement with A.A. eventually become the strongest supporters of this program. A.A. offers an excellent referral source within the community once the patient has completed whatever rehabilitation program with which he or she has come in contact.

CONCLUDING REMARKS

Alcoholics Anonymous is more than an organization of people who have decided to terminate their drinking behavior. Rather, A.A. represents a complete or nearly complete philosophical approach to the process of daily living. In many respects this organization is religious in nature. Living the A.A. life-style simply renders the individual incapable of drinking. While not developed as a form of treatment, A.A. has nonetheless significantly contributed to the ongoing sobriety of countless numbers of formerly hopeless alcoholics. Alcoholics Anonymous provides help for more than just the alcohol-addicted family member. The fellowship of A.A. includes separate programs for the spouse and children of the alcoholic. In actuality Alcoholics Anonymous is a family-oriented approach to the resolution of the problem of alcoholism and problem drinking. What is so strikingly profound about this organization is its simplicity and yet its success. A great deal of the benefit genetic to A.A. has to do with the human relatedness and acceptance of the organization. To A.A. members this is simply referred to as the "fellowship" of Alcoholics Anonymous. Professional personnel have been somewhat reluctant to acknowledge the therapeutic nature of this organization. It is my feeling that A.A. represents the example par excellence of a therapeutic community. Members share their common experiences in a manner which readily conveys to the "outsider" that personal concern and support are the *modus operandi* of A.A. Very often the only place certain individuals have to turn is A.A. A significant number of such unfortunates do attain their sobriety through learning to live the A.A. program. Alcoholics Anonymous is oriented toward personality growth and change, as well as learning self-acceptance. The A.A. serenity prayer exemplifies this attitude:

God grant me the Serenity to accept the things I cannot change
Courage to change the things I can
and Wisdom to know the difference.

Chapter 9

TREATMENT IV
RESIDENTIAL TREATMENT

IN essence, residential treatment refers to those treatment approaches which attempt to provide rehabilitation services for the alcohol-addicted individual on some form of inpatient basis. In many cases residential treatment may mean a brief period of hospitalization in which the patient is seen simply for detoxification. Patients requiring residental treatment along the lines of detoxification are typically quite sick, both medically and psychologically, and require immediate intervention. Individuals of this type display characteristics of excitement, manifested by ataxia, peripheral vasodilation, slurred speech and combativeness; or coma, which is manifested by vascular relaxation, fall of blood pressure, loss of reflexes, pallor and shallow respiration. At this stage the patient must be treated for withdrawal symptoms which include (a) delirium tremens, marked by constant tremor, vivid auditory and visual hallucinations and a general lack of reality orientation; (b) acute hallucinosis, marked by extreme auditory hallucinations; and (c) acute brain syndrome, marked by confusion, generalized psychomotor agitation ("shakes") and sensory impairment.

Presently a rather standardized treatment procedure is employed for cases involving detoxification. This procedure includes (a) polyvitamin therapy with a heavy concentration of Vitamin B; (b) intravenous and oral fluid ingestion to counteract dehydration; (c) psychotropic maintenance; and (d) the initiation of a high protein, high carbohydrate diet. This constitutes residential "treatment" for many alcoholics. While inpatient treatment for "drying out" is highly successful from the medical standpoint, it is notoriously unsuccessful as a measure for initiating and maintaining long-term sobriety. This has been recognized for forty years or more. Within many communities there exists a small segment of people who may receive such residential treatment for their alcoholism three or four times a year for any number of years. Although detoxification is for the most part unsuccessful as a measure for establishing and maintaining long-term sobriety, it does provide a means whereby countless numbers of alcoholics are simply kept alive. Without such medical intervention and treatment the number of annual alcohol-related fatalities might be increased as much as 15 percent. Residential treatment limited to the basic medical process of detoxification usually involves from one to two weeks of hospitalization and has very little to do with ongoing treatment for the problem of alcoholism. The patient who enters such a detoxification treatment program is usually brought for treatment by relatives or friends when in a state of complete physical and psychological deterioration. Unfortunately, serious motivation to terminate drinking is often not a part of this particular individual's makeup at this time. As a result, the patient is "detoxed" only to return to his or her pathological pattern of consumption within a matter of hours or days after release from the hospital.

A more comprehensive residential approach to the treatment of alcoholism and problem drinking involves both detoxification and short-term rehabilitation efforts directed more specifically at initiating long-term sobriety. This form of treatment is frequently provided by the psychiatric unit of the hospital or specific alcoholic rehabilitation services provided within state and federal psychiatrically oriented agencies. Once detoxification has been completed and the patient is medically cleared he begins a specific alcoholic rehabilitation program which has the explicit goal of initiating long-term sobriety. While these programs may vary considerably in length of treatment time, most involve from two weeks to two months of inresident treatment. Such programs also vary a good deal with regard to services provided, follow-up and overall treatment philosophy. At worst, such approaches amount to a period of confinement within a locked hospital ward where the patient is indoctrinated into A.A., forced to attend "group therapy" and whatever other "treatment" procedures which happen to be a part of the rehabilitation program. While such an approach may sound rather undemocratic and doomed to failure, one must realize that such measures may represent the only practical means of dealing with a particular segment of the gross alcoholic population. Those familiar with the Veterans Administration can surely appreciate this. At a more optimal level this approach means hospitalization in a private or semiprivate alcoholic rehabilitation center for a period of a month or two. Here the patient can probably come and go as desired, after a week or two on a closed ward. He will in all probability be exposed to A.A. on a voluntary basis and will also be involved in such other rehabilitation services as individual and group psychotherapy, marital counseling, and possibly Antabuse maintenance.

Obviously there is a good deal of program overlap between these two settings. The essential point of similarity lies in the extended duration of treatment with the specific rehabilitation goal of establishing long-term sobriety. Practical considerations render most hospital settings capable of only short-term detoxification; those settings providing detoxification and ongoing alcoholic rehabilitation services are state, government or privately operated. It should be noted that although the services provided by facilities geared more toward the ongoing rehabilitation of the alcoholic and problem drinker are basically the same, there are often significant differences of a more psychological and sociological nature which I suspect relate to treatment outcomes and program success or failure. The fact that one has been "committed" to a hospital for treatment of a psychiatric nature may be of significance from a number of perspectives. Forced treatment, as opposed to self-referral, remains an unclear issue with regard to treatment prognosis. It would appear that the majority of patients seen within most alcoholic rehabilitation centers of an inresident variety are overtly, if not covertly, "forced" into treatment.

At any rate, once the individual has completed the inresident treatment program he is hopefully referred to local A.A. programs, in addition to being encouraged to continue in outpatient therapy via the original hospitalization facility provided it offers such treatment. Patients may also continue with individual or group psychotherapy on a private basis. In the recent past, community mental health centers have provided excellent follow-up services for alcohol-addicted patients. If we have learned anything in the field of alcoholic rehabilitation, it would surely be that the successful treatment of most alcoholic patients is very much contingent upon adequate follow-up and ongoing treatment procedures.

A community-oriented approach to residential treatment which is currently in vogue is the "halfway house" model. This form of treatment for the alcoholic and problem drinker has received a good deal of attention both by professionals in the area of alcoholic rehabilitation and interested lay personnel. Partly as a result of the growing interest in the halfway house as a treatment modality, as well as other more pragmatic reasons, many communities have readily accepted the idea of maintaining the alcoholic within the community via the halfway house. Essentially, the halfway house provides a therapeutic atmosphere in which the patient can receive various forms of treatment during the evenings and weekends, while at the same time continuing to be vocationally functional during the day. This basic attempt at maintaining the patient within the community rather than hospitalization within the state hospital alcoholic ward or some other remote treatment setting is in accord with the community mental health philosophy. This approach stresses the importance of maintaining the patient within the community rather than isolating him within some pseudotherapeutic community, only to eventually face the social and interpersonal shock inherent in the process of reentry into the original setting from which he was removed. It has been recognized that this issue is of paramount importance in the successful rehabilitation of most psychiatric patients. How many psychiatric patients have been "successfully" treated within the confines of the hospital only to undergo a marked decompensation upon release? Frequently, readmission occurs shortly after the reentry into the family and community. Much of the therapeutic gain afforded by the halfway house setting has to do with the partial elimination of this social reentry trauma. Rather than progressing from the sheltered environment of a hospital setting to the "real world" in a matter of minutes or hours, the halfway house enables the patient to undergo a continual process of gradual reentry into society. Within such a setting the patient never loses complete contact with the ongoing social reality of his or her personal community. Such an arrangement reinforces the patient's movement in the direction of community engagement, while simultaneously helping to extinguish dependency needs focused around the therapeutic atmosphere of the halfway house.

Actual treatment within the halfway house is usually very similar to that provided by most ongoing inpatient programs. It has been noted that variability in treatment services offered is often determined by funding and other monetary factors. The typical halfway house setting involved in the process of rehabilitating the alcoholic and problem drinker provides some form of group therapy, at least limited individual therapy, an Alcoholics Anonymous program and hopefully some type of structured referral process for those patients requiring medical attention. Patient self-government programs have been central to the halfway house model. In many respects this type of program amounts to milieu therapy to include an occupational or vocational involvement eight hours a day. In this regard, many communities which have established successful ongoing treatment facilities, à la the halfway house model for the alcoholic and problem drinker have found that vocational rehabilitation services have often proved highly beneficial to the rehabilitation process. Another tremendous source of potential gain within the halfway house setting has to do with a spiritual emphasis. While this approach may not appeal to the majority of patients involved in treatment, it is my experience that a significant number of those patients who eventually recover do so explicitly as a result of their spiritual "awakening." This may become possible through their personal discovery of a "higher power"; it may be linked to a direct or specific spiritual experience or perhaps to the reestablishment of some type of religious commitment. The point is that spiritual measures, whatever, form they might happen to take, can be a source of inner strength for many individuals and as such are a potentially vital aspect of the halfway house milieu.

As is apparent from the discussion thus far, the halfway house approach to alcoholic rehabilitation is somewhat selective with regard to patient selection for the rehabilitation program. Most halfway houses providing rehabilitation for the alcoholic and problem drinker require the patient to maintain some type of vocational engagement in order to remain in the rehabilitation program. In short, this means the halfway house caters to the marginally functional patient. Patients with an extended history of unemployability, extreme apathy with regard to returning to the world of work or in whatever other capacity are unable to become at least minimally employed are felt to be unacceptable candidates for the halfway house. While some might feel this last statement might apply to most "alcoholics," it should be emphasized that although this may seemingly be the situation, in many instances nonetheless it is not the case in terms of potential. Excluding marked organic brain syndrome and extreme personal psychopathology, the vast majority of individuals labeled "alcoholic" or problem drinker do manifest significant vocational potential. Age is another factor which must be taken into account in this regard. It is the potential or probability for successful engagement in the world of work, as well as the resolution of one's addiction, that determines both acceptance and duration of treatment in many halfway house settings.

It should be noted that some professionals well versed in the field of alcoholic rehabilitation have advocated the development of what might be termed "three-quarter-way houses." In essence this approach seems to be based upon the assumption that a sizeable segment of the alcoholic population will never be capable of maintaining prolonged sobriety, let alone becoming vocationally functional in the absence of some form of ongoing, supportive environment. This being the case, it is advocated that such "three-quarter-way houses" be established within the community so that the alcoholic with limited rehabilitation potential might at least remain minimally engaged in the community. I can personally think of many cases in which this minimal goal seems to reflect a realistic assessment of rehabilitation potential. Uniformly this seems to be the case with older (fifty to sixty-five), extremely passive-dependent alcoholics who are either unmarried or who, for all practical purposes, have no family ties. Over and over again I have seen this type of individual attain sobriety and become vocationally functional upon entering the halfway house milieu, only to again fail on both of these accounts upon leaving the halfway house. Existentially I am of the opinion that these individuals as a group have very little to live for in the absence of some form of meaningful involvement in life. The halfway house seems to be capable of providing this meaning to the extent that the patient at least remains sober and functional; if indeed this is practically all we can provide should this not be our ultimate goal via the "three-quarter-way house"?

While these and other residential approaches to the treatment of the alcoholic and problem drinker may vary considerably from setting to setting, an essential point of similarity rests in the establishment of environmental control of the patient. Indeed, the degree of environmental control may approach the level of total control within such settings as the Veterans Administration locked ward. In many individual cases it seems as though this has become the only pragmatic means of deterring further deviant behavior precipitated by alcohol consumption. Within other settings this degree of environmental control is much less apparent. Certainly the alcoholic "receiving" treatment within a private psychiatric facility geared toward alcoholic rehabilitation has a much greater "say so" in the nature of his or her confinement. There can be little doubt that one's freedom in the sense of being an alcoholic or problem drinker in treatment is influenced by the type of residential setting in which one is receiving treatment. At some particular point in the drinking history of most alcoholics it becomes imperative that residential treatment be initiated. The type or form of residential treatment the patient receives will vary considerably from facility to facility. When this point has been reached society has very often become directly involved in the patient's alcoholism. It is at this·point that most individuals are officially "labeled" alcoholic, if they have not already been identified as such by family, friends and their immediate community.

Unfortunately, many alcohol-addicted individuals initiate a new "career" which frequently becomes permanent after the experience of extended residential "treatment." It is this "career" which I now wish to explore.

THE REVOLVING DOOR

Granted, residential treatment is both effective and needed as a treatment modality germane to the problem of alcohol addiction. However, residential treatment is not without its pitfalls. Experienced personnel in the field of alcoholic rehabilitation are all too familiar with that segment of patients who seem to initiate a new "career" upon experiencing residential treatment. This new "career" amounts to nothing more than becoming a long-term patient within the residential treatment facility. Finding the residential treatment facility to his or her liking, the patient simply makes a career of remaining in this environment. The dynamics of this process are easily enough understood: having a place to sleep and three meals a day, limited work demands, personal attention and a long list of similar variables amounts to a very potent dose of secondary gain. While this list may alienate or in other ways seem somewhat less than meaningful to those of us who have successfully met these basic needs, it is these very essentials which many alcoholics have lost in the process of becoming addicted. In fact, many of these individuals may have never experienced the security of knowing that they had a place to live, plenty to eat, etc. Once these needs are met or partially met there is a great deal of reinforcement to remain in the phenomenal field which has provided such "goodies." While conditioning conducive to remaining within the residential setting as long as possible may require a number of hospitalizations encompassing a prolonged time span for most patients, a surprising number of patients need only two or three conditioning trials to initiate their active movement in the direction of long-term hospitalization. Veterans Administration and state hospital personnel are well aware of this phenomenon.

What does all this eventually add up to with regard to the

effectiveness of the residential treatment approach to alcoholism and problem drinking? Unfortunately, such facilities often become caught up in the "revolving door" phenomenon, which in my opinion becomes a socially significant reinforcer of alcohol addiction. What this amounts to is a pattern of continual readmission to the residential center for detoxification and "rehabilitation." Many intact patients have a history of as many as ten to fifteen admissions to the same residential treatment facility for "rehabilitation" of their alcoholism. By "intact" I make reference to those patients who are physically and intellectually competent to the extent of being potential candidates for the labor force, etc. They simply could be successfully rehabilitated. These patients are not suffering from marked organic brain syndrome, they are not necessarily fifty or sixty years old, and they do not manifest significant medical complications. They are not psychotic or markedly sociopathic. Being aware of this process is certainly not a new thing for the behavioral scientist. While we have been most cognizant of this global process for a long time, we have nonetheless been extremely unsuccessful in the initiation and development of corrective alternatives. As is apparent, I have avoided the intrapersonal effect of this process upon the individual patient involved in the revolving door phenomenon. The basic understanding of why the individual patient becomes engaged in this "career" of being involved in residential treatment, and thus the revolving door process, is rather elementary. It would seem to me that the potential for modification of this process lies for the most part in the hands of those most responsible for shaping patients' behavior — those who control such residential programs. These individuals are responsible for program structure and development. It seems most apparent to me that these individuals must initiate new machinery, i.e. new therapeutic strategies, to more effectively deal with this self-reinforcing process of alcohol addiction. New or significantly modified reinforcement contingencies must be brought to bear on the career alcoholic or problem drinker. The revolving door must somehow be eliminated. The process of patient release this morning and subsequent intoxication this afternoon must be extinguished if we are to stop the revolving door.

By now the reader must be saying to himself, "I agree with all of this, but how are you going to bring about such change?" Unfortunately there is no definitive answer. However, some testable ideas and theoretical solutions will be offered as potential change contingencies. It is my feeling that the revolving door phenomenon and the role of the career alcoholic can be extinguished first and foremost vis-à-vis the residential treatment center itself. This is potentially the case regardless of the type of residential treatment facility, i.e. V.A., private alcoholic treatment center, state hospital, etc. Every effort must be made to assure continued involvement in some form of ongoing treatment once the patient leaves the residential treatment milieu. The alcoholic or problem drinker simply cannot remain abstinent in the absence of such ongoing therapy. At present, the only forms of ongoing therapy I know of, that will maintain patient sobriety are group or possibly individual psychotherapy, Alcoholics Anonymous or a firm religious commitment. Residential treatment staff should rely upon virtually any workable means possible to guarantee continued patient rehabilitation. Patients who, for all practical purposes, are legally forced into the residential setting for "alcoholic rehabilitation" can be likewise engaged in a behavioral contract to continue outpatient treatment once residential treatment is completed. Failure to continue outpatient treatment, whatever such treatment might be contracted to include, should result in some form of legal follow-up geared to "push" the patient in the direction of continued engagement in the rehabilitation process. This in particular should be consistently and strongly reinforced in the matter of multiple offenders, particularly those involved in auto accidents and other personal injury offenses. The family or possibly friends should be engaged in some form of contract to reinforce the patient's continued treatment. This may amount to seeing the entire family together weekly upon termination of the patient's residential status. Employers should be a part of this behavioral paradigm. The clergy should also be engaged as an additional source of reinforcement. What I am attempting to convey to the reader is that once the patient has completed whatever program of treatment the residential treatment center has to offer, the center staff should actively make effort to insure the patient's involvement in some form of ongoing treatment. The potential sources of ongoing treatment within the patient's community must also be actively engaged in the process of assuring the patient's involvement in such endeavors. While this may seem an arduous or impossible task, particularly for the larger residential treatment centers, I maintain that it is not. Granted the initial development of a proper machinery to guarantee such total push in the direction of continued patient treatment will be most difficult. Once this process becomes established and well developed it will prove most economical from all perspectives. This type of total push program might be the only measure capable of producing large-scale success rates for the general alcoholic and problem-drinking population. A fragmented approach to the treatment of alcoholism is doomed to failure. Punishment-oriented measures have a long history of dismal failure. Successful rehabilitation of the alcoholic patient must involve the totality of his or her living community. Every potential source of nondrinking reinforcement within the community becomes grist for rehabilitation purposes. However, it is the behavioral scientist engaged in the rehabilitation effort of the individual patient who must actively work to bring these contingencies to bear upon the process of extinguishing the patient's addiction. The general theme of this proposal is certainly not new or particularly innovative. It is felt to be an antidote to the revolving door, the alcoholic "career" and the generally poor results which "alcoholic rehabilitation" has historically provided.

CONCLUDING REMARKS

Residential treatment approaches to alcoholism and problem drinking are quite varied, both with regard to treatment measures and goals. In essence residential treatment refers to any inpatient program of rehabilitation. Relative to alcoholism this may include simple detoxification, or it may apply to any number of hospital environments which provide ongoing rehabilitation services for the alcoholic and problem drinker. Such is the case with the state psychiatric hospital, the Veterans Administration and the private alcoholic rehabilitation hospital. The half-way house and similar facilities providing partial inpatient services are viewed as residential treatment. While simple detoxification is usually felt to be of little benefit in the initiation and maintenance of long-term sobriety, such procedures do in fact keep many alcoholics alive. It should also be remembered on this account that sobriety must begin somewhere. Lack of both adequate follow-up and treatment of an ongoing nature are usually cited as causative factors in the overall lack of effectiveness of detoxification and other short-term, medically oriented measures directed at the alcoholic patient. Regardless of setting, residential treatment oriented toward the establishment of long-term sobriety usually includes individual and group psychotherapy of various sorts, an Alcoholics Anonymous program, family-oriented treatment and proper medical support. Marital couples' therapy, recreational therapy and other therapeutic adjuncts may be a part of the rehabilitation program.

The revolving door phenomenon and the "career" alcoholic were discussed briefly in this chapter. It is my opinion that, while residential treatment is essential in many cases, such facilities may often unwittingly become involved in a process of reinforcing patient-addictive behaviors. The career of "alcoholic" is most apparent in those cases of continual entering and leaving the residential treatment center. It is strongly suggested that this entire pathological process can be significantly altered by better coordination and regulation of services provided by residential treatment facilities. A large part of this responsibility rests in the hands of the program "controllers" or directors. This can only be accomplished through total community involvement. While most residential treatment centers purport to have adequate follow-up and community involvement, such has not been the case in my experience. Fragmentation seems to be the rule upon closer evaluation of services provided by most alcoholic rehabilitation centers. We must actively engage every potential source of gain within the patient's functional life space. Aside from engaging the various service agencies in a well-coordinated manner, we must involve family, friends, employers and other potentially significant contingencies of reinforcement.

Chapter 10

TREATMENT V
BEHAVIOR THERAPY*

$\mathbf{B}$EHAVIOR therapy techniques have recently received a good deal of attention in the treatment of alcohol addiction. While many of the principles of current behavior therapy models differ very little from the initial Pavlovian, Watsonian and Skinnerian approaches, the focus of a good deal of the recent clinical and experimental work with alcohol addiction has been along the lines of aversion therapy. Central to any behavior therapy model are the fundamental learning theory principles; positive and negative reinforcement, generalization, extinction, discrimination, avoidance, etc. In order to both understand and appreciate the complexity of behavior-oriented strategies of alcoholism treatment, it is imperative that one first be familiar with learning theory. This particular model of treatment is based upon an extensive body of experimental evidence derived largely from animal studies. The fundamental assumption of behavior therapy is that the patient, who was earlier well but now having developed pathological behavior, has "acquired" these new disturbed patterns of behavior. These new faulty behaviors are viewed as the result of learning. As these behaviors were learned, so can they be unlearned. In theory, the essential difference between behavior therapy strategies and the more traditional reward and punishment paradigms rests in the empirical knowledge, understanding and systematic application of such data in order to shape and modify behaviors in a more predictable and controlled fashion.

Meyer and Chesser (1970) state,

> the principle underlying treatment (aversion therapy) is the

---

*The Applied Social Learning Theory section of this chapter was contributed by J. H. Evans, Ph.D., and L. E. "Frank" Wellman, M.S.

creation of a conditioned aversion to the undesired habit either by applying a noxious stimulus when the act is performed or by pairing a noxious stimulus with the cues which usually evoke the behavior. The rationale of aversion treatment is that a conditioned anxiety response will become associated with the undesired behavior and its cues will lead to the establishment of an incompatible response.

In this chapter we shall discuss three primary forms of aversion therapy used in the treatment of alcoholism and problem drinking. Chemical, electrical and verbal forms of aversion therapy will be reviewed in addition to a brief discussion related to Antabuse maintenance. Applied social learning theory treatment strategies will also be considered.

CHEMICALLY BASED AVERSION THERAPY

Historically the emetic drugs, ematine and apomorphine, have been the most frequently used aversive stimuli. While recent research has concentrated upon aversive faradic stimulation and verbal aversion therapy, more patients have been treated by chemical aversion therapy than by other aversive methods. Stated very simply, the goal of chemical aversion treatment is the establishment of a conditioned aversion to alcohol ingestion through the pairing of drinking with drug-induced nausea and vomiting.

In one method the alcoholic is taken into a room in which there is a bar with bottles of liquor prominently displayed. He is given an injection of emetine hydrochloride (the emetic), pilocarpine (to induce sweating and salivation) and ephedrine (to prevent any dangerous fall in blood pressure). He is also given an oral dose of emetine in saline which is supposed to cause gastric irritation and to increase the quantity of fluid in the stomach to be regurgitated. When the patient starts to feel sick he is urged to smell and taste a selection of his favorite drink, particularly when the nausea reaches its height. A large vomiting bowl is provided. Aversion treatment sessions are usually given daily at first, followed by "booster" treatments at irregular intervals to try to prevent relapse. Between treatment sessions, the patient is encouraged to take soft drinks freely, so that discrimination between alcohol and nonalcoholic beverages is established.

Some therapists have used this procedure in the treatment of groups of alcoholic patients (Meyer and Chesser, 1970).

Lemere and Voegtlin (1950) conducted the most extensive chemical aversion program ever reported. Some 4,000 fee-paying patients received "conditioned reflex therapy" over a thirteen-year period. This investigation involved emetine and generally followed the earlier noted procedure. Patients received from four to six treatments over a mean period of ten days of hospitalization. Booster treatments were provided upon patient request and routinely six months after the initial program was begun. While this investigation included no control group, the authors report unspecified follow-up data to the effect of an overall abstinence rate of 51 percent. In spite of the lack of a control group and other design inadequacies, this overall outcome is most impressive when compared with other treatment modalities. Beaubraum (1967), using chemical aversion therapy and involvement with Alcoholics Anonymous, reports that 77 percent of the patients involved in this treatment regimen remained totally abstinent for a minimum of two years. These results suggest a synergistic interaction between emetic treatment and A.A., in addition to providing a relatively new research frontier. Miller, Dvorak and Turner (1960), Franks (1966), Bandura (1969) and Rachman and Teasdale (1969) report success in the use of chemical aversion therapy with alcohol-addicted patients. Miller, et al. (1960) report success in the application of chemical aversion therapy within a group therapy context. Rachman and Teasdale (1969) indicate that sound chemical aversion treatment results in one-year abstinence for 60 percent of those treated.

While these figures are most impressive, it must be emphasized that the experimental basis for such data has been less than sound. Inadequate follow-up, lack of control groups and variable interaction are but a few of the major flaws evident in the literature relative to chemical aversion treatment. Moreover, Rachman and Teasdale (1969) have noted a number of practical as well as theoretical difficulties involved in the process of chemical aversion therapy. Practical issues include the extremely unpleasant nature of chemical aversion treatment, which may precipitate staff ambivalence to the program, in addition to patient resistance. As a result of the need for close support, possibly including medical personnel and the need for highly trained supervision, chemical aversion therapy is for the most part not a feasible outpatient treatment modality. Individual differences with regard to the speed and extent of drug reactions render the process of conditioning difficult to control. These factors have served to limit the use of chemical aversion therapy within most alcoholic rehabilitation settings.

AVERSION THERAPY BASED ON ELECTRIC SHOCK (NOXIOUS FARADIC STIMULATION)

Rachman and Teasdale (1969) indicate that few studies of the effects of aversive shock treatment with alcohol-addicted patients have been reported. An early report by Razran (1934) in which subjects received strong shock to both hands upon being presented with the sight, smell and taste of alcoholic beverages resulted in a 70 percent abstinence rate for periods ranging from three weeks to twenty months after treatment. Only three of ten control subjects employed in this investigation remained sober for longer than ten days. The recommended shock device should apply to relatively high voltage (85-150 volts), and deliver a very low constant current of 0.005 amps or less (Fried, 1967). Typically, discomfort and pain threshold levels for electrical stimulation are determined prior to each treatment session. Intensities between these thresholds are employed as the noxious stimulus. McCance and McCance (1969), in an experimental evaluation of aversive shock treatment, delivered shock to the patient's hand as he sniffed his favorite alcoholic beverage. The experimental procedure employed in this study involved sitting down to drink, smelling it and presumably anticipating its consumption. This procedure was repeated five times during each of twenty-four treatment sessions which were conducted within a six-week time interval. The aversion treatment procedure was compared with biweekly group psychotherapy effect. McCance and McCance (1969) concluded that no differences were found between the results of group psychotherapy and aversive shock therapy in follow-up studies conducted at six- and twelve-month intervals.

Vogler, Lunde, Johnson and Martin (1970) in an experimental investigation of electrical aversion treatment in which shock termination was contingent upon spitting out alcoholic beverages, provided weak support of the effectiveness of this treatment modality in the resolution of alcoholism. It is well to note that this particular investigation was conducted according to rigorous experimental design. Davison (1972) recently paired shock with alcohol delivery until the patient terminated responding for the alcohol. Although over 30 percent of the sample originally employed in the investigation failed to complete the research project, Davison reported that five of the fifteen patients completing treatment were successfully rehabilitated. In addition to successful vocational employment, three of the five were abstinent during the year following treatment and the other two were reportedly controlled social drinkers. Blake (1965, 1967), employing a similar conditioning procedure, reported results much in accord with those of Davison. However, the over-all experimental design of Blake's study renders it not amenable to clear interpretation.

It has been suggested that electric shock may prove a more useful and practical method of aversive treatment for alcoholism than other aversive techniques (Rachman and Teasdale, 1969b). As was pointed out earlier, precise temporal control is virtually impossible to achieve in most chemically oriented aversive strategies. This is not at all the case with aversive faradic treatment. Furthermore, intensity adjustment is easily regulated according to individual differences. Aversive faradic treatment is not arduous; in addition, the number of conditioning trials per session is not limited. As the electrical procedure does not demand drug administration and close medical supervision, the program can be administered by a trained technician.

In contrast to the practicality of the aversive faradic treatment modality, its lack of effectiveness in the case of alcoholism and problem drinking renders it a questionable rehabilitation procedure. Elkins (1973) succinctly makes this point in a recent article on aversion therapy in the treatment of alcoholism: "Considered as a whole, clinical and experimental attempts to modify alcoholism through aversion therapy based on shock have produced disappointing results . . . available information provides little support for clinical applications of currently existing shock procedures to alcoholism treatment."

VERBAL AVERSION THERAPY
OR COVERT SENSITIZATION

It is apparent from the discussion of aversion strategies presented thus far that these particular forms of behavior therapy are questionable forms of treatment for the problem of alcoholism. This general skepticism applies to treatment procedures as well as outcomes. While some authors have suggested further research of a more rigorous design as perhaps the solution to this dilemma, others have been less optimistic about aversive behavioral methods and have even questioned the value of continued clinical and experimental application of these techniques. A recent innovative rebuttal to such skeptics of the aversive procedures has been the development and experimentation with verbal aversion techniques. This approach has also been designated as "covert sensitization." Essentially, verbal aversion therapy attempts to induce nausea by verbal suggestions rather than through chemically or electrically induced methods. Needless to say, verbal induction of nausea eliminates many of the practical problems associated with the other aversion therapy methods. For this reason Rachman and Teasdale (1969), as well as other authors, have recommended the verbal strategy of aversion therapy as a promising alternative. Cautela (1970) has described the procedure of covert sensitization in an explicit manner. The goal of this strategy is the establishment of a conditioned aversion to alcohol whereby nausea is induced by simply thinking about drinking. The extinction of feelings of nausea is contingent upon rejecting the alcoholic beverage. Cautela (1970) initially determines the patient's preferred drink and drinking habitat. After teaching the patient deep muscle relaxation à la Wolpe (1958), he is told to imagine that he is about to drink his favorite beverage in his typical drinking environment, becomes nauseous and vomits. This behavioral sequel is totally contingent upon verbal induction. Nausea can be produced in a few trials and is felt to be essential to successful treatment. This procedure also involves ten scenes pairing the intention to drink with vomiting. These ten scenes are then alternated with ten relief scenes in which the patient imagines the desire to drink, becomes mildly nauseous and then decides not to drink, which facilitates an immediate extinction of the feelings of sickness. Cautela (1970) teaches his patients to practice this procedure on their own twice daily. It is of significance to note that this author feels that the successful resolution of alcohol addiction dictates some six to twelve months and requires multiple treatment techniques.

It is well to point out that while "covert sensitization" is a verbal aversion technique, it is somewhat different from the verbal aversion therapy per se of Anant (1967). In addition to Anant's stages of treatment, his method of treatment differs from that of Cautela (1970) in that the relaxed patient is initially told to imagine the actual consumption of an alcoholic beverage. At a second stage the patient imagines vomiting upon himself, a girlfriend or within some other strongly emotional context. During the third stage the patient no longer imagines actual drinking but rather imagines that the smell of alcohol makes him sick. In the fourth stage the imaginary alcohol is omitted. The final stage involves learning to differentiate between alcoholic beverages and soda. While these stages seem to be marginally defined, the author does note that each stage of treatment involves only one or two sessions. Inasmuch as these differences may appear to be rather erudite to those not well versed in learning theory and clinical behavior therapy, it is well to emphasize that such differences may be of major significance in therapeutic outcome. Only continued research in this newly developed treatment modality will provide us with data relative to issues such as these. As could also be expected, the relative effectiveness of verbal aversion treatment methods remains to be seen. The newness of the technique has not rendered it subject for extensive evaluation. Anant (1968) has reported individual and group aversion therapy research as well as follow-up data on a small sample of alcoholic patients.

While his rates of abstinence were high, his lack of a control group and other flaws of design render his overall research difficult to accurately evaluate. Nonetheless, a number of investigators seem to be enthusiastic about the potential treatment value of the covert sensitization and verbal approaches to aversion therapy with alcohol-addicted patients (Rohan, 1970; Elkins, 1973).

ANTABUSE TREATMENT

An effective alcohol-antagonizing treatment modality is Antabuse (disulfiram) maintenance. Antabuse treatment was first introduced in 1948 and has since enjoyed a rather widespread use, including general hospitals, alcoholic treatment centers, psychiatric facilities involved in the treatment of alcoholism and problem drinking. The actual basis for this approach lies in the process of having the alcoholic ingest a drug which, combined with alcohol, will precipitate an extremely adverse physiological and psychological reaction. The patient, knowing the consequences of alcohol consumption while taking the drug, will abstain from drinking to protect himself. Ingestion of alcohol while taking Antabuse produces extreme nausea, vomiting, fall in blood pressure, extreme headache, blurred vision and breathing difficulties. Prior to placing the patient on an Antabuse maintenance program a complete medical examination should be completed. Patients with cardiac or other significant medical problems are not acceptable candidates for Antabuse treatment (Cahill, 1972). Antabuse is effective for several (four to five) days after it has been taken daily for one week, thus maintaining sobriety for brief periods of time in the absence of daily consumption of the drug. The standard dosage schedule for Antabuse therapy consists of one tablet daily (0.5 gm) for five consecutive days followed by a daily 0.25 gm maintenance dose. There seems to be no medical time limit for Antabuse therapy; some patients have taken the daily maintenance dose for as long as twenty years without complication (Caster, 1978).

Research evaluating the effectiveness of Antabuse treatment

indicates success rates over a prolonged period of time to approximately 50 percent (Milt, 1969). It has been found that a significant number of patients do reestablish old drinking patterns upon termination of Antabuse therapy. Clinical experience indicates that when patients no longer receive enough reinforcement to remain sober, regardless of what that reinforcement might be, they quickly return to drinking. This is the case with Antabuse treatment. Holding pills under the tongue and self-induced vomiting to remove the Antabuse from the stomach are only a part of the alcoholic's behavioral repertoire designed to eliminate the effect of Antabuse maintenance. It has been hypothesized that the ritualistic nature of the Antabuse procedure meets specific needs of the obsessive-compulsive personality, and as such, patients with an accentuation of this particular character structure do quite well on the Antabuse program. It has also been a rather standard procedure for certain therapists to follow up the aversion treatment of alcoholism with Antabuse maintenance therapy.

Considerable lack of understanding surrounds Antabuse treatment. Patients often come to the alcoholic rehabilitation center wanting a prescription for "that pill that takes away the urge to drink." The public has heard so much about the pill that "stops you from drinking." While there is some truth to such ideation, in many respects such notions are grossly distorted. Presently we have no "magic." Antabuse does not take away the desire to drink; it simply reminds the patient of the consequences of further drinking. In this respect it has been emphasized that Antabuse treatment is doomed to failure in the absence of auxiliary therapy and support, proper follow-up and similar "control" measures.

APPLIED SOCIAL LEARNING THEORY

There exists today a rehabilitation approach for the treatment of alcohol abuse that is based upon the emperical findings of social learning theory. Although learning theory techniques have existed and have been demonstrated to be efficacious over the past thirty years, these procedures are familiar to and accepted by only a small number of workers in the field today. This section includes a discussion of the basic principles of the learning theory approach, general therapeutic techniques, and a detailed discussion of some specific therapeutic techniques.

In order to understand the applied social learning theory approach, it is necessary to operationally define learning. Hilgard and Bower (1966) define learning as "The process by which an activity originates or is changed through reacting to an encountered situation, provided that the characteristics of the change in activity cannot be explained on the basis of active response tendencies, maturation or temporary states of the organism (e.g. fatigue, anxiety, etc.)." A more easily understood definition of learning is provided by Coleman (1976) who defines it as the "modification of behavior as a consequence of experience."

Thus, a treatment approach based on learning principles views "behaviors that may be detrimental to the individual or that depart widely from accepted social and ethical norms, not as manifestations of an underlying pathology, but as ways which the person has learned of coping with environmental and self-imposed demands" (Bandura, 1969). When discussing the learning of behaviors, it is important to understand that learning takes many forms and often occurs in uncontrolled situations. Learning normally takes place within one of two basic paradigms. These paradigms are the classical conditioning model based upon the work of Pavlov and Watson, and the operant or respondent conditioning model, based upon the work of Thorndike and Skinner.

Classical conditioning is concerned with learning based upon conditioned reflexes. In this paradigm a neutral stimulus is paired with an unconditioned stimulus that elicits an unconditioned response. After numerous pairings of the neutral stimulus and the unconditioned stimulus, the neutral stimulus alone comes to elicit the unconditioned response. The neutral stimulus is then called a conditioned stimulus and the response is called a conditioned response. Thus, the focus is on what precedes the response in the environment.

The second basic model of learning asserts that learning

takes place as a result of behaviors or behavioral patterns being reinforced. This model holds that if an organism acts in a certain manner and as that act is reinforced, it is likely that the rate of behavior will be modified. Therefore, the focus is on what follows the response in the environment. The types of reinforcement vary from the addition of something pleasant (giving food, money, praise, etc.) to the removal of an adverse situation (discontinuing an electrical shock, removing the threat of harm, alleviating anxiety, etc.) and to the addition of an aversive stimulus (spanking a child, receiving a traffic ticket, etc.). A behavioral counseling approach applies both types of learning to the counseling situation. The methods of therapy may be based on either of the two described models or on a combination of both.

Applied social learning theory makes three primary assumptions regarding deviant behavior: (1) all voluntary behavior is learned, (2) since behavior is learned, it can be "unlearned" or extinguished, and (3) the problem area is the maladaptive behavior (Wellman, 1977).

The first assumption that all voluntary behavior is learned is central to an applied social learning theory approach. Individuals throughout their lives learn both appropriate (normal) and inappropriate (maladaptive) behaviors that help them deal with their environment. There is no definitive answer as to how early learning begins, but it has been demonstrated that a fetus *in utero* has been taught to respond to a tactile stimulation of the mother's abdomen (Spelt, 1948). It has also been demonstrated that an organism can learn to control a number of autonomic behaviors such as rate of heartbeat, constriction of blood vessels, respiration rate, etc.

The second basic assumption of an applied social learning theory approach states that since behavior is learned, it can be "unlearned" or extinguished. It then follows that if an individual is experiencing difficulty due to some maladaptive behavior, e.g. relieving anxiety by drinking alcohol, it is possible to eliminate the problem area by eliminating the problematic behavior. It is important to note, however, that the maladaptive behavior that is unlearned or extinguished should be replaced with a more socially acceptable behavior. For example, an alcoholic could be taught to use relaxation techniques to reduce the anxiety. (More discussion of this assertion will be included in the section on therapy techniques.)

The third assumption regarding an applied social learning theory approach is that the maladaptive behavior is the *primary* problem area to be dealt with in the counseling situation. This model of therapy does not view maladaptive behavior as being a manifestation of a deep underlying emotional problem. It views maladaptive behavior as learned responses and nothing more. A behavioral therapy approach thus does not utilize the medical model or "disease" concept of behavioral problems (Evans, 1977).

Application of Learning Theory Approaches

A learning theory approach to treating the alcohol abuser offers many advantages over the more traditional and dynamic treatment modalities. Some of the advantages of the behavioral techniques are discussed by Franks (1967), who thinks behavioral approaches are more efficacious because (1) behavior therapy is more practical as the effectiveness may be greater and the duration of treatment shorter and more goal directed; (2) behavior therapy can be carried out by a trained technician, leaving the professional free to concentrate on overall strategy and preparation of new procedures; (3) behavior therapy is appropriate for all individuals, not just the verbal, intelligent and educated members of society; (4) clients can work with any technician; there does not have to be the establishment of rapport; and (5) the methods are empirically demonstrated to be efficacious, and reliable statistical data can be maintained through treatment.

In addition to the advantages listed above, behavior therapy enables the client to play an active role in his therapeutic process. He learns about the processes of learning in his life, and he is taught techniques that help him control his environment. He is able to see progress very soon in therapy, and this progress in itself becomes reinforcing to the client.

General Treatment

An applied social learning theory approach asserts that the treatment of alcoholism consists of two primary goals: (1) the alleviation of the drinking and (2) the increase of socially acceptable alternative activities. The first three steps used to accomplish these goals by the therapist and client are (1) the definition of situations in which drinking occurs; (2) the definition of conditions which make for socially acceptable and unacceptable drinking behaviors; and (3) the specific conditions leading to an increase of socially acceptable behaviors (Ullman and Krasner, 1969).

If an individual has an alcohol problem it is necessary to delineate exactly the situations and conditions that lead to the drinking behaviors. The therapist will seek to learn from the client the places he prefers to drink, i.e. at home, in a bar, etc.; the therapist will also attempt to ascertain whether the client prefers to drink alone or with other individuals, what he drinks (beer, wine, whiskey, etc.), whether he mixes his drinks and what conditions normally precipitate his drinking. Factors that preceded a drinking episode are extremely important as they may give the therapist clues as to how to approach the treatment of the client. For example, if the client tends to drink excessively after having a fight with his wife, the therapist will include as a part of the therapeutic program some training relative to more appropriate ways of dealing with this particular type of situation. What is often found is that any stress-producing situation may lead to a drinking episode, and a primary focus of most treatment will be in the areas of anxiety reduction and stress management. (This is covered in the sections on relaxation and assertive training.)

One of the problems faced by counselors who work with alcohol-dependent individuals is the widespread use of alcohol in our society today. Adults in this society are conditioned to drink and are often ostracized if they do not drink. It therefore becomes one of the goals of the therapy session to either help the client learn how to appropriately participate in drinking or to teach him to be a nondrinker in a drinking society. This last goal is the one most often used by the behavior therapists as it is very hard for an individual who has a severe alcohol problem to learn appropriate drinking behaviors.

Contracting

One of the general techniques that is used by behavioral counselors is that of contracting with the client. During the initial session with the client, the counselor and client together discuss the goals and duration of the therapy and will enter into a contract surrounding these areas. The conditions of the contract are very explicit and usually will contain provisions for the termination of therapy by either the counselor or the client. The contract will also delineate exactly what is expected of the counselor and the client.

DURATION OF TREATMENT. A typical contract between the counselor and client will include a time limit for the therapy process, e.g. the contract may state that therapy will last for twelve, one-hour sessions. At the end of the twelve sessions, the therapy is evaluated by the therapist and client, and the therapeutic relationship is severed. However, many counselors like to include an option in the contract that will allow the therapy to continue if both the client and therapist think it would be beneficial. If this option is included, at the end of the original contract, the therapy is evaluated and a decision is reached as to whether or not to continue. If continued, a specific number of sessions will be agreed upon by the therapist and the client.

The advantage of being very specific as to the duration of the treatment is that it lets the client know exactly what to expect in terms of time in treatment. It also has a secondary advantage of often encouraging a client to work harder in therapy as he knows that he has a limited time to take advantage of therapy.

GOALS. Included in the treatment contract is an explicit listing of the goals of therapy. The goals are normally expressed in the form of target behaviors as opposed to very general statements; e.g. one goal may be for the client to go from drinking a case of beer a night to drinking only a total of six beers each week.

Normally in dealing with the alcohol abuser, one of the goals will deal directly with his drinking. There will also be other target behaviors that will be worked on as they contribute to the drinking behaviors. For example, an individual may drink excessively after having an argument with his wife. The target behavior may be for the client to substitute relaxing (through progressive relaxation techniques) for his usual drinking behaviors, or to learn to assert himself with his wife so that anxiety is minimized. It is not unusual for a contract to include five or six goals to be worked on during the therapy sessions.

TERMINATION OF CONTRACT. One other area that is normally outlined in the treatment contract is the provision for premature termination of the contract by either the therapist or the client. The termination option is usually very specific as to what behaviors will constitute a breach of the contract, and the contract may be terminated by either party. One condition included in all contracts is that the client will not be intoxicated or under the influence of alcohol when he comes for treatment. If a client violates this condition twice, therapy is terminated. The therapist may consider negotiating a new contract if the client expresses an interest at a later date to reenter treatment.

HOMEWORK ASSIGNMENTS. Another condition of the contract may be that the client will complete any homework assignments agreed upon by the client and therapist. Homework assignments are an integral part of a behavioral treatment approach. By the proper use of homework assignments, the therapist can help the client to experience new ways of controlling his environment.

Some behavioral therapists believe that the most important part of therapy takes place between the therapy sessions, and homework assignments help to encourage progress between sessions. Noncompletion of homework assignments is another valid reason for premature termination of therapy.

Specific Techniques

In addition to the aversive treatment models presented earlier, there are many applied social learning theory approaches that are effective in dealing with alcohol abuse. In this section, there will be a discussion of models of relaxation training, assertive training, prosocial modeling and multimodality approaches.

Relaxation

Analogue research indicates that alcohol is a general depressant acting both on the peripheral and central nervous systems (Horsey and Akert, 1953). Masserman, Jacques and Nicholson (1945) demonstrated that alcohol decreases the chance of cats developing experimental neurosis when subjected to conflicting fear and hunger motivation. In 1956, Conger advanced the knowledge of Masserman et al. by demonstrating that an injection of alcohol into animals served to resolve a simple approach-avoidance conflict while controlled animals continued to hesitate in approaching the feeding box where they had previously received an electrical shock. Conger concluded that the resolution of this conflict was produced by a reduction of the fear response rather than a heightening of the approach response.

"At the human level," the first effect of alcohol on the brain is usually the anaesthesia of the higher centers. These centers inhibit and control behavior; thus, their narcotization results in a pharmacological depression of the drinker's tension and anxieties. Above all, alcohol reduces or abolishes conditioned fear or anxiety responses (Lazarus, 1965). A theoretical application of the Dollard and Miller (1950) drive model uses the idea of anxiety reduction to explain the excessive ingestion of alcohol.

Conger (1951) states that the drinking response becomes habitual because it leads to a reduction in drive (anxiety). To the extent that alcohol reduces tension, worry and anxiety, it serves as a source of reward or reinforcement to the individual. Conger then argued that the differential reduction of fear is the crucial reinforcement which makes the learning of drinking responses so efficient. If we assume that drinking is learned because it is reinforced, then it would appear that one obvious exception would be the man whose drinking is, at least socially, more punishing than rewarding. However, two characteristics of the reinforcement would be considered here. The first characteristic is the immediacy of the reinforcement. *Immediate* reinforcements are more effective than delayed ones (Reynolds, 1968). The immediate reduction of anxiety more than compensates for any later socially administered punishment. The second reinforcement characteristic of importance is the amount of drive or its *magnitude*. The personal anxiety reducing effects of alcohol may, if the anxiety is great enough, constitute a greater magnitude of reinforcement than any competing social punishment.

Paul and Bernstein (1973) state that maladaptive behaviors are learned and maintained to alleviate or avoid inappropriate, conditioned anxiety reactions. These problem behaviors also involve escape and avoidance behaviors such as drug and alcohol abuse. Any habitual source of relief from anxiety may become excessive and maladaptive, particularly when multiple reinforcement is obtained.

Eysenck (1959) warned against the partial cures which might result should only the motor reactions (alcohol consumption) be extinguished and the historically earlier conditioned autonomic drive (anxiety) be ignored. The majority of alcoholics would appear to require treatment of the conditioned autonomic drive (anxiety) as well as their drinking behavior if relapses are to be avoided (Lazarus, 1965).

Thus, many of the established techniques designed to reduce physiological arousal (relaxation training, meditation, hypnosis and biofeedback) are appropriate tools for therapy if an individual patient's drinking and other maladaptive behaviors are secondary to or in fact are in any way potentiated by anxiety. The routine use of relaxation therapy techniques in a treatment regime also may serve as a positive introduction to psychotherapy, thus paving the way for the patient's acceptance of therapy, self-examination and ultimately significant changes in his behavior.

Assertive Training and Prosocial Modeling

The clinical rationale for teaching a problem drinker to express anger, to be able to give positive feedback, to learn to stand up for his own rights and to be able to confront others without anxiety is of obvious therapeutic value.

The often-overlooked family member who has socially withdrawn over a period of five to twenty years normally is not considered for assertive training. However, for these individuals the ability to express their feelings, to stand up for their own rights and to do so without anxiety often gives them the strength to make changes in their own behavior and to respond appropriately to their drinking family member. While the goals of assertive training are specific to the individual who is undergoing assertive training, the benefits to other members of the family are of importance.

Eysenck and Rachman (1965) stated in their review of aversion conditioning that sometimes it is not sufficient to eliminate only the unsuitable behavior; "The aim of aversion therapy should be twofold; we should attempt to generate satisfactory alternate forms of behavior." This necessity for generating alternate forms of behavior is not often encountered in the treatment of behavior disorders such as alcohol dependency. Wolpe (1952) states that assertive responses are used against anxieties arising out of the individual's immediate relationships with other individuals. The patient for whom assertive training is applicable has unadaptive anxiety response habits in interpersonal relationships, and the evocation of anxiety inhibits the expression of appropriate feelings and the performance of adaptive acts. The most common class of assertive responses invoked in a therapeutic regime is the expression of anger and resentment. The term *assertive behavior* is used to cover all socially acceptable expressions of personal rights and feelings (Wolpe, 1969).

While factor analytic studies have attempted to ascertain the factors leading to an individual's becoming an alcoholic, researchers have never agreed upon a set of characteristics of inability to express emotions adequately, high level of anxiety in interpersonal relationships, emotional immaturity and sex-role confusion have been popular factors reported in most ex post facto studies of alcoholic personality types (Clinebell, 1956). Catanzaro (1968), in discussing alcoholic personalities, describes part of their characteristics as follows: alcoholics find it very difficult to talk out their feelings, and therefore, "either hold them inside or explosively let them out in an argument or fight. His previous training has taught him to bottle up his feelings." These patients may be assisted in this regard by means of behavioral-reversal, a special form of modeling in which the patient's outward expression of resentment can be systematically released by enacting imagined interpersonal encounters (Lazarus, 1965).

Unfortunately (or fortunately), assertive behaviors are not the sum of all social behaviors necessary for an individual to be successful in his environment. Of general belief among therapists is the fact that individuals dependent upon alcohol often lack the basic social skills necessary to get what they need from their environment without harming themselves or others. Thus for many individual patients the need to learn new behaviors or social skills must accompany the modification of existing behaviors.

One of the fundamental means by which new responses are acquired and existing behaviors are modified entails modeling and vicarious processes (Bandura, 1969). Research (Bandura, 1969; Bandura and Walters, 1963) demonstrates that almost all learning phenomena resulting from direct experiences can occur on a vicarious basis as a result of observation of other individuals' behaviors and the consequences of that behavior. Bandura states that modeling procedures are ideally applicable for affecting the reduction of excessive fears and inhibitions and the social facilitation (acquisition) of interpersonal behavioral patterns (social skills). The use of videotape feedback for behavioral rehearsal and modeling of prosocial behaviors greatly enhances the acquisition of many of the behaviors necessary for positive interpersonal relationships.

Biofeedback

A recent treatment entry into the field of the addictions is that of biofeedback. Although the work published specific to the use of biofeedback and autogenic training in the treatment of alcohol and drug dependency is limited at this time, there do appear to be two distinct treatment applications to this complex set of behaviors. The majority of the work in this area (Green, 1973; Green, Green, and Walters, 1974; Kurtz, 1974; Gosling, 1975; and Steffen, 1975) utilizes some form of biofeedback (electromyograph (EMG), electroencephalograph (EEG), thermoster, etc. as a technique of enhancing relaxation procedures.

EEG, the recording of electric potential in various areas of the brain by means of electrodes placed on the scalp, is used to monitor brain wave activity in terms of different patterns (Alpha, Theta, Beta) which are believed to be correlated with states of relaxation. EMG, the recording of the electric potentials developed in muscles, is employed to monitor and give feedback specific to the level of physiological arousal in a patient. To the extent that the anxiety or physiological arousal is diminished, the more successful the biofeedback training is. Thus, if anxiety, or the unsuccessful control of excessive anxiety, is central to why an individual drinks excessively, then these techniques are direct approaches of training the patient to reduce and control anxiety which has lead to chemical abuse.

The other application of biofeedback techniques in the treatment of alcohol and drug dependency is to teach patients to naturally achieve alternate states of consciousness (Naitoh, 1973). The rationale for this intervention is based on the hypothesis that many individuals learn to, and continue to abuse substances because they get "high," or "mellow" or whatever. Based on the reinforcement characteristics, secondary to altered states of consciousness, it is not difficult to see a connection between use and immediate positive reinforcement. EEG is used in this approach with the treatment goal being to teach the patient to achieve through cognitive processes an alternate state, alpha, without the aid of substances.

At this time, the state of the science is such that no wealth of clinical data exists, which is empirically based, to support the indiscriminated broad application of biofeedback techniques. Although no evidence has been published that suggests the existence of contraindications or negative side effects as the direct result of the application of biofeedback techniques to an addicted population, caution should be exercised with these procedures. Application should be under the supervision of trained professionals.

Multimodality Approaches

In addition to the specific techniques already discussed, many therapists are developing behavioral approaches that incorporate several principles and techniques of applied social learning theory.

One such program has been developed at the New Jersey Neuropsychiatric Institute (Cheek and Mendelson, 1973). This program is different from other learning theory approaches such as aversive conditioning or token economies in that the treatment is geared toward teaching the client self-control and modification of behavior without the use of external control or rewards.

The program consists of two, ninety-minute group sessions per week over a four-week period. Each client also receives individual sessions to help in understanding how the program might be useful for him or her.

During the program, clients are taught seven basic behavioral techniques. The skill first learned is relaxation, and the clients are encouraged to practice this skill frequently. Each of the preceding sessions is then begun, with a relaxation exercise. The second technique utilized is desensitization aimed at helping the client reduce the anxiety of tension-producing situations. Third, the clients work on self-image training. In this session, clients are asked to imagine themselves in an anxious situation they can realistically expect to occur in the near future and then to visualize themselves handling it well and to think how they would look, act and feel after successfully handling the situation. The fourth skill the clients learn is termed *behavioral analysis*. Clients are instructed in the basic principles of learning theory, and playlets are used to illustrate the principles. The fifth technique is behavior control, where clients are taught how to apply the principles learned in the previous session to modify the behaviors of their spouses or close associates. Assertive training is the sixth skill learned, and clients are taught to be assertive without being offensive. Role playing is used in this session to help facilitate the learning process. The seventh and final skill clients learn is rational thinking. In this session, the focus is on common errors in thinking and techniques to overcome them. Some common thinking errors discussed are stereotyping, dichotomous reasoning and excessive reliance on other people's judgement.

There are two other unique aspects of this therapy program. The first is that all staff members involved in the program undergo the same type of group sessions as the clients, but the goals of the sessions are oriented toward staff problems. There are also two additional sessions for the staff, one focusing on the history of the program and the other giving instructions on how to set up and administer a behavior modification program. The second unique characteristic of this program is that there is extensive use of volunteers participating in the treatment sessions. The volunteers are not used as co-therapists or aides but as group leaders.

Another behavioral approach to the treatment of alcohol abuse is based on the work of Albert Ellis and his Rational Emotive Therapy (RET). According to this theory, the first step in changing the alcohol abuser's behavior is to focus on changing his distorted perceptions of himself and his environment. According to RET, it is not people or events in themselves that are upsetting, but rather the way in which the event is perceived by the individual (Ellis, 1961).

One program using RET in the treatment of alcohol abusers is the Problems of Daily Living Clinic at Sinai Hospital in Detroit, Michigan (Hindman, 1976). The focus of the treatment program is on changing the client's behavior by examining the cues which precipitate his heavy drinking. The clinic encourages changes in behavior as opposed to gaining insight into the underlying reasons for drinking. Clients are taught to analyze the cues that precipitate drinking and then to either develop a plan to avoid future problem situations or learning alternative behaviors if the situation cannot be avoided. By focusing on precipitating cues, clients learn to perform their own crisis intervention by properly dealing with situations that might otherwise lead to intoxication. The program at the clinic places a great deal of personal responsibility on the client. Each client is required to set three goals during the initial sessions, and a contract between therapist and client is developed. At the end of eight weeks, progress of the client is evaluated and treatment may either end, the goals may be changed or the client might be referred elsewhere. One unique aspect of this program is that it does not insist that total abstinence be a goal for every client. In the next and final portion of this chapter, a study that set controlled drinking as a primary goal will be discussed.

Individual Behavior Therapy for Alcoholics

The question of whether or not an alcoholic can relearn social drinking is a hot and volatile issue in the field today. In 1962, a great furor was raised when Davies reported that out of a population of ninety-three clients treated for alcoholism, seven clients resumed "normal" drinking on their own during the seven-to-eleven year follow-up period. This was the beginning of the heated debate that continues up to the present. Today there are numerous references indicating that some alcoholics can and do return to nonproblem drinking. Sobell and Sobell (1975) reported in their address to the American Psychological Association that they had collected seventy-one references documenting the possibility of controlled drinking.

In 1972, Patton State Hospital instituted a research project that was based on the principles of learning and had a goal of controlled drinking for selected subjects. The treatment sessions during the experiment dealt directly with the inappropriate behavior of excessive drinking and emphasized a subject learning alternative, more appropriate responses to stimulus conditions which had previously functioned as setting events for his heavy drinking. The treatment took into account the learning history of each individual patient, and treatment was specifically tailored to meet each patient's needs. The program was called Individual Behavior Therapy for Alcoholics (IBTA).

The experiment as reported by Sobell and Sobell (1972) included seventy male, voluntary, alcoholic inpatients. All seventy of the subjects met with the criteria to be classified as a Gamma alcoholic (Jellinck, 1960). That is to say, they had all experienced some withdrawal symptoms, damage to their physical health, finances and social standing as a result of excessive drinking. The subjects were screened for medical and psychiatric problems, and a thorough social and drinking history was obtained on each subject. Subjects were then either assigned to a treatment goal of either controlled drinking or nondrinking (abstinence), on the basis of a majority of staff opinion. A treatment goal of controlled drinking was usually based on the criteria that some form of nonproblem, limited drinking was desired by the subject, that the subject could reasonably be expected to learn new drinking behaviors, and that the environment to which the subject would return would be supportive and conducive to nonproblem drinking. No subject was ever denied a treatment goal of abstinence if requested. Within each of the two treatment goal groups, subjects were then randomly assigned to either a control group receiving only conventional state hospital treatment oriented toward abstinence or to an experimental group receiving seventeen experimental treatment sessions in addition to the conventional treatment. Thus, only the controlled drinker experimental subjects received treatment oriented toward a goal of controlled drinking. The subjects in each of the experimental groups (controlled drinking, abstinence) received seventeen behavioral treatment sessions. The sessions were designed so that they could be individually tailored to meet a client's specific needs. Central emphasis was placed upon specifically defining prior setting events for heavy drinking and training the subject in alternative, socially acceptable responses to those situations. All preceding events had to be operationally defined, and vague terms such as "depression" or "anxiety" were not allowed. Rather, the specifics such as "losing a job" or "a fight with my wife" were listed as the events preceding heavy drinking.

The first two sessions of treatment consisted of a videotape of the subject while intoxicated. During these sessions, each client was allowed to consume up to 16 ounces of eighty-six proof liquor, or its equivalent, in a three-hour period. These treatment sessions took place in a simulated bar. The final ninety minutes of each session were videotaped.

Sessions three through seventeen took place either in the simulated bar or in a simulated living room depending upon where the subject did the majority of his heavy drinking. Session three was educational, and the client was instructed as to the nature of his treatment program and the rationale for the program. During this session, clients were evaluated for electric shock pain threshold and were trained in alternative responses to drinking. Sessions four through sixteen were the actual treatment sessions. Sessions four and five consisted of viewing the videotape made during sessions one and two. Session six began with the clients being administered a failure test (a series of plausible, but impossible tasks). The results of the tests were then discussed with the client focusing on how he had responded to failure previously. Sessions seven through sixteen involved the aversive conditioning utilizing electrodes attached to the fingers of the subjects. During these sessions, alcoholic beverages of all types were available to the clients. During these sessions (except the probe sessions, eight, twelve, and sixteen), inappropriate drinking behaviors were punished by electric shocks. Controlled drinking subjects were punished for inappropriate drinking behaviors, and subjects who had abstinence as a goal were punished for any drinking behavior. An avoidance schedule was utilized, and a variable ratio schedule of two was used. During probe sessions, shock contingencies were not in effect and electrodes were not connected. The purpose of the probe sessions was to assess whether the drinking patterns manifested during the contingency sessions could be expected to generalize to situations where there was no punishment delivered for inappropriate drinking. The last thirty minutes of session sixteen were also videotaped. Session seventeen was a summary and no alcohol was offered. During this session, the videotape from session sixteen was contrasted with the tape of sessions one and two. Each subject's progress was discussed, and the subjects were presented a card with a list of "do's" and "don't's" specific to each individual's treatment. Subjects were then free to be discharged from the hospital, and almost all did so within two weeks.

The results of the experiment indicate that, at least with some individuals, it is possible for Gamma alcoholics to return to a state of controlled drinking. Of the twenty subjects in the controlled drinking experimental group, 85 percent functioned well in the first year posttreatment as compared to only 31.58 percent of the control subjects. Similar results were formed for clients who had abstinence as a goal with 86.67 percent of the experimental group functioning well one year posttreatment as compared to 26.67 percent of the control group. In both cases, the differences were significant at the 0.05 level (Sobell and Sobell, 1973).

Summary

In 1934, the first systematic application of learning theory was utilized in the treatment of alcohol abuse by Kantorovich when he paired electrical stimulation with the presence of alcohol. Since that first systematic application, there have developed numerous treatment approaches with therapeutic techniques based in the empirical findings of social learning theory. Thus, in order to facilitate an understanding of these techniques, it is essential to have a basic understanding of learning theory. The applied social learning theorist uses techniques developed from the two basic paradigms of learning; classical and operant conditioning. Classical conditioning places the major focus on what precedes the response in the environment, while operant conditioning places the major emphasis on what follows the response in the environment.

An applied social learning theorist makes three assumptions regarding deviant or maladaptive behavior: (1) all voluntary behaviors are learned; (2) since behavior is learned, it can be "unlearned" or extinguished; and (3) the maladaptive behavior is the primary problem area. In the field of alcoholic treatment today, the most well known of the learning theory approaches are the aversion techniques.

The most comprehensive work in this area has been done by Voegtlin and Lemere (1950), who over a ten-year period worked with more than 4,000 patients. Their success rate for these patients averaged 57 percent (Bandua, 1969). However, if the patients returned for follow-up treatment during the first year after treatment, the success rate increased significantly. As can be seen, aversive techniques can be efficacious in the treatment of alcohol abuse. However, many workers in the field view this treatment approach as "inhumane" and as a result, the techniques are not widely accepted as a viable treatment modality.

Over the past five years, several other learning theory techniques have been successfully applied to the treatment of alcohol abusers. Some of these techniques include the use of behavioral treatment contracts, goal setting, homework assignments and behavioral reversal. Two of the more promising behavioral techniques for treatment of alcohol abuse are relaxation and assertive training. A great number of substance abusers have problems with severe anxiety; therefore, the proper application of these procedures enables the patient to deal with his problems in a socially acceptable manner and with less harm to himself (Forrest, 1977).

It seems that the applied social learning theory approaches are more effective when multiple behavioral techniques are used, for a behavioral approach views that if one succeeds in getting an individual to give up alcohol, the alcohol abuse must be replaced with a more appropriate behavior. By applying a combination of the procedures discussed in this chapter, the goal may be accomplished. A critical review of the research indicates that many advances have been made in the therapeutic application of social learning theory in the field of substance abuse. These techniques, when appropriately applied, have been demonstrated to be efficacious. It is believed that many aspects of these techniques can' be selectively utilized by all workers in the field.

CONCLUDING REMARKS

Behavior therapy as a global concept encompasses a number of specific techniques and therapeutic strategies. Central to the totality of these measures is the role of learning theory. Regardless of the particular strategy of a behavior therapy method, be it covert sensitization, flooding or assertive training, the underlying rationale of the technique has to do with basic learning theory. In this chapter we have discussed behavior therapy, aversive therapy and the applied social learning theory based behavioral strategies of treatment. Of all the techniques and systems of behavior therapy, the aversive approach has received most attention in the treatment of alcoholism and problem drinking. Certainly we can anticipate more clinical and experimental investigation into the other forms of behavior therapy as they apply to the problem of alcoholism. Behavior modification and behavior-oriented therapeutic communities for the alcoholic and problem drinker will receive growing attention in the future.

Aversive methods have proven beneficial in the treatment of alcoholism. However, this approach as well as other behavior-oriented treatment modalities has fallen short of initial optimistic expectations. Those familiar with the history of psychotherapy seem to tacitly share the opinion that particular schools or approaches to therapy seem to be most effective when they are new or still in the novel stages. This seems to be the case with behavior therapy. The cure rates initially presented by Wolpe (1958) seem to have undergone a progressive regression toward the 65 to 70 percent rate of remission proposed by Eysenck (1965). Regardless of the causative factors seemingly involved in this process, behavioral approaches to the problem of alcoholism constitute a glimmer of hope and promise for those involved in alcoholic rehabilitation efforts. Certainly continued research and investigation are indicated. It is interesting to note that, while behavior therapists have been rather quick to recommend their strategies of treatment for phobic and compulsive disorders, in general, there seems to be a reluctant feeling about the use of these same techniques as an explicit method for treating alcoholism and problem drinking. Most behavior therapists seem to agree with Bandura's (1969) opinion that the successful treatment of alcoholism (prolonged sobriety) dictates a combination of treatment procedures. In accord with this I feel that as behavioral scientists we are all well aware of the fact that one's phenomenal field presents a multiplicity of reinforcement contingencies potentially useful in the process of extinguishing addictive behaviors. Perhaps at some future time we may possess the knowledge and skills which could conceivably render alcoholism and problem drinking amenable to one specific form of treatment. At present we do not. As such, it would seem that behavior therapy strategies represent but one facet of the therapist's "bag of tricks." To be able to successfully draw upon one's interpersonal skills and training to the extent of helping facilitate behavioral change in the realm of drinking remains the central issue in alcoholic rehabilitation work. The use and understanding of behavior therapy principles constitutes one viable aspect of this potential for helping to facilitate change.

Chapter 11

TREATMENT VI
MARITAL AND FAMILY THERAPY

MARITAL and family therapy techniques are very new additions to the armamentarium of the psychotherapist. Gurman and Rice (1975) indicate that almost all of the relevant material dealing with marital and family therapy has been published since 1960. Historically, clinical work with couples has been referred to as marriage counseling in the literature. Marriage counseling is a rather global term which does not at present adequately take into account the various treatment strategies employed by most therapists in their clinical work with the marital dyad. The vast majority of professional psychotherapists who practice marital and family therapy are identified primarily with such professions as clinical psychology, psychiatry and social work. Olson (1975) points out that the field of marital therapy has been retarded in the development of clinical research and theory and the organization of professional training centers. Furthermore, this author indicates that the "field has been seriously lacking in empirically tested principles, and it is without a theoretically derived foundation on which to operate clinically." Much of the clinical literature dealing with marital and family therapy focuses on clinical practices and techniques, with empirical research being a very rare commodity. The field of family therapy is actually much more recent in development than that of marital treatment.

Perhaps the most significant clinical contribution made to date by the marital and family therapists has been their emphasis upon marital and family relationships per se. Most clinicians and psychotherapists have stressed the importance of intrapersonal conflict and psychopathology in their work with emotionally disturbed individuals. In direct contrast to this position, marital and family therapists emphasize the interpersonal or relationship aspects of emotional disturbance. Such a stance is congruous with my own clinical experience and writings (Forrest, 1975; Forrest, 1978) specific to the realm of psychotherapy and rehabilitation work with alcoholic patients. Marital and family therapists tend to view the marriage and family from a systems perspective. Pioneers in the field of family therapy found that their patients who had successfully been treated and returned home consistently became symptomatic in a short interval of time after family "reentry." The family system was viewed as being responsible for such a regression. Sometimes, it was another family member who evidenced symptomatic behavior. Family therapists believe that their patients usually come from a disturbed family and that a problem child or adolescent is a symptom of a conflicted family. It is significant that family therapists generally view the schizophrenic family member as a unique result of a severely disturbed family relationship. Accordingly, the total family unit is believed to be pathogenic. A good deal of the work which has been accomplished to date in the field of family therapy has been limited to family systems in which at least one family member has been identified as floridly schizophrenic.

In spite of the fact that it can be said that neither marital nor family therapy has its own history, body of commonly accepted concepts and tenants, or an underlying framework of research findings, these terms can be clinically defined. Marital therapy can be defined as any strategy of psychotherapy which is fundamentally employed in order to modify the marital relationship. Modification of the marital dyad encompasses patterns of communication, transactional patterns, the dyadic management of feelings and the totality of other variables specific to the marital relationship. Olson (1975) states that the "goal of marital therapy has usually been defined as assisting a couple to better understand their reciprocal marital interaction and attempt to find ways in which their needs can be mutually satisfied so that the growth and development of each partner can be maximized in the relationship." Marital therapy techniques vary considerably. Marital group therapy, conjoint marital therapy and marital behavior modification are but a few of the primary strategies utilized to alter the marital relationship. Marriage counseling or marital therapy focuses mainly upon problems related to the marital (interpersonal) relationship, and these terms will be used interchangeably in this chapter. My own approach to marital therapy with the alcoholic is essentially conjoint. Therefore, the chapter is generally limited to the conjoint approach to marital therapy. I think it is accurate to say that conjoint marital therapy is at present the most widely utilized strategy of marital therapy. The conjoint approach to marital therapy involves seeing the marital couple during *all* treatment sessions. Within the last few years, it has become rather common for the psychotherapist to work with unmarried couples using the conjoint therapy approach. Social change relating to family and marital structure can be viewed as having facilitated this occurrance. The conjoint treatment method has proven clinically useful in the management of marital difficulties for a number of reasons. Leslie (1964), indicates that the conjoint approach to marital therapy is effective for identifying and working through distortions, for objectifying conflict, for dealing with transference and countertransference problems, for focusing upon the here-and-now of the marital relationship and for modifying the transactional style of the marital couple. Male and female therapist teams have been advocated as being beneficial in the conjoint treatment process due to the modeling effect provided by this procedure.

Family therapy has been defined by Zuk (1967) as, "the technique that explores and attempts to shift the balance of pathogenic relating among family members so that new forms of relating become possible." It is apparent that this definition is congruous with the viewpoint that the family is a homeostatic system in which change upon the part of one family member is likely to effect change within the family system. Family therapy is even more recent in development than marital therapy. The techniques and procedures of family therapy are, for the most part, centered around viewing the family as a system. Jay Haley (1962), one of the mavericks in the field of family therapy, states that psychopathology in the individual is a product of the way he deals with his intimate relations, the way they deal with him, and the way other family members involve him in their relations with each other. Further, the appearance of symptomatic behavior in an individual is necessary for the continued functioning of a particular family system. Therefore, changes in the individual can occur only if the family system changes, and resistance to change in the individual centers in the influence of the family as a group.

Family therapists attempt to alter the immediate social environment of the disturbed family member, i.e. the family system. According to the family therapist, it is fruitless to remove the symptomatic family member from the family system, attempt to change him and then return him to the same family environment. Satir (1964) points out, "the parents are the architects of the family, and the marriage relationship is the key to all other family relationships. When there is difficulty with the marital pair, there are more than likely problems in parenting." Perhaps the most striking feature of the field of family therapy today is the diversity of forms of family treatment. Conjoint family therapy involves one or two therapists working with *all* of the members of the nuclear family during all treatment sessions. The multiple impact therapy approach utilizes a team of therapists to work with family members on an individual basis and in various family member combinations. This approach to family therapy (MIT) is intensive and short term. Some family therapists (kin network therapists) work with not only the nuclear family and extended family but also include close friends and even neighbors. Generally speaking, family therapists emphasize family system change rather than individual change. In addition to a variety of "normal" evolutionary changes affecting the field of psychotherapy, certainly the development of family therapy during the past decade has been facilitated by the social *Zeitgeist* (Erickson and Hogan, 1976). Many social scientists have written about "the breakdown of the family" and family restructuring in recent years. Most assuredly, a plethora of social factors have contributed to the emergence of both marital and family therapy. Today's practicing clinician who is skilled and experienced in the realms of marital and family therapy is in demand.

A cursory review of the clinical and research literature dealing with any of the marital and family psychotherapy approaches reveals a total lack of data specific to the treatment of the alcoholic marriage or the alcoholic family system. This situation could be easily predicted. None of the "established" schools of counseling and psychotherapy have been developed via primary clinical experience with alcoholic persons. Thus, psychoanalysts, reality therapists, rational emotive therapists, orgone therapists and so on simply have not written about their treatment experiences with alcoholic patients. This chapter entails a discussion of the author's clinical observations and experiences associated with some seven years of work with alcoholic family systems and alcoholic marriages. Psychodynamic issues specific to the alcoholic marriage and the alcoholic family system are elaborated upon. Specific treatment strategies for working with alcoholic marriages and family systems are discussed. These matters are initially considered within the framework of the alcoholic marriage and working with the alcoholic and nonaddicted spouse within the confines of marital therapy. Later in the chapter, these same issues are addressed as they apply to clinical work with the alcoholic family system.

Much of the work with alcoholic persons has been delegated to the para-professional, lay person and self-help organizations. It is my observation (Forrest, 1975; 1976; 1978) that professional behavioral scientists, of whatever specific discipline, have for the most part been less than interested in and involved with the field of alcoholism. Certainly, there are noteworthy exceptions to this statement. The Alcoholics Anonymous community (Alcoholics Anonymous, Al-Anon, Alateen and Ala-Tot) has historically concerned itself not only with the welfare and well-being of the person who is addicted to alcohol but with the families of these individuals as well. Herein lies the secret to the success of Alcoholics Anonymous in working with alcoholic persons. Alcoholics Anonymous (the A.A. Community) provides active family treatment for the alcoholic family system. The Alcoholics Anonymous community has historically recognized alcoholism as a "family disease" and thus has worked to provide self-help treatment for the spouse, children and even extended family of the alcoholic. Consistently in the A.A. literature one finds an emphasis upon the family nature of alcoholism, yet the depth of this emphasis leaves much to be desired. Within A.A. circles, as well as within alcoholic treatment settings, we often hear something along the lines of "the spouse of the alcoholic is just as *sick* as the alcoholic." Clinicians who work with alcoholics soon realize that the spouse and children of the alcoholic frequently, if not always, are in need of some kind of psychological help. Marital and family therapy are needed, but such services are typically not adequately available within most alcoholic treatment facilities. Alcoholics Anonymous does not provide marital or family therapy per se. In short, everyone recognizes the fact that the alcoholic, the alcoholic marriage and the alcoholic family system must *all* be changed. I would venture to say that virtually every professional change agent involved in the actual treatment of alcoholic persons continuously attempts to change the alcoholic, the alcoholic marriage and the alcoholic family system. The same can be said of the Alcoholics Anonymous community and other self-help groups which work with addicted individuals. In view of the fact that the professional change agent and self-help worker involved in treating alcoholic marriages and families have essentially no clinical guidelines or parameters of marital and family treatment techniques available to them, I think this chapter will be quite beneficial in these areas.

MARITAL THERAPY WITH THE ALCOHOLIC

The Alcoholic Marital Relationship: General Clinical Observations

The marital relationship involving a chronic alcoholic and his (her) spouse is diffusely and chronically conflicted. Heavy drinking or chronic alcoholism has been central to the adjustment style of one or both parents of the couple entering psychotherapy as a result of alcoholism and extreme marital conflict in over 60 percent of the cases I have treated. Prior to marriage, both the alcoholic and nonaddicted spouse have experienced considerable emotional conflict. The nonaddicted spouse will often deny any "personal problems" prior to marriage. However, I have found that within a few hours of marital therapy, we often times quickly "discover" that such has not been the case. Over 80 percent of the alcoholic couples that I worked with have been able to vividly recall being intoxicated before, during and after the wedding ceremony. This pattern applies to both the alcoholic and nonaddicted spouse. Many nonaddicted spouses report "knowing" their spouse was an alcoholic prior to marriage. I believe that alcoholic marriages frequently involve a selective process of pathological mate selection. The nonalcoholic spouse does not "randomly" select an alcoholic mate, nor does an alcoholic randomly or by chance alone select a marriage partner. From what I have already stated, it is apparent that very often an alcoholic interpersonal history can be one predisposing factor in the choice pattern determining an alcoholic marriage. Feelings of inadequacy, overdetermined dependency needs and poor social skills characterized many of the alcoholic *couples* which I have treated. In other words, both the alcoholic and his (or her) spouse tend to feel insecure, inadequate, and in other ways *share* a number of common psychological conflicts. Narcissistic injury is clearly central to the interpersonal histories of the alcoholic and nonaddicted mate. Furthermore, I have observed that both partners often have a rather clear-cut history of "heterosexual conflict" prior to marriage. In other words, both partners have found dating and courtship to be emotionally difficult; both partners have found it difficult to "relate" to the opposite sex and, quite honestly, there is very often a conscious history of dislike for the opposite sex. Many of my patients, both alcoholic and spouse, have expressed feelings to the effect that their marital choice had to do with finding someone who would at least "put up with me." Like so many couples, the alcoholic and his (her) spouse expect to change the "bad habits" of each other following the wedding ceremony. Preconsciously and unconsciously each expects the other to magically change as a result of being married. Some alcoholic marriages seem to take place as a result of the naivety of one or both partners. Not uncommonly, I have worked with a wife of an alcoholic who, at the time of marriage and before, had absolutely no understanding of the various ramifications surrounding her "to be" spouse's drinking behavior. Women who marry military alcoholics often fit this pattern. A brief period of courtship during which neither spouse really develops an opportunity to know the other, heightened sexual intimacy, and a good deal of drinking and "socializing" before the marriage characterize many military marriages involving alcoholism. The nonaddicted spouse frequently realizes she has "made a mistake" or even knows that she has married an alcoholic within a matter of months. In my clinical experience, the wife has chosen very early in the marriage to continue to live with her addicted husband in spite of the difficult and ongoing conflicts in which this choice results. Typically, she understands well what many of the problems related to this choice are, and yet, tragically she cannot begin to comprehend what difficulties the addiction process will eventually create. If the nonaddicted spouse has in fact been parented by an alcoholic, she (in the case where the alcoholic is the husband) primitively believes that she can magically undo her husband's alcoholism and thus rescue him from his addiction. Women who have been parented by an alcoholic father unconsciously and sometimes consciously "blame" their mother for the father's addiction. Therefore, such a woman primitively believes that if she can be what her own mother "should have been" in her relationship with her father, what the daughter believes she will be in her relationship with her husband, her own father would not have been an alcoholic, and therefore her husband cannot become an alcoholic. All too soon the wife realizes the fact that she cannot behave differently in her relationship with her alcoholic husband; in other words, she cannot make him stop drinking! As her mother was trapped, as she was trapped during her formative years, so she is trapped as an adult within the marital and parenting relationship. The more she consciously realizes and understands her dilemma in living, the more depressed and intrapersonally conflicted the wife of the alcoholic becomes. It is important to point out that the alcoholic marital relationship becomes progressively more pathological and dysfunctional. As the addiction process unfolds, both marital partners manifest a growing number of psychological symptoms. In choosing to live with an alcoholic, the nonaddicted spouse, in essence, chooses to be symptomatic. *Ipso facto* the alcoholic chooses to be interpersonally and intrapersonally disturbed by actualizing the addiction symptom choice.

As the alcoholic marriage deteriorates, both partners become progressively more angry. Indeed, the rage and hostility associated with the alcoholic marital dyad usually takes on an overtly sadomasochistic flavor. The alcoholic and his (her) spouse become so enraged at each other that they virtually cease to communicate in any manner which is not essentially hostile, resentful and hateful. Communication in the alcoholic marriage is limited, parataxic and steeped in rage. On the surface, one is impressed with the near total lack of verbal communication between the alcoholic and the nonaddicted spouse. Closer clinical scrutiny reveals an ever-present communication style constructed around feelings of rage and anger. During the initial months and perhaps years of the alcoholic marriage, conflict and marital discord are generally more overt. Both parties confront, challenge, and attack each other verbally and quite possibly physically. The alcoholic marriage of fifteen or twenty-five years duration often is characterized by a form of more pathological noncommunication. In these marriages verbal and physical attacks are less frequent but far more poorly controlled and destructive when they erupt. I have worked with couples of this variety who not uncommonly refused to talk to each other for as long as two months following a major "blow-up." This was the case in spite of the fact that the couple ate together at least twice a day, slept together almost every night and in a multiplicity of other ways were involved in a marital relationship. Alcoholic marriages which persist in this form involve a basic struggle for psychological and physical survival upon the part of both partners. At the more primitive levels of conscious awareness, as well as at the conscious level of awareness in some cases, the sadomasochistic dimensions of the alcoholic marriage involve the wish upon the part of each spouse to destroy the other. I believe this situation pertains to the nonalcoholic spouse as well as the alcoholic. Survival in a strictly physical sense (see Chap. 7) can mean to the alcoholic or the nonaddicted spouse "winning." As she anxiously awaits for her alcoholic husband to return home at three o'clock in the morning, the nonaddicted wife hopes that her spouse will be killed in an automobile accident on the way home. The next minute she feels guilty over thinking "such thoughts" and prays that God will somehow get her alcoholic husband home safely. Likewise, the alcoholic harbors many ambivalent sentiments about his spouse and the marital relationship. At one moment the communications and interactions of the alcoholic within the marital relationship clearly are violent and destructive. Hours or even minutes later, the alcoholic attempts to communicate feelings of concern and love for the nonaddicted marital partner. The alcoholic literally and figuratively attacks his (or her) spouse via a plethora of communication strategies. The same can be said of the spouse of the alcoholic. Much of the communication within the alcoholic marriage is in the form of threats. It seems as if the alcoholic and nonaddicted spouse are forever threatening and blaming each other about everything. First and foremost in the "battle" of communication threats is the matter of divorce. Audaciously, the alcoholic declares to his (or her) "friends" that he has "had it" with his wife (or husband) and is "getting divorced." The nonaddicted spouse has threatened the alcoholic with divorce on hundreds of occassions and has never followed through on this divorce threat. Divorce threats constitute a type of mutually destructive communication.

Communication patterns, transactional interactions and, indeed, the alcoholic marital relationship per se, in an overdetermined fashion, involve the basic issue of control. Just as the alcoholic is intrapersonally and interpersonally "out of control" a good deal of the time, so is the alcoholic marriage "out of control." Emotions and affect rule and pathologically determine behavior within the context of the alcoholic marriage. The alcoholic persistently attempts to control his (or her) wife (or husband) vis-à-vis the totality of the marital relationship. The nonaddicted spouse attempts to control the alcoholic's drinking behavior as well as numerous other vicissitudes constituting the adjustment style of the addicted mate. Struggles pertaining to the issue of control within the alcoholic marriage frequently are related to rule setting. Such matters as who pays the bills, who is primarily responsible for parenting, how money is spent, how much liquor is consumed and the management of sexuality in marriage are but a few of the conflicted areas in the alcoholic marriage which involve power and control struggles. Rules which maintain these transactions are not effectively established in the alcoholic marriage. When the alcoholic feels like buying a new car or television set, he may do so without discussing this decision with the spouse. While an alcoholic husband may believe that such a transaction only demonstrates "who wears the pants in this family," obviously the lack of a mutually agreed upon rule to discuss such major decisions in the marriage can only result in a sense of powerlessness and feelings of hostility upon the part of the wife.

The alcoholic marriage is chameleonlike in many ways. In certain respects, the only stability of the alcoholic marriage is its instability. Emotional vacillation, ambivalence and chaotic turmoil describe rather well the disequilibrium basic to the alcoholic marital relationship. I have observed that many of the alcoholic couples I have worked with appeared much older physically than their actual ages. It is difficult and in numerous ways psychologically damaging to remain within the alcoholic marriage. Pathological dependency needs and self-system fragmentation are factors which operate to maintain the alcoholic marriage in spite of the tremendous pain which such marriages created in the lives of both spouses. Identity conflict or ego deficit sometimes plays a crucial role in the decision to remain within an alcoholic marriage. In spite of these psychodynamic factors, as well as other clinically relevant sources of psychopathology which "feed into" the alcoholic marriage, a significant relationship variable in many alcoholic marriages is love. In spite of the global psychopathology genetic to every alcoholic marriage, there is a great deal of concern, love and mutual caring in many of these marriage relationships. Marital therapy consistently fails in alcoholic marriages devoid of underlying feelings of love and concern. When the addicted partner is actively entrapped in the addiction process, the marital relationship clearly lacks a sense of mutual respect, dignity, love, concern and commitment. The bipolar character structure of the alcoholic manifests itself within the marital context, and the marital relationship takes on a bipolar or dichotomous dimension as the addiction process unfolds. In some alcoholic marriages, there is never direct physical violence or the uncontrolled expression of hate, rage and vengence in spite of the florid presence of the addiction process. It can be exceedingly difficult for the therapist to facilitate change in such marriages. The couple maintaining a reasonably healthy or positive relationship in spite of one spouse's addiction can be extremely resistant to both relationship change and pattern of consumption change. At the other end of the continuum, the clinician is confronted with the task of working with couples who consistently attack and attempt to annihilate each other. Chronic and intense "double binding" (Bateson et. al., 1956) is central to the transactional and communication styles of such couples. The essential conditions for creating a double bind follow:

> The individual is involved in an intense relationship; that is, a relationship in which he feels it is vitally important that he discriminate accurately what sort of message is being communicated so that he can respond appropriately . . . (second) the individual is caught in a situation in which the other person in the relationship is expressing two orders of messages and one of these denies the other . . . (third), the individual is unable to comment on the messages being expressed to correct his discrimination of what order of message to respond to i.e., he cannot make a metacommunicative statement (Bateson et al., 1956).

Obviously, double binding includes victimizing and scapegoating. Roles, transactions and communication patterns which serve the interpersonal purpose of placing an individual in a "not-OK" stance are generally psychologically destructive.

Severely disturbed alcoholic marriages sometimes involve pseudomutuality, where there is an overwhelming emphasis on fitting together *as a family* at the expense of adequate or healthy self-differentiation. The marital schism (Lidz et al., 1957) is basic to all severely disturbed alcoholic marriages. Schism refers to families in which there is chronic undercutting of the other spouse and generalized severe marital difficulties. This marital pattern frequently includes a husband with little prestige in the family, and a wife who is emotionally cold and sexually aloof. When the alcoholic marriage involves an actively alcoholic husband and an actively alcoholic wife, treatment is extremely difficult, if not impossible, in my experience. Likewise, it is virtually impossible for the psychotherapist to work effectively with an alcoholic couple who, in addition to the alcoholism of one spouse, are both floridly sociopathic.

I have found that even within the confines of the severely disturbed alcoholic marriage, positive behavioral and transactional change can often be effected by the psychotherapist. An almost inherent psychodynamic characteristic of most alcoholic marriages is that of role reversal or ongoing role "slippage." In other words, the alcoholic is not the only one who is a scapegoat or victim in the alcoholic marriage. Nor is it always the nonaddicted spouse who is placed in the double bind situation. The role reversal and role slippage process are such in these marital relationships that both spouses are from time to time victimized and scapegoated. This process is clearly a neurotic one; yet, I believe that it is adaptive in the sense that it operates to deter a psychotic decompensation upon the part of either spouse. Ongoing role reversals in the alcoholic marriage create guilt conflicts, depression, rage and various other interpersonal and relationship disturbances. However, I view the role slippage process as a defense against psychosis in the alcoholic marriage. This process also neurotically reinforces persistence within the alcoholic marital relationship.

It is important to touch upon the sexual problems of the alcoholic couple. This is an area which is poorly understood in clinical circles as well as among paraprofessionals and self-help groups working with alcoholic persons, their spouses and families. In my clinical experience with alcoholic couples, the most common variety of sexually oriented conflict specific to these couples involves sexual acting-out. As the addicted spouse deterioriates into the middle and later stages of the addiction process, almost invariably there is a loss of control in the sexual realm. The alcoholic who early in the addiction process has been involved in a few extramarital affairs suddenly becomes polymorphously involved in any number of extramarital sexual liaisons. The spouse of the alcoholic may come home from work only to find the addicted partner in bed with a best friend. The alcoholic may attempt to seduce a completely uninterested neighbor. While intoxicated, the alcoholic may seduce or attempt to seduce a daughter or son. Sexual relationships between an alcoholic father or step father and daughter are not at all uncommon in my experience. Alcohol-induced loss of control is a common denominator in virtually all of these distorted sexual transactions. From time to time, I have worked with couples in which the nonaddicted spouse had been aware of the sexual involvement of the alcoholic with a son or daughter for years, but had done nothing to deter such a relationship. For the most part, the nonaddicted spouse who is aware of an overt incestuous sexual relationship between the alcoholic and a son or daughter and fails to do anything about such a relationship for months or years is severely disturbed and needs extended individual psychotherapeutic treatment as well as conjoint therapy or family therapy. A number of pathogenic factors create such a family relationship. It is also not uncommon for the clinician to encounter in treatment a married alcoholic who acts-out homosexually while intoxicated. This pattern may be unknown to the nonaddicted spouse until the alcoholic enters the later stages of the addiction process. I should point out that less than 10 percent of the alcoholic persons I have worked with fit this pattern or, for that matter, were primarily homosexual in sexual object choice. In spite of this fact, every alcoholic suffers with chronic and intense identity conflicts. This issue is discussed at length in my most recent text (Forrest, 1978).

Aside from the overdetermined sexual acting-out and promiscuity of the alcoholic, the clinician who works with alcoholic couples will be confronted with the entire gamut of other "classical" sexual dysfunctions. Frigidity, premature ejaculation and the inability to sustain an erection are but a few of the dysfunctions which pertain to the alcoholic couple. Chronically alcoholic males of fifty or sixty years of age not atypically have sustained such physical damage from the ingestion of alcohol that their sexual performance may be permanently impaired. It is imperative for the psychotherapist to focus upon the relationship aspects of sexuality when working with the alcoholic couple. The marital relationship is affected directly and in a multiplicity of ways by sexual acting-out upon the part of the alcoholic or the nonaddicted spouse. If the nonaddicted spouse is impotent, frigid or sexually disinterested, the marital relationship is directly affected as a result. An obsession upon the part of one or both marital partners with fellatio or cunnilingus influences the marital relationship. Sexuality is relationship and, therefore, by definition a matter to be explored by the therapist in his work with the alcoholic couple (Uraa, 1978).

With this admittedly truncated discussion of the basic psychopathology of the alcoholic marital relationship in mind, let us turn to the issue of psychotherapy with the alcoholic couple. The essential strategies of effective psychotherapeutic work with the alcoholic marital couple will be considered in this section.

Strategies of Psychotherapy for Working with Alcoholic Marriages

A major initial and continuing treatment objective for the clinician working with the alcoholic and his (or her) nonaddicted spouse must always be the continued sobriety of the alcoholic spouse. Psychotherapy is usually of little benefit in cases where the chronic alcoholic spouse continues to remain intoxicated. The alcoholic, during the initial stages of marital therapy, blames the marital relationship (among other things) for his (or her) alcoholism. Directly as well as by inference and inuendo, the alcoholic states that he (or she) would not drink alcoholically were it not for the spouse: "If you weren't such a son-of-a bitch I wouldn't *have* to drink the way I do" is how one of my patients explained her feelings. The alcoholic does *not* drink alcoholically as a result of the adjustment style and behaviors of the nonaddicted spouse. The psychotherapist must emphasize this position again and again to the alcoholic and nonaddicted spouse. If the addicted spouse drinks while in treatment, he (or she) exercises choice in the decision to drink. Very often, the *modus operandi* of the alcoholic in the marital relationship has been to make the spouse feel guilty for his or her drinking. As the therapist explains to the nonaddicted spouse that he or she is not to blame, i.e. he or she has not caused the alcoholism of the addicted spouse, guilt conflicts and depressive symptoms begin to be resolved. The therapist should point out to both spouses that if the alcoholic continues to remain intoxicated the marital relationship will, in all probability, continue to worsen or deteriorate. In making this point, the therapist provides a significant reality input for the couple. This can in particular become a threatening issue for the nondependent spouse as she (or he) is faced with the reality of *choosing* an increasingly conflicted adjustment in the event the addicted spouse chooses to continue to be intoxicated. Psychotherapy with alcoholic couples is in part a process of teaching both partners how to actualize more rational life and relationship choices.

An explicit goal of therapy with alcoholic couples cannot be "saving the marriage." Many alcoholic couples seek treatment as a last resort in order to keep their marriage together. In the case of the alcoholic marriage, it is often only one spouse who manifests this attitude toward therapy. Surprisingly, it is frequently the alcoholic spouse who "pushes" for the couple to enter marital therapy. In this situation, a marital crisis is usually the driving vector behind the alcoholic's desire to enter a marital therapy relationship. More specifically, the marital crisis may occur when the nondependent spouse physically separates from the alcoholic or actually initiates a divorce. This process most typically takes place after a number of years of marriage. During the early months and years of marriage, it is the nonalcoholic spouse who tries to initiate marital therapy, but at this stage in the marriage and the addiction process, it is the alcoholic who "refuses" treatment. When the alcoholic couple enter therapy, a basis for change has been established. This is true regardless of the overt and underlying factors resulting in treatment engagement. Successful psychotherapy with the alcoholic couple can yield any number of outcomes. Radical relationship change including sobriety is certainly one optimal treatment outcome. While in marital therapy and with sobriety, many alcoholic couples come to realize that they cannot live together happily and productively. In such cases, the rational management of a legal separation or divorce can be viewed as an outcome related to a successful psychotherapy relationship. It is important for the psychotherapist to point out to the alcoholic couple initially in the treatment relationship that therapy is not a panacea which will guarantee a "forever after" blissful marital relationship. Marital therapy can and often does result in a divorce or separation, and the couple entering a marital therapy relationship should be made aware of this reality. Divorce can be a psychologically adaptive and beneficial process for one if not both spouses. The alcoholic spouse may decide to remain intoxicated in spite of therapeutic treatment. In the event the nonaddicted spouse in such a case is better able, via the psychotherapeutic process, to either leave the alcoholic or in a multiplicity of other ways live more rationally and effectively, psychotherapy has been successful. Many times marital therapy with the alcoholic couple creates significant relationship changes which enable the couple to live together constructively. Commitment and work within the confines of the marital therapy relationship upon the part of both spouses can be tantamount to radically positive relationship change.

It has been my rather consistent clinical experience that the alcoholic couple decides early, either as a couple or individually, whether or not to make a commitment to the treatment process. Brief or short-term marital psychotherapy is of little benefit to the alcoholic marriage. Optimal relationship change for the alcoholic couple generally dictates long-term and multifaceted treatment engagement. After the alcoholic couple has made a commitment to marital therapy, and the alcoholic, in a congruous manner, is committed to sobriety, the initial treatment task of the psychotherapist is to begin a process of facilitating communication within the marital relationship. I have always been amazed by the inability of the alcoholic couple to simply talk to each other. Some of the couples I have worked with have established a pattern of not talking to each other for weeks and months at a time. It is imperative for the counselor or psychotherapist to foster "talk communication" within the context of marital therapy with the alcoholic couple. Talk communication usually occurs spontaneously between the alcoholic couple when they are seen *with* the therapist in the treatment situation. I have found that the early sessions are taken up with angry, hostile verbal exchanges. As mentioned earlier in the chapter, "blame" oriented verbal confrontations are central to the early stages of marital therapy with the alcoholic couple. The angry verbal exchanges between alcoholic and spouse are therapeutic and represent but one phase in the treatment process. In spite of the parataxic aspects of hostile "talk communication" between the alcoholic couple early in the marital therapy process, at least the couple begins at this point to relate verbally. The therapist must operate as a "buffer" and controlling agent during this stage of treatment. When one spouse begins to overly attack or dominate the other spouse, the therapist intervenes in order to reinforce rather than block further marital communication and interaction. Catharsis can be an important source of treatment gain for both spouses at this stage in the treatment process.

Therapists who work with alcoholic couples must actively intervene in the marital relationship. Once the couple begins to verbally communicate, the therapist begins to point out to both spouses the irrational and pathological aspects of their patterns of communication. Juxtaposed to the therapist's active process of identifying and pointing out communication distortions is the work of associating emotional or affective disturbance with verbal and interactional patterns. This procedure usually begins to be effective following ten to fifteen hours of conjoint psychotherapy. Counselors and psychotherapists who attempt to focus primarily upon the feeling dimensions of the alcoholic couple, especially during the initial therapy hours, will find their efforts to be in vain. Furthermore, the alcoholic couple often responds to this strategy of treatment by terminating contact with the therapist. Rational strategies of marital therapy which eventually attempt to integrate reason with feeling and affect prove most effective in the treatment of the alcoholic couple. As the therapist experiences the alcoholic marriage via his relationship with the alcoholic couple he perceives, experiences and participates in the relationship pathology of the couple. The scapegoating, victimizing and "double binding" transactions of the alcoholic couple are most typically quite apparent to the therapist during the initial hours of marital therapy. I believe that it is therapeutically most efficacious to progressively and sometimes even only obsequiously deal with these transactional pathologies with the alcoholic couple. Pointing out, confronting and therapeutically attempting to resolve the transactional and communicative scapegoating behaviors of the alcoholic and nonaddicted spouse constitute the work of the middle and advanced stages of marital therapy. The establishment of a productive and enduring therapeutic alliance is the basic precursor to this form of therapeutic work. In the absence of a working therapeutic relationship, the various intervention strategies of the psychotherapist prove to be untimely and impotent. After some ten to fifteen hours of marital therapy with the alcoholic couple, the therapist must directly focus his treatment efforts upon the destructive double binding, scapegoating and victimizing interactions of the couple. Very often the therapist will find it necessary to "side" with one of the spouses. In so doing, the therapist is better able to provide direct interpersonal and behavioral feedback to the spouse who is *at that time* sabotaging the other spouse and the marital relationship (Walker, 1977). When the alcoholic couple begins to communicate and interact in more rational, honest and straightforward ways, each spouse begins to feel stronger and more integrated in a psychological sense. Likewise, the marital partners begin to treat each other with a sense of personal dignity, worth and respect. During the middle stages of the marital treatment process, roughly between twenty and forty hours of therapy, I have found it productive to assign homework tasks to the alcoholic couple. The most basic ingredient in such tasks is that the couple mutually participate in the activity or the task. Although it might be suspected that participating in a mutual task would be easy for the alcoholic couple, such is not the case in my clinical experience. One task which I suggest is simply going out to eat together. An activity such as this involves an hour or perhaps two at most. Spending an evening attending a movie or structuring an explicit hour or two each week for the purpose of talking with each other are other task assignments which I "assign" the alcoholic couple. Most typically, I have found that the alcoholic couple returns to therapy the week after receiving such an "assignment" rather frustrated. This is especially true with regard to the initial homework tasks. Processing and working through the conflicts and affect created by the attempt of the alcoholic couple to complete the homework task can productively facilitate the work of the psychotherapeutic process. The relationship conflicts of the alcoholic couple are brought to the fore in all situations which demand working and interacting together. Once the alcoholic couple has been able to complete or productively work at accomplishing a few therapist-initiated homework assignments, it is important for the couple to begin to develop their own weekly homework assignments. A contractually oriented, problem-solving approach to this process at least tangentially involving the therapist is optional.

Paradoxically, the alcoholic couple, prior to entering treatment, functions poorly together or as a marital couple, and yet every alcoholic marriage which persists for a number of years is steeped in overdependence, ego fusion, and pseudomutuality. During the middle and later stages of the treatment process the therapist must help the alcoholic as well as the nonaddicted spouse with the process of establishing a more adaptive sense of individuality and independence. A good number of the wives of alcoholics with whom I have worked were unable to drive a car when they entered therapy. While this may seem to be a rather inconsequential bit of clinical data, it significantly symbolizes the pathological dependency needs of the nonaddicted spouse. Not having a car or not being able to drive pragmatically means being dependent upon one's spouse or significant others for transportation to the grocery store, school, etc. Anger, resentment and a host of other sentiments and conflicts accompany such a state of pathological dependence. Pointing out and exploring the symbiotic dependency needs of the alcoholic and nonaddicted spouse in therapy exacerbate feelings associated with dependency. A concrete point of emphasis for the therapist is that the patient must behave differently in order to be both less dependent and feel differently relative to the matter of being dependent. In the case of spouses who are unable to drive, I actively explore the psychodynamic issues basic to this reality while at the same time reinforcing and supporting the movement of the patient in the direction of deciding to learn how to drive. A major goal of the psychotherapeutic process with alcoholic couples is that of fostering healthy individuality within the marital relationship rather than pathological dependence and overdetermined mutuality. Should one spouse indicate that attending church is an activity which he (or she) has given up due to the other spouse's refusal to participate in this particular activity, I reinforce the point that it is important for the patient to attend church on his (or her) own. Many of the alcoholic couples I have worked with were actively involved in Alcoholics Anonymous and Al-Anon. Attending these meetings separately as well as together can be therapeutic in the sense that individuality and independence are reinforced via the process of A.A. and Al-Anon involvement. Both the alcoholic and nonaddicted spouse fear independence and separateness. When the nonaddicted spouse attends church, a therapy session or an Al-Anon meeting, the alcoholic in a paranoid fashion accuses the spouse of "having an affair" or "running around." Not atypically, the drinking alcoholic husband accuses his wife of a homosexual attachment in her Al-Anon group. This is a clinically significant projection designed to reinforce the dependence and symbiotic needs of the nonaddicted wife. It can be most helpful for the therapist to simply let such a wife know that it is "OK" for her to continue her involvement with activities outside the marriage. In a very real sense, the therapist reinforces individuality by giving the nonalcoholic spouse permission to be a person outside of the marital relationship. The alcoholic couple can learn how to function effectively without always having to pathologically depend upon each other.

The alcoholic marriage has many sadomasochistic components (Forrest, 1978). Generally speaking, it is the alcoholic spouse who is physically and psychologically most abusive within the context of the alcoholic marriage, although the nonaddicted spouse can be every bit as violent as the alcoholic from time to time. I always make it clear to both spouses that physical abuse from the other spouse is not to be tolerated. Some alcoholic marriages seem to have always included bruises, black eyes and batterings. The most typical pattern involves a nonaddicted spouse who permits such assaults. This pattern of abuse can be extinguished by the therapist's messages to the effect that such assaults are not to be tolerated and by the active utilization of legal intervention if necessary. Nonalcoholic spouses have been conditioned by the alcoholic to feel ashamed and guilty at their feeble attempts to secure outside legal assistance in such matters. It is completely appropriate for the nonaddicted spouse to initiate a "restraining order" upon the abusive alcoholic, and the therapist should make this point known to both spouses. From time to time, I have had to support and help the spouse of an alcoholic effect this very process. Working through the irrational and yet very understandable guilt feelings which this process precipitates upon the part of the nonalcoholic spouse constitutes important grist for the psychotherapeutic relationship. Feelings of anger, rage and resentment are created in the alcoholic caught up in such a situation. Working with these feelings with the couple is of paramount importance, and this is perhaps the only way to modify the overtly abusive pattern of marital adjustment. Some alcoholics or, for that matter, the spouses of the same alcoholics become overtly abusive and violent weeks or a few months after the establishment of sobriety. Therefore, the explicit clinical management of interpersonal rage or violence can be germane to our work with the alcoholic couple at various points in the treatment process.

Counselors and psychotherapists working with alcoholic couples invariably come to understand some of the sexual conflicts of these couples vis-à-vis the treatment relationship. Frankly deviant sexuality upon the part of one spouse may result in a therapeutic focus upon the sexual adjustment of the alcoholic couple during the initial hours of marital therapy. Most alcoholic couples, in my experience, are uncomfortable with the issues of sexual adjustment and at least obsequiously attempt to avoid dealing with this matter in therapy. Therapists who are uncomfortable with the realm of human sexuality or their personal sexuality tend not to deal with sexual issues in therapy and, as a result, can unwittingly reinforce the sexual adjustment difficulties of the alcoholic couple. After spending fifteen or twenty hours in marital therapy, the alcoholic couple should hopefully be able to openly discuss and work on their areas of sexual concern. As noted earlier, promiscuous sexual acting-out upon the part of the alcoholic is a major dimension in many alcoholic marriages which must be managed in the therapy relationship. Affairs which have taken place years previously can be a major source of resentment and hostility which literally erode the present marital relationship. In this area as in so many others, the therapist must stress the here-and-now of the marital relationship. Sexual transgressions of the past cannot be undone. They can only be understood, accepted and lived with more rationally in the present. I believe that it is important for the therapist to be able to help the alcoholic couple examine the totality of their historic relationship, yet this task also encompasses the rational and reality-oriented integration of relationship historicity with the present. Alcoholic couples tend to "live in the past" and the future. In reality all of us can only experience life on a moment-to-moment or here-and-now basis. The past experiences, including sexual experiences, of the alcoholic and the nonaddicted spouse are, in fact, the precursors of present relationship disturbance. Providing basic sex information can be an integral part of our work with alcoholic couples. One alcoholic couple with whom I have been working (the husband is a professional man with some seven years of sobriety) quite recently entered therapy because of the husband's inability to maintain an erection after vaginal penetration. The husband had not, in fifteen years of marriage, attempted to manually stimulate his wife. Oral sex was perceived by the patient as bizarre and totally repugnant. His wife had been highly desirous of having oral-genital sex for years and had on a few occasions suggested that he manually stimulate her. Obviously, basic sex information was needed in the treatment of this couple as well as an exploration of the underlying psychodynamic issues pertaining to the sexual problems in the marital relationship. The spouse of the alcoholic often feels sexually "used." Improvement in the marital relationship is contingent upon the alcoholic and the spouse changing such feelings. Sobriety can result in any number of new realities in the realm of the sexual adjustment of the alcoholic couple. These realities are not "new" but rather more overt, concrete and imposing interpersonal "facts" which the alcoholic couple must face.

The later stages of marital therapy with the alcoholic couple involve a process of ongoing synthesis. Following thirty-five or forty hours of successful weekly marital therapy, I have found myself and the alcoholic couple involved in a process of creatively synthesizing the clinical data of earlier hours. Viewing previous material somewhat differently or from a relatively different perspective, attaching less affect to this material and integrating the content of past therapy hours into the present characterize the final stages of marital therapy with the alcoholic couple. Clearly, the marital relationship of the alcoholic couple changes in that both spouses are better able to consistently apply the learning facilitated by the therapeutic process into a relationship framework which is transactionally, communicatively and affectively more adaptive. The marital history of the alcoholic couple is no longer a spector which compulsively dictates relationship conflicts in the present and future. It is critically important for the therapist to reinforce sobriety in his work with the alcoholic couple throughout the treatment process. The most necessary but not sufficient condition for continued marital growth and development in the case of the alcoholic couple is sobriety upon the part of the alcoholic spouse. I have observed that it can be easy for the alcoholic couple to regress into old patterns of interaction and communication. Congruously, old behaviors precipitate old feelings; therefore, during the final stages of marital therapy, the psychotherapist needs to explore relationship and behavioral maintenance alternatives with the alcoholic couple. I recommend to the couples with whom I work an extended process of therapeutic disengagement rather than an abrupt treatment termination. We schedule bi-weekly sessions, then monthly sessions, and finally make arrangements to meet when the couple feels a need to do so. Ancillary to this method of treatment termination, I have found it efficacious to suggest that couples actively involve themselves with the Alcoholics Anonymous community during and most importantly after completing marital therapy. Some couples reject the A.A. community. In any event, during the later stages of marital therapy, the therapist must explore with the alcoholic couple activities which they can engage in together. Consolidating and reinforcing interpersonal sources of gain for the alcoholic couple is an important area of therapeutic work to be accomplished prior to treatment termination. When the alcoholic and the nonaddicted spouse have given up pathological patterns of interaction and communication, the matter of treatment termination should be integrated into the marital therapy process. A simplistic and yet useful clinical barometer of relationship change for the alcoholic couple is that of assessing the degree to which one or both spouses *resentfully* lives in the past of the marital relationship. Alcoholic couples living and experiencing their marital relationships in the here-and-now with sobriety and after successful marital therapy experiences have worked through the anger and resentments which formerly cemented their relationships in a past orientation toward life.

As mentioned earlier in the chapter, uncoupling can be one outcome of marital therapy with the alcoholic couple. Obviously, such a process differs in many clinical respects from that of marital therapy with the couple who chooses to persist in a marital relationship as a result of positive and creative changes which have taken place in the relationship due to therapeutic intervention. The process of marital therapy with couples deciding to uncouple is beyond the scope of this chapter.

In summary, marital therapy with the alcoholic couple aims at fostering positive and mutually adaptive relationship changes within the explicit context of the marital relationship. In order for marital relationship change to occur, the alcoholic must first quit drinking. Marital therapy is a process which demands committment and work upon the part of the alcoholic couple. Patterns of interaction and communication must be significantly modified between the alcoholic and nonaddicted spouse if marital therapy is to be successful. A major task of the marital therapist is that of helping to extinguish destructive patterns of scapegoating and victimizing between the alcoholic and nonaddicted spouse. Working through feelings of anger, hostility and resentment is central to the work of marital therapy with the alcoholic couple. Power struggles and attempting to control one another are clinical matters which the marital therapist must continually deal with throughout the course of therapy with the alcoholic couple. Sobriety must be stressed throughout the process of marital therapy. A number of strategies of therapeutic intervention are discussed in this chapter. Unfortunately very little has been written to date relative to the process of marital therapy with the alcoholic couple. I have found that working with alcoholic couples can be a very rewarding, although always difficult, clinical experience. Brief marital therapy is of little value in the case of alcoholic couples. I have found that weekly, one-hour sessions for some eight to twelve months are required to facilitate significant relationship change for most alcoholic couples who have been married for ten or more years.

THERAPY WITH THE ALCOHOLIC FAMILY

General Clinical Considerations

The alcoholic family system is diffusely conflicted. Many of the conflict typologies discussed in the previous section dealing with the alcoholic marital relationship can be associated with the global adjustment style of the alcoholic family system. Yet, the alcoholic family system is generally more conflicted than the alcoholic couple if for no other reason than the interpersonal impact and interaction effect of three or more people living together as opposed to only two people living together. In order to avoid redundancy, I will not for the most part focus upon the relationship pathology of the alcoholic couple considered in the earlier section of this chapter.

In a recent extensive clinical examination of alcoholism and family psychodynamics (Forrest, 1978), I have characterized the alcoholic family system as chaotic and violent. Furthermore, the alcoholic family system interacts and communicates in a number of pathological ways. Scapegoating, victimizing and "double binding" are central to the interactional and communicative style of the alcoholic family system. Members of the alcoholic family system frequently reverse roles in their family interactions. A regressive ego fusion takes place within the alcoholic family system which creates a symbiotic family ego. This process results in ego deficit upon the part of all family members living in an alcoholic family system for an extended interval of time. Living in an alcoholic family system creates feelings of guilt upon the part of each family member. Guilt feelings precipitate many neurotic behaviors. Family or collective guilt accompanies the experience of living within an alcoholic family system.

Alcoholism is a multifaceted, progressive disorder. Living in an alcoholic family system quite simply results in progressive and multifaceted emotional disturbance for all of the members. Unfortunately, there has been virtually no clinical or research data available on this subject to date. Euphemistically, counselors and paraprofessionals who have worked with alcoholic families indicate that the spouse or children of the alcoholic are often "just as sick" as the addicted family member. The emotional conflicts of each family member evolve as a direct result of the family interaction and family relationships. It is important to view the alcoholic family from a systems perspective. Alcoholics are often identified by the mental health worker via their children or the nonaddicted spouse. Family conflicts do not cause the alcoholism of a family member, yet family conflicts invariably synergize the drinking behaviors of the alcoholic family member. The children of an alcoholic parent or parents frequently manifest serious emotional problems. For these and a plethora of other reasons, I view chronic alcoholism as a family disorder. Axiomatically, it therefore behooves the psychotherapist to always include the family in any treatment or rehabilitation strategy involving an alcoholic. In the event that the alcoholic family member rejects treatment, the therapist will not uncommonly find himself working with the nonaddicted family members. Such a treatment enterprise can prove extremely beneficial to the entire family system including the alcoholic in some cases.

A good deal of the chaos basic to every alcoholic family system stems from the perpetual role reversal which takes place in these families. Role reversal and "role slippage" processes also involve scapegoating, victimizing and "double binding" in the alcoholic family system. The alcoholic family system has no homeostatic equilibrium other than instability. Unlike the schizophrenic family system, the alcoholic family system is not transactionally constructed around a particular family member's perpetual role involvement as the family scapegoat. Roles change rapidly and fluidly within the alcoholic family system. On the surface, it often appears that the alcoholic is the only scapegoat or victim in the alcoholic family system. Clinical work with alcoholic families reveals the fallacy of this superficial appearance. Roles continuously change within the alcoholic family system in a *quid pro quo* manner. The alcoholic places himself in the role of family scapegoat for perhaps a day, week, or even longer. Behaviorally, the alcoholic chooses to be the family scapegoat. When the addicted family member behaves himself into the role of family scapegoat or victim, other family members actively reinforce the scapegoat role of the alcoholic. In a neurotically adaptive fashion, the alcoholic family member soon assumes a familial role other than scapegoat. When this role reversal takes place, another family member becomes the scapegoat. Within the alcoholic family system, the children periodically form an alliance against the alcoholic parent, the nonalcoholic parent and each other. The alcoholic parent and the nonalcoholic parent frequently form an alliance against the children or a particular child. In this context "against" means that one or any number of the family members interact with another family member in a manner which victimizes or scapegoats another family member. I suspect that guilt plays an important role in the timing of interfamilial role reversals within the alcoholic family system. A primitive sense of when to place self or another family member in the role of family victim or scapegoat can be viewed as an interfamilial process which serves the purpose of guarding against the outcropping of a schizophrenic symptom choice upon the part of any particular family member. In this way, the "role slippage" which constantly takes place in the alcoholic family system is neurotically adaptive.

Chronic, overdetermined role reversal, involving every member in the alcoholic family system, precipitates feelings of anger, hostility and frustration upon the part of each family member. Clear-cut and consistent patterns of communication and interrelationship are lacking in the alcoholic family. The homeostatic equilibrium in the alcoholic family system is one of disequilibrium. Ambiguity and uncertainty result in violence and angry acting-out within the alcoholic family system. Obviously, transactional and relationship chaos can be associated with such a style of family living. Rage, anger and hostility within the alcoholic family system are relationship-determined affects as well as intrapersonally oriented and determined feelings. One family relationship interaction effect of living with an alcoholic is to be angry. As the alcoholic is angry, so are the nonaddicted spouse and children. Furthermore, each member in an alcoholic family system can only be marginally in control of feelings of rage and hostility. Physical and psychological acting-out against each other constitutes one *sine qua non* of the alcoholic family system. Progressively and systematically, the alcoholic family system becomes out of control. It is not just the alcoholic family member who "looses control." Physical violence and assaults, as well as poorly controlled psychological attacks, eventually involve every member living in the alcoholic family. The alcoholic physically and psychologically "abuses" the nonaddicted spouse and the children. Children living within an alcoholic family system ruthlessly attack their parents and sometimes go so far as to actually murder a parent, typically the alcoholic. The nonaddicted spouse attempts to destroy the alcoholic psychologically and sometimes physically as well. Child abuse and neglect are very often basic to the alcoholic family system. Understandably, survival in a physical and psychological sense is frequently a paramount matter of concern for every member living in an alcoholic family system.

As each family member persists within the alcoholic family system, the more the family system, as well as each individual family member, becomes dependent upon this symbiotic relationship choice. The spouse of the alcoholic becomes increasingly dependent upon the alcoholic in a multiplicity of ways. The alcoholic, over an extended number of years of marriage and family living, becomes more and more dependent upon the nonaddicted spouse and children. Children who grow up within an alcoholic family system are often pathologically attached to the family system. It would seem logical to assume that the children and nonaddicted spouse of the alcoholic would try in every way possible to escape or leave such a family system. Alcoholics constantly threaten their spouses and children with leaving, separation or divorce. I have found in my clinical work with alcoholic family systems that these families remain together as a result of pathological family ego fusion. Alcoholic marriages and families which have somehow endured for fifteen or twenty years generally continue to endure in spite of all else. The identity of each separate family member is fused with the family system. Such a process of family ego fusion reinforces symbiotic dependence and persistence within the alcoholic family system. This process also reinforces the actualization of an eventual alcoholic symptom choice upon the part of children growing up in an alcoholic family system and likewise can be associated with the re-creation of alcoholic family systems by those family members who leave the original alcoholic family system. As the alcoholic family becomes isolated and removed from other families and healthy extrafamilial interpersonal relationships, the various members of the alcoholic family system are pushed into a pathological family coalition in order to survive. It should be pointed out that in some alcoholic family systems, one or more family members will adaptively terminate their family involvement and intrafamilial relationships.

Sexually oriented relationship conflicts are very often a part of the alcoholic family system. As noted earlier in the chapter, promiscuous sexual acting-out by the alcoholic family member is a rather common source of family conflict within the alcoholic family system. Children growing up in an alcoholic family are cognizant of the marital and sexual struggles of their parents. At the time of adolescence these children of alcoholic families begin to act-out pathologically in numerous ways to include rebellion against and outright rejection of the sexually promiscuous alcoholic parent. By the same token, the child or children who have grown up in an alcoholic family system may act-out against the nonaddicted parent at the time of adolescence. Invariably, children who grow up within the confines of an alcoholic family system are hurt and abused psychologically, if not physically. I have found that as a means of retaliation against their parents many children who have grown up in an alcoholic family system act-out sexually and aggressively. In the event one or both parents in an alcoholic family system are pathologically promiscuous, their children experience role and identity conflicts specific to the issue of sexuality. This is but another primary area of family confusion and chaos. The parent who models inappropriate or bizarre sexual behavior within a family constellation may profoundly effect the sexual development of his or her children. A parent who is sexually aloof, cold and rejecting can obviously affect and influence the sexual adjustment style of his or her children. Sexual conflicts are always relationship conflicts in varying ways and degrees. As the alcoholic family relationship is invariably disturbed, it is only logical to surmise a sexual dimension to be a part of the family relationship disturbance, and it has been my clinical experience that this is very often the exact situation.

With regard to familial sexual psychopathology at the more

floridly deviant end of the continuum, it has been my observation that the actual seduction of a daughter by an alcoholic stepfather is not an uncommon occurance. While I was employed by the military (Army) as a clinical director of two comprehensive addict treatment centers, this family dynamic was a frequent issue in the treatment of military alcoholic family systems. More rarely the alcoholic husband may, while in a state of intoxication, homosexually assault his son. Intrafamilial sexual deviation, in my clinical experience, usually involves adolescents but from time to time may involve even young children. Very few alcoholic families are willing to work on issues of this variety in an extended family therapy relationship.

These pathological issues of family living constitute the primary sources of relationship disturbance within the alcoholic family system. The members of an alcoholic family system are forever "blaming" each other for their individual difficulties in life as well as family problems. Although the nonaddicted spouse tends to assume many of the responsibilities associated with parenting and family living, each member in the alcoholic family system in many ways attempts to avoid or rejects matters of personal responsibility. Let us turn to a consideration of the strategies of family therapy which I have found useful in working with alcoholic family systems.

Strategies of Psychotherapy for Working with Alcoholic Families

The global alcoholic family relationship style or pattern must be significantly modified. In other words, the family psychotherapist must, in his or her relationship with the alcoholic family system, function in a manner conducive to facilitating transactional, behavioral and communicative changes within the family interrelationship. In sum, this amounts to the task of extinguishing the various psychonoxious dimensions operational within the alcoholic family system. Congruent with this process, the family therapist actively teaches and reinforces new and more adaptive patterns of family living.

Exactly how can these monumentous therapeutic goals be accomplished? The work of family therapy with the alcoholic family system is accomplished via the therapist's relationship *within* the family. I have found that this work can be most efficaciously conducted by including in the treatment relationship the alcoholic family member, the nonaddicted spouse and all other primary family members above the age of ten who are living within the alcoholic family system. Children below the age of ten who are living in an alcoholic family system are generally not to be included in the family therapy relationship for a number of reasons pertaining to their relative levels of emotional, cognitive and interpersonal development. In the event the child or children in an alcoholic family under the age of approximately ten exhibit psychopathological symptoms, a referral for individual therapy should be made as soon as possible. From time to time I have worked with alcoholic family systems including a parent or relative of one of the spouses who was residing within the alcoholic family constellation. In one such case, the mother-in-law and the identified alcoholic drank together no less than three or four nights each week. Obviously, this was an issue of primary clinical importance which dictated the involvement of the mother-in-law in the family therapy process.

Modification of the alcoholic family system begins with a focus upon the drinking behavior of the addicted family member. The chaos, violence and relationship pathology within the alcoholic family system can in large measure be associated specifically with the alcoholic adjustment style of the addicted family member. Invariably, when the alcoholic family member terminates his or her addiction the family system changes rather significantly from a relationship perspective. Attempting to conduct family therapy while the alcoholic family member is intoxicated in the treatment session is inappropriate and can result in any number of iatrogenic outcomes. A basic groundrule for the family therapist to establish with the alcoholic family in the first treatment session is that the alcoholic family member will attend all sessions *completely* sober. I strongly suggest that the alcoholic terminate his or her drinking behavior during the first family therapy session; in the event the alcoholic is unable to accept this position, I make it quite clear that treatment sessions will not be held in the event that the alcoholic has been drinking on the day of the scheduled family therapy session. All drinking while in family therapy is grist for the treatment process. It is also efficacious to point out very early in family therapy that successful treatment demands work, commitment and a good deal of *family* effort. Although the family therapist cannot "guarantee" a particular treatment outcome, he can indicate that "success" in whatever context is contingent upon family and relationship change. As is true with regard to the initial session or sessions for the marital therapist, the family therapist must deter the occurrence of violent and uncontrolled family confrontations early in the treatment process. Usually such an attack involves the spouses, although the adolescent family member may attempt to initiate such a transaction against one or both parents during the initial treatment sessions. In the event the initial treatment session or sessions become overly affective and "out of control," a particular family member or the entire family system will often terminate treatment. The family therapist frequently assumes the role of a "buffer agent" within the alcoholic family system. This is concretely so within the family therapy situation, but once a productive therapeutic alliance has been established with the alcoholic family system, the therapist imago becomes a controlling or buffer factor external to the explicit treatment situation. Each family member learns very quickly that his or her behavior and various interactions within the family system will be openly discussed in the family therapy process. This simple factor can operate to stabilize and facilitate interpersonal control within the relatively more adjusted alcoholic family system.

During the early family therapy sessions each family member attempts to demonstrate to the other family members as well as the therapist just how victimized he or she has been by the family system. Often this amounts to blaming other family members and whining about "poor me" and "ain't it awful." The alcoholic family member blames the spouse and children by stating, "if you would only do such and such, I wouldn't drink the way I do." The nonaddicted spouse complains about "all the bills," "the children just won't behave" and asserts that "it's all your (the alcoholic's) fault." Children living in these family systems are confused. They may blame the alcoholic one minute, the nonaddicted spouse the next, and finally themselves. Everybody in the alcoholic family system expresses a wish to be out of the family relationship, and each is quick to let the other and the therapist know that he or she is "fed up with it all." Clearly, these family as well as individual feelings and transactional communications are in large measure a function of the pervasive victimizing, scapegoating and "double binding" processes operational within the alcoholic family system. One of the most arduous tasks confronting the family therapist is that of helping to facilitate change in the realm of these transactions within the alcoholic family system. The process of family therapy with alcoholic families consistently involves this matter from beginning to end. In order to modify or extinguish interfamilial victimizing, scapegoating and similar transactions ("double binding" and persecuting), the family therapist must consistently identify and point out such transactions when they occur in the therapy process, explore the various psychodynamic issues underlying the transaction, make active interpretations specific to the transaction, and explore and help the family members involved in each specific transaction actualize specific alternatives to the transaction. When a family member is victimized or feels victimized in a family therapy session, the treatment strategies just indicated are implemented. It is important to spend adequate time processing with each family member how it feels or how it felt to be victimized. In certain respects, the family therapist strives to teach each family member what victimizing (and similar pathological family transactions) is, for what purposes such a procedure is carried out by a family member, how to immediately identify a victimizing transaction and finally, how to avoid being victimized and how not to victimize other family members. It is important to explore in the therapeutic fashion just delineated familial victimizing transactions which take place outside of the family therapy sessions. I know very well how difficult it is for the family therapist to continuously actualize and employ the strategies of intervention which I have just proposed. It must be remembered that successful family therapy with the alcoholic family is not a process or set of therapeutic interventions limited to five or ten hours of work with the family. The family therapist cannot abreactively attempt to radically change the alcoholic family system overnight. Nor can the family therapist expect the alcoholic family system, as a result of his therapeutic interventions, to change dramatically following a few short hours of family therapy. As each family member becomes increasingly adept at understanding the particular transactions and communications which pathologically occur and are employed in his or her unique alcoholic family system, the family therapist will begin to see treatment-facilitated changes taking place. Members of the alcoholic family system likewise begin to perceive and experience positive change in their interpersonal relations. Just as the alcoholic family system has historically interacted in a progressively more pathological manner, so can the alcoholic family system in therapy begin to synergistically interact in any number of different and more adaptive ways.

As the alcoholic family system vis-à-vis the family therapy process begins to interact, communicate and behave more appropriately and adaptively, the family system in essence stabilizes. As I pointed out earlier, prior to being involved in family therapy the alcoholic family system is "out of control" in the sense of having a chronically disturbed familial interrelationship. When family members begin to terminate their parataxic patterns of interfamilial communication and behaving (scapegoating, role reversal, persecuting and victimizing, etc.), I have observed a concomitant modification of rage, anger and resentment-oriented transactions within the alcoholic family system. Invariably, the alcoholic family system including a drinking alcoholic is a very violent family. When people interact and behave according to the pathological paradigms discussed thus far with regard to the alcoholic family system, feelings of anger and resentment result. The family therapist must begin to work with the angry and violent transactions of the alcoholic family system early in the treatment process. It is not uncommon to find in the course of family therapy with alcoholic families that physical assaults, beatings and violent acts have occurred or are even presently occurring in the family with which the therapist is working. Exploring the historical acts of violence within the alcoholic family system is important to the familial process of working through in family therapy. Tragically, childen are very often physically abused and always psychologically abused in the alcoholic family system. When these violent transactions have occured in the alcoholic family system, parents feel guilty and angry at themselves or each other. Children are deeply hurt, confused and angry. The non-addicted spouse of the alcoholic is usually angry, hostile and resentful, yet the children living in an alcoholic family system are just as resentful and angry at the spouse or the alcoholic. Each year many adolescents living in an alcoholic family system either choose to prematurely leave home or more tragically take the life of a family member, usually that of the alcoholic. Poor controlled rage and anger cause family members to confront and attack each other. Members of the alcoholic family system attack and ventilate feelings of anger and resentment against the family scapegoat. As the family scapegoat or victim is from day to day and week to week a different family member, each member in the alcoholic family system knows that "his or her day will come" with regard to being on the receiving end of familial persecution transactions. As each family member understands very well the various feelings of stress and uncomfortableness associated with the role of family scapegoat, the family therapist can point out and reinforce more adaptive patterns of family living which each family member can practice. This process frequently results in another very important source of treatment-facilitated gain. After a family member or the family system victimizes and persecutes another family member, guilt is experienced. Individual or family guilt is experienced under these circumstances. The alcoholic family system is neurotically encapsulated in any number of vicious circles, this being but one explicit example of an ongoing family adjustment style which is chronically unresolved and pathological. When the alcoholic family system becomes significantly stabilized with regard to role vacillation, there is no longer a need for the family members to experience marked guilt in their interpersonal relationships. This process further synergizes healthy and more adaptive patterns of family living. Familial stabilization with regard to a decrease in pathological "role slippage" results in less family chaos, less violence and angry acting-out in the family system and finally, guilt and other intrapersonal affective disturbances are significantly decreased. It may be necessary or even manditory for the family therapist to effect a legal intervention in the alcoholic family system in the event that he becomes aware of physical abuse and violent confrontation within the alcoholic family. Such an intervention may be critically important to the process of family therapy, particularly if the alcoholic spouse resumes drinking or goes on a "binge" while in treatment. Violence within the alcoholic family system, in my experience, can often be directly associated with the drinking behavior of the alcoholic family member or is alcohol facilitated.

The family therapist working with an alcoholic family system from time to time is faced with the problem of familial incest. This issue may result in the family decision to enter therapy or more often constitutes the reason for referral to the family therapist. In the event a family is referred for therapy due to the explicit matter of incest, the family therapist should immediately concentrate on this issue in the initial treatment sessions. Covert pathological sexual alliances, not involving frank sexual acting-out upon the part of any of the family members, can contribute greatly to the global relationship disturbance of the alcoholic family system. When the therapist suspects such an alliance within the alcoholic family system, it must be dealt with and openly discussed in the therapy situation. It is generally inappropriate for the family therapist to assume a probing, interrogating stance with regard to *suspected* sexually oriented psychodynamic issues pertaining to the alcoholic family system. A working therapeutic alliance must be established with the alcoholic family system prior to the therapeutic exploration of highly emotional sexual issues involving the family. The timing of interpretations and confrontations is of crucial importance in the matter of dealing with familial sexual pathology. Should the therapist find out in the process of family therapy that an overt sexual liaison has existed or currently exists between family members, he will be confronted with a number of difficult treatment decisions. In many states, the therapist who is made aware of this form of information by a patient or family member must divulge this same information to the appropriately designated agency. In my own clinical experience, frank sexual acting-out in the alcoholic family system has almost always involved an alcoholic father and his early adolescent stepdaughter. The stepfather has initiated such encounters while intoxicated. In these cases, it can be important for the family therapist to play an active role in the process of securing a family placement (outside of the alcoholic family) for the stepdaughter. Family therapy is certainly one of the few viable treatment procedures available for dealing with interfamilial sexual object deviation. In addition to maintaining the adolescent stepdaughter in family therapy once such a disclosure has been made in the context of family therapy, I work with the stepdaughter in individual psychotherapy. I have found that many alcoholic fathers terminate family therapy once such a disclosure has been made. Even under these circumstances, family therapy should be continued with the remaining family members. In the event that the alcoholic father terminates family therapy following an incestuous familial disclosure, every effort should be made to engage the father in some form of psychotherapy. Familial incest, as well as more covert familial sexual pathology, facilitates relationship disturbance, confusion, anger and virtual plethora of other difficulties for each member in the alcoholic family system.

Initially in his work with alcoholic families, the family therapist will observe many familial and relationship conflicts involving the matter of control. The middle and later stages of family therapy with the alcoholic family system involve going over and over this issue. Following some fifteen to twenty hours of work with an alcoholic family, I have found myself continuously dealing with the neurotic attempts upon the part of one family member to control another family member or the entire family system. The alcoholic parataxically controls the alcoholic family system via his or her addiction. The nonaddicted spouse attempts to neurotically control the drinking behavior of the alcoholic as well as the acting-out behaviors of the children. Assuming responsibility for the global process of family living is in many respects adaptive, and yet this same process is paradoxically neurotic and maladaptive on behalf of the nonaddicted spouse. Children in an alcoholic family system parataxically control or attempt to control their parents and the family system via retaliation and acting-out behaviors. The family therapist must stress the point that family members cannot in reality control or be responsible for each other. Ultimately, the spouse and children of the alcoholic cannot control the drinking behavior of the alcoholic. They cannot choose "for the alcoholic" not to drink. Adolescent children who grossly misbehave within and outside of the alcoholic family system generally cannot be "controlled" by the wishes or beatings of their parents. The children of the alcoholic, by the same token, cannot be responsible for the irresponsible behaviors of their parents. As the alcoholic family system is "out of control," we can view the distorted attempts of each family member to control other family members and the family system as maneuvers which are prototaxically carried out in order for the person to feel in control of himself or herself. When one family member feels he can control another family member, or the family system, he feels more in control of himself. A sense of personal security, certainty, predictability and a diminishment of ambiguity constitute some of the primary underlying psychodynamic reasons for the control struggles basic to every member living in an alcoholic family system.

One pathological control maneuver utilized frequently by the spouse of the alcoholic family member is that of "setting the alcoholic up" for further intoxication. This process may occur during the early and middle stages of family therapy; however, such a family tactic of interaction often takes place later in the family therapy situation, especially if the nonaddicted spouse is beginning to consciously feel and realize that things are not radically improved in the family realtionship. I have come to view such familial transactions as a form of sabotage. In effect, the spouse and children of the alcoholic can obsequiously, if not overtly, reinforce further drinking by the alcoholic. The alcoholic family system, by effecting such a regressive process, chooses to live with the various conflicts thus far discussed. When the alcoholic responds to familial messages and feedback suggesting intoxication by resuming his alcoholic drinking, he is at once "the one" responsible for *all* of the family problems. Family therapists who treat alcoholic family systems will find that immediate exploration and examination of this dynamic when it is suspected can be therapeutically most efficacious. Spouses who begin to drink a good deal more following the sobriety of the alcoholic family member frequently sabotage the family therapy process. When the children or spouse of the alcoholic family member begin to suggest that "two or three" drinks "wouldn't hurt" the alcoholic, the family therapist should confront the family system with the distorted nature of such messages. Many of the families I have worked with told the alcoholic family member in no uncertain terms that "things were better when you were drunk." Such interfamilial messages are extremely destructive and reflect a familial need for a scape-goat. Furthermore, when family members begin to communicate along these lines, I suspect they are attempting to avoid the real work, responsibility and personal committment required of effective family therapy.

The later stages of family therapy, after perhaps thirty or forty hours of work, consist of reinforcing the areas of gain facilitated by earlier treatment efforts. Covering old material in less emotional and distorted ways is central to the final working through process in family therapy with alcoholic families. I find that homework tasks involving the entire family are more easily actualized by the family later in the treatment process. Dealing with feelings associated with interfamilial concern, warmth, love and even anger assumes an increasingly important role in the later stages of family therapy with alcoholic families. Family decision making becomes possible later in treatment. Some spouses rationally decide not to continue living together while in family therapy. This decision significantly impacts upon the entire family system. When such a decision takes place late in the treatment process, the family can more rationally determine the process of family living effected by divorce.

In summary, family therapy with the alcoholic family system must be directed at the modification of the familial relationship. As the family therapist behaves and interacts within the alcoholic family system, he actively points out the transactional, behavioral and communicative distortions taking place in the family. The alcoholic family member must terminate his or her drinking in order for positive familial relationship change to take place. In my own experience, family therapy should include all family members above ten years of age, and in certain cases it is quite appropriate to include extended family members in the treatment process. A more adaptive homeostatic equilibrium must be established within the alcoholic family system. This therapeutic goal can be accomplished by extinguishing the scapegoating and victimizing transactions which occur in the alcoholic family system. The sabotaging, controlling and other familial adjustment patterns touched upon in this chapter must be modified if the alcoholic family system is to be successfully treated in family therapy. It is important to avoid family "blow-ups" early in the treatment process. Family therapy requires continued work and commitment upon the part of each family member. Successful family therapy can result in divorce or a change in the family structure. An important objective for the family therapist is that of helping the alcoholic family system to reengage itself with the larger community. I suggest to the families that I work with an involvement with the Alcoholics Anonymous community (A.A., Al-Anon, Alateen). Even in the realms of family sexual pathology, violence and dependency conflicts, the active involvement of each family member within the Alcoholics Anonymous community can result in both individual and familial change. Alcoholism is a cancerous familial disorder.

This chapter is admittedly limited in scope, both with regard to strategies of treatment and psychodynamic formulations. Nevertheless, it is an important contribution to the field of alcoholic treatment and rehabilitation. To date, very little has been written about marital and family therapy involving the chronic alcoholic. Marital and family therapies with an alcoholic are difficult clinical enterprises. These particular strategies of intervention require rather long-term commitments upon the part of all parties involved, including the therapist. The field of alcoholic rehabilitation sorely needs a comprehensive textbook devoted to the topics of family and marital therapy involving the alcoholic. Successful marital and family therapy with an alcoholic spouse or family member begins with the establishment of sobriety upon the part of the alcoholic. Hopefully, the reader will be able to gain from this chapter a better perspective about the processes of alcoholic marital and family therapy. Chronic alcoholism is always an interpersonal process. By definition this pathological process always categorically affects the significant others in the immediate life space of the addicted person, hence the marital and familial relationships of the alcoholic are invariably disturbed. The marital and family therapist who works with alcoholic marriages and families must always strive to effect marital and family relationship change.

Chapter 12

TREATMENT VII
THE RECOVERY ISSUE

To discuss alcoholism or problem drinking from the perspective of "recovery" is in certain respects congruous with accepting the medical model or disease concept specific to alcohol addiction. Thus far I have attempted to avoid this area of debate. In chapter two it was pointed out that the disease model of alcoholism fits well with the concept of developmental stages relative to drinking behavior. However, to avoid the "recovery" issue seems to be a gross avoidance of a very relevant matter. Every alcoholic or problem drinker I have known who has successfully terminated his or her drinking behavior has been confronted in a very real and meaningful way with this issue. In reality this statement may apply to virtually every individual experiencing difficulty as a result of problem drinking or alcohol addiction. Perhaps it is only the person who eventually attains sobriety who consciously and meaningfully deals with the recovery issue. "Have I recovered?" "Am I still recovering?" and "Will I ever be fully recovered?" are the types of ongoing questions which I hear these individuals asking. Unfortunately, those of us who purport to be expert in the field of alcohol addiction really have no definitive answers to questions such as these. Hopefully this situation might change within the next decade or two. Nonetheless, these are questions which we are forced to come to grips with presently on a day-to-day basis. While there are virtually no "hard" data relative to the recovery issue, and for that matter the problem of alcohol addiction *in toto,* I would like to share some of my observations and feelings regarding this general matter.

First of all let me point out that I am not particularly concerned with the relationship between the recovery issue and the medical model or disease model of alcohol addiction. In my work with people experiencing difficulty in the process of daily living which stems in large part from their drinking behavior, I am foremost concerned with helping them terminate this specific behavior. I have found that viewing the patient's alcoholic behavior as a disease helps me very little as a therapist. In fact, viewing the patient's addictive behavior as a disease and communicating this to him may well serve to reinforce his drinking behavior — it gives him another excuse! While some might simply argue against verbally communicating such information to the patient, I am of the utmost certain opinion that such feedback literally oozes out of the therapist's every pore. It is my opinion that therapist behaviors communicating "You have a disease, you are an alcoholic" amount to nothing more than "You are not responsible for your behavior," which in effect means "Continue to drink." At the same time we must realize that alcoholism and problem drinking may in fact be disease oriented. Genetic and hereditary factors may eventually be identified as primary precipitants or causative determiners of alcohol addiction. Moreover, within the therapeutic context there may be occasion to reap "gain" from the usage of the disease concept. The analogy of the diabetic has often been used in this context. Patients taking Antabuse have probably heard this frequently: "If you had diabetes you would take insulin wouldn't you? — if you have 'alcoholism' then, doesn't it make sense to take Antabuse?" While this analogy may be somewhat inappropriate, if it in fact works, most of us — spouse, children, therapist, etc. — are happy with the patient's behavior. In short, therapeutic gain may well also be a potential by-product of the disease model concept. Certainly the therapeutic management of guilt and depression is made easier by a strong emphasis upon the disease model of alcohol addiction.

I have observed active members of Alcoholics Anonymous with as many as ten to fifteen years of total sobriety consistently refer to themselves as "recovering" alcoholics. In general, I would prefer to use this same approach in explaining or handling the recovery issue with patients. The "recovering" concept encompasses personal responsibility for one's drinking behavior, as well as providing for more global human growth potential. Initial sobriety is contingent upon interpersonal growth. Ongoing sobriety is just as contingent upon continual interpersonal growth and in all probability is an impossibility in the absence of such movement. The point at which the "recovering" alcoholic stops changing and growing interpersonally is the point at which he once again becomes intoxicated. In this respect recovery means an ongoing process of learning new and more effective patterns of behavior. When this stops the patient may well have only one behavioral alternative — to return to the bottle. Prior learning, conditioning and behavioral programming dictate this to be the case. Another related source of gain offered by the "recovering" concept has to do with the reinforcement of an ongoing awareness of what things were like prior to the termination of drinking. In a real fashion this amounts to a constant reminder of what things were like before. As most alcoholics and problem drinkers have a history of numerous attempts to stop drinking prior to actual success in this difficult matter, it also helps them remember what happened at those points when they either viewed themselves as recovered or able to drink socially again. Unfortunately, reaching this point means entering an experiential hell once again for the vast majority of alcoholics and problem drinkers. I suspect the magic of the repetition compulsion to be at work here as well. Getting sober via A.A. usually means a rather thorough conditioning to the "recovering" concept. Once sober, the compulsive dynamism of the alcoholic character structure accounts for the repetition of whatever behaviors might happen to be associated with the positive experience of sobriety. Indeed, this magic often "works" for the remainder of the individual's life. Alcoholics Anonymous often becomes a source of magic for many formerly addicted individuals; in fact, many have suggested this amounts to no more than switching addictions. While it can scarcely be argued that this may essentially be true, most would be reluctant to condemn this change in addiction or compulsion. This is most certainly the case as long as the change in addiction "works" or, in other words, successfully helps maintain the individual's sobriety.

Recovery as a concept describing the fact that a given individual or a particular group of people do terminate their alcoholic behavior seems to me to be an extremely important social and interpersonal reality. Viewed from this perspective, recovery from alcohol addiction simply means that people do terminate their drinking behavior. In my experience the termination of drinking is usually accompanied by a termination of numerous other "crazy" behaviors. It is imperative that we as change agents work to inform the general public that this form of "recovery" is the fate of thousands of alcoholic and problem-drinking individuals each year. "Once an alcoholic, always an alcoholic," has been the stereotype most people have accepted as truth. This simply need not be the case. Expectancies such as these only maintain social and interpersonal reinforcement contingencies which serve to perpetuate the alcoholic trap. In this sense we must stress the point that alcoholics and problem drinkers do "recover." This also applies to the philosophical orientation of alcoholic rehabilitation personnel and agencies. It is my feeling that we must continually emphasize to patients the fact that recovery is and has been the fate of countless numbers of alcohol-addicted persons. As I mentioned earlier, it is my feeling that models (other individuals who have experienced the same alcoholic process and have been sober for extended periods of time) serve the most effective means of communicating the reality of recovery or change potential.

I am well aware of the tenuous nature of "recovery" from alcohol addiction. This seems to be particularly true during the initial six or eight months of sobriety. It is during this interval that "slips" or regressive phenomena are rather common. In my experience, once the addicted individual has been able to establish this much total sobriety, his potential for remaining sober on a continued basis is quite good. Patients who do initiate drinking once again after such a prolonged period of abstinence usually respond favorably to further treatment. Should such a regression take place after seeming success in the rehabilitation effort, it is imperative that every effort be exerted to reengage the patient and significant others in the treatment program. Unfortunately, it is just at this point that many patients, families and even therapists often give up. The gamesmanship of the wife who asserts "See, I told you so," is all too familiar to those experienced in alcoholic rehabilitation matters. At this point, immediate treatment reengagement must be the goal. Clinically, I feel it is important to acknowledge and understand the reality of this regressive potential. In so doing, it becomes possible to recognize situational and ongoing lifestyle presses which help facilitate the patient's alcoholic behaviors. Dealing with these issues prior to the slip or drinking bout becomes of paramount importance to the process of maintaining the sobriety of given patients at particular points in the therapeutic enterprise. Moreover, there would seem to be a good deal of practical education inherent in the awareness that recovery in essence means an ongoing struggle. Being around A.A. brings this entire aspect of the recovery issue into focus. Too many individuals with ten or fifteen years of total abstinence seemingly overnight end up drunk again. It is for this reason that ongoing "treatment" of some type seems to be indicated for most alcoholic and problem-drinking patients completing a rehabilitation program. While A.A. is allegedly not a treatment-oriented group, it is my strong feeling that treatment is indeed the *modus operandi* of this organization. As such, I recommend involvement with this organization as a form of community follow-up. This is most obviously appropriate in the absence of community mental health services.

In short, recovery is an experiential reality for many alcoholics and problem drinkers. "Once an alcoholic, always an alcoholic" is an untruth which those of us involved in the alcoholic rehabilitation field must actively work to dispel. The simple fact is that countless numbers of alcoholic and problem drinking individuals have terminated their addiction. This is the reality of the "recovery" issue. At the same time recovery is acknowledged as tenuous. Long-term sobriety is contingent upon working at being sober. In essence, this means continual interpersonal growth. When formerly alcohol-addicted patients quit growing and changing interpersonally, they frequently return to the one behavioral alternative thev have learned so well: the bottle. Recovery has historically been associated with medically oriented phenomena. This need not be the case with regard to alcohol addiction. Recovery in the sense of being sober is significantly enhanced through ongoing contact with other human beings and organizations which are oriented toward a nondrinking life-style.

Chapter 13

TREATMENT VIII
TOWARD A CAUSATIVE THEORY
OF ALCOHOL ADDICTION

IN reality we know very little about the causes or possible causes of alcohol addiction. In this chapter I have chosen to discuss briefly some of the current theoretical determinants relative to the problem of alcohol addiction. In addition, I have included a good deal of theoretical material based upon my work and clinical experience with alcohol-addicted individuals. I suspect this chapter may impress the reader with just how inadequately we understand the basics of alcohol addiction. Rather than responding to this reality in a depressive or avoidance manner, hopefully the reader might feel some source of challenge, stimulation and engagement in this present situation.

Heredity has historically been championed as a primary determinant of a wide variety of aberrant behaviors. Unfortunately, biological science has been unsuccessful to date in its attempts at proving or disproving the role of hereditary influence upon interpersonal and social behaviors. While this general situation may be reversed in the immediate future, we must nonetheless deal with the scientific givens of today. This exact situation characterizes the problem of alcohol addiction (Von Wartburg, 1971). Jellinek (1945), evaluating the results of a number of studies including a total sample of some 4,000 alcoholics, found that 52 percent of these subjects had at least one alcoholic parent. It is significant to note that Jellinek reports that 35 percent of the sample manifested some form of psychiatric deviance in common with their parents. Rather than concluding that alcoholism is hereditarily determined, Jellinek (1945) supports the position of hereditary influence via constitutional instability to the social risks of inebriation. Bleuler

(1955), investigating upper-class alcoholic patients seen in a psychiatric clinic, reported similar findings. Other investigators have either indicated a lack of evidence of a hereditary factor in the etiology of alcoholism (Roe, 1945) or have minimally supported such a position (McCord and McCord, 1960; McCord, 1972). It is apparent that we simply do not know the extent, if any, that genetic factors play in the development of alcohol addiction and problem drinking.

A related causative explanation of alcohol addiction has been associated with endocrine disorder. Smith (1950, 1951) proposed that alcoholism was caused by pituitary deficiency which resulted secondarily in adrenal-cortex exhaustion. As with others who have attributed alcoholism to endocrine disorder, Smith failed to provide scientific evidence in support of his theory.

The nutritional theory of alcoholism asserts that a metabolic defect results in cellular requirement for alcohol ingestion. This basic premise of nutritional theory, as well as other divergent theories based upon the nutritional concept, has proved unsound and unsatisfactory.

An even less accepted theory is that of alcoholism as an allergy. In essence, the "allergy" theory of alcoholism maintains that a particular body chemistry results in addiction or loss of control for the allergic individual upon alcohol ingestion. While it would seem possible that certain individuals with a peculiar constitutional sensitivity to the ingestion of alcohol might experience an increased desire for alcohol once its effects have been experienced, this general theory has been criticized (Haggard, 1944) as supported only by analogy, metaphor and connotation.

All of these body physiology or physically oriented theories of alcohol addiction are tangentially, if not directly, related to the disease model or theory of alcoholism (Jellinek, 1960; De-Lint, 1971). This theory of alcohol addiction has certainly received more recognition than those previously discussed. Alcoholics Anonymous is constructed around the validity of the disease model of alcoholism. While the disease model has, in general, achieved a good deal of professional and paraprofessional acceptance, many vehemently oppose this explanation of alcoholism. There is in actuality significant dissonance among those accepting this general model. This situation is most apparent with regard to the specifics of the disease process. The "unitary disease" concept (Milt, 1969) advocates that the differences in the psychological and behavioral manifestations of the alcoholism are secondary if not irrelevant. The disease process is the uncontrollable, addictive drinking behavior per se. More globally, the disease model of alcoholism (Edwards, 1970) posits that when certain predisposed individuals come into contact with alcohol they initiate a disease process which ultimately results in all the characteristics and symptoms specific to the diagnosis of alcoholism. Central to this theory is the developmental behavioral progression as well as the ultimate tissue and general medical condition of the addicted individual. As is true of the earlier discussed theories of alcohol addiction, research procedures to date have been grossly unsuccessful in proving the validity of the disease model of alcohol addiction. One of the most heated areas of current debate among alcoholic rehabilitation personnel is that of accepting or rejecting the disease model of alcohol addiction. I suspect this exact situation may still prevail ten years hence.

Alcohol addiction and problem drinking have also been extensively explained via numerous environmental-psychologically oriented theories. Generally speaking this type of explanation begins with an evaluation of parental and other primary environmental reinforcers of behavior and extends to include individual personality characteristics, internal psychodynamics and eventually incorporates global psychiatric considerations. Within this environmental-psychological rubric one finds a great deal of theoretical data relative to the role of parental influence upon the development of alcoholism and problem drinking in offspring. A good deal of this type of information is based upon patient reports of parental behavior and status. With the exception of the studies of McCord and McCord (1960), Robin et al. (1962) and McCord (1972), we have very little longitudinal data to support the "like father, like son" model of alcoholism (Weiner, Tamerin, Steinglass and Mendelson, 1971). These authors report that children who eventually became alcoholics were products of families of low social status; they had inadequate parents who themselves displayed antisocial behavior; and more precisely they had experienced a particular family constellation in which the father held very little esteem for the wife, the mother herself was overtly a social deviant, and both parents consistently failed to provide clear-cut, responsible, male-role expectancies for the boy. It is apparent that generalizations such as these might well be applied to most psychiatric patients.

Data inferences of a more extended environmental type are even more difficult to support. It is relatively well established that growing up in a slum or ghetto district sets some rather potent limits and barriers regarding occupational, educational and socioeconomic potential. These areas also seem to enhance the potential for becoming a psychiatric patient, an alcoholic or simply a social outcast or deviant. To ferret out the cause-and-effect relationship of such an interaction is a virtual impossibility. It must also be remembered that individuals respond to environmental presses in an individual as well as collective manner. We can most assuredly surmise that the effect tendency of particular total environmental press systems may well be in the direction of enhanced probability of becoming alcohol-addicted for given individuals.

One environmentally oriented psychological model of alcohol addiction which has received growing stature and acceptance among professionals is based upon learning theory. While the essentials of learning theory have been applied to alcoholism and problem drinking for quite some time, recently the "new twist" of behavior modification, behavior therapy, operant conditioning and aversion techniques has accounted for a resurgent interest in this method of explanation as well as treatment. Although different learning theorists tend to emphasize somewhat different specifics of learning theory, they are in strong agreement that alcoholic behavior is learned behavior. One general model of learning theory applied to alcoholism and problem drinking is that of anxiety (as well as other noxious affective states) — alcohol ingestion — relief from the unpleasant affective state. Within this paradigm the anxious individual learns that he can effectively extinguish his uncomfortable emotional state by ingesting alcohol. This process is practiced and repeated to the extent of becoming highly overlearned. Upon becoming anxious the individual simply begins to drink. It is apparent that this process might become a continual endeavor for the chronically anxious person. Indeed, it might become akin to a conditioned reflex. It should also be noted that the reinforcement, or escape from the unpleasant emotional state, is immediate. This also serves to enhance the probability of the same behavioral sequence occurring in similar circumstances. Moreover, the drinking response tends to progressively preempt other potential response contingencies. This is understandably the case as long as it extinguishes or partially blocks the unpleasant affective state. While this particular explanation of learning to become addicted to alcohol includes a wealth of other complexities, many of which we only partially understand, it does explain the behavior of a great number of alcohol-addicted individuals.

This general approach to the explanation of alcohol addiction is based on the results of extensive animal research. Most would agree that generalizing the findings of animal research to include human behavior, with all of its complexities, is a rather precarious enterprise. This approach in many respects amounts to an explanation of "psychological addiction." Psychological addiction, in this context, can be simplistically defined as a learned response (ingestion of alcohol) which is reinforced by the reduction of tension. It is significant that this general theory of alcohol addiction and more particularly the concept of anxiety as it relates to alcoholism, does have a sizeable body of experimental and clinical data to support the theory.

More intrapersonally oriented psychological models of alcohol addiction have focused upon the internal psychodynamics of the individual alcoholic. Aside from the anxiety variable, insecurity, dependency-oriented conflicts, unresolved Freudian psychosexual issues and global personality considerations have been proposed as models of explanation for alcohol addiction. Often concepts such as these have been used in combination to explain the problem of alcoholism or problem drinking. In my experience such attempts at general or total explanations of alcohol addiction have been notoriously inadequate. While the primacy of certain of these psychological issues may be apparent in the pathological drinking behavior of a given individual, these same dynamics may be of limited use in the explanation of a significant segment of the general population of alcoholics and problem drinkers. Very often it is just at this point that we have turned to "psychiatric" exploration of the problem of alcoholism. It is my feeling that this approach is just as futile, if not more so. In fact, the essence of any psychiatric evaluation has to do with the exact likes of such psychological concepts as we have already discussed. What does happen as a result of psychiatric evaluation is that the alcoholic often tends to be viewed as manifesting other, more primary, psychopathology and is labeled as such. This amounts to viewing drinking as a secondary symptom of such clinical syndromes as paranoid schizophrenia, psychopathic personality, chronic depressive personality, etc. Indeed, it is the opinion of many psychiatrists that nearly every case of alcoholism contains an underlying or concomitant psychiatric illness. This line of reasoning supports the position that alcoholism is not a specific disease, but rather a particular symptom associated with any number of other illnesses or syndromes.

These ideas or theories as to the etiology of alcoholism are admittedly somewhat truncated and fragmented. Certainly other theories relative to the etiology of alcoholism have been advanced (Truitt, 1970; Steinback and Blumenthal, 1970; Keller, 1972). Nonetheless, they are felt to be "living examples" of where we are now with regard to understanding the "whys" of alcohol addiction. What is perhaps most frustrating is the lack of benefit those of us involved in treatment and rehabilitation efforts have received from such theoretical data. Our groping efforts at rehabilitation surely have not been positively facilitated by such past and present inadequate explanations of why people become addicted to alcohol. What I want to construct now is a simplistic explanation of why people become alcohol addicted, which will serve as an adequate base for effective treatment and rehabilitation strategies. The fact that such an approach to the etiology of alcoholism and problem drinking provides a workable treatment rationale is the crucial issue in my opinion. Moreover, this treatment approach has been found to be highly effective in the rehabilitation of alcohol-addicted individuals.

A PRACTICAL, TREATMENT-ORIENTED EXPLANATION OF ALCOHOLISM

Most theoretical explanations of alcohol addiction and problem drinking include a treatment regimen. If not explicitly so, such is surely alluded to. Thus, the nutritional theory of alcoholism suggests that this condition might be modified by dietary manipulation. The psychiatric position suggests that treating primary psychopathology will result in the resolution of the secondary symptom of alcoholism. The psychological theory of alcoholism based upon the primacy of anxiety posits that counter-conditioning or other anxiety-alleviating techniques will extinguish the alcoholic behavior. And so it goes with the other theoretical explanations of alcoholism and problem drinking.

Throughout the text of the treatment-oriented chapters in this book I have attempted to convey some basic methods of relating to alcohol-addicted individuals which I have clinically found effective in the process of helping such individuals to extinguish their drinking behavior. These methods have included what we have traditionally referred to as psychotherapy. Underlying these various treatment strategies, or, in fact, the basis for any of the treatment methods thus far advocated, are a number of fundamental beliefs related to the etiology of alcoholism. Again these are my personal convictions, based upon extensive review of the literature, clinical experience, research findings, etc. Let me point out that the process of becoming addicted to alcohol is exceedingly complex; certainly we may never possess the totality of knowledge relative to the successful interpersonal and societal resolution of this problem. I point this out lest the reader feel I have grossly oversimplified the entire issue of alcoholism. What I wish to now discuss are a few crucial constructs, not necessarily new or innovative constructs within the behavioral science field I might add, which I have found to be ever present realities in the lives of alcohol-addicted individuals. The realities of these constructs relative to the problem of alcohol addiction have been such that I have consistently felt them to be the essence of much of that process we have come to designate as etiology.

Interpersonal Failure

Early in my therapeutic work with alcoholics and problem drinkers I was impressed with the failure that these individuals as a group had experienced. As this initial experience included some two years as the clinical director of a military halfway house, I felt that perhaps this continual bombardment with the failure issue was skewed to this population. Subsequent experience with community agencies, Alcoholics Anonymous, various hospital settings and other facilities involved in rehabilitation measures directed at the alcoholic and problem drinker convinces me that "failure" may be the single most important behavioral issue in the developmental pathology of alcohol addiction. Other behavioral scientists have indicated the primacy of failure in the development and maintenance of various forms of pathology. Certainly Glasser (1965) has been one of the more recent supporters of this position. In a very cogent manner, Glasser has focused upon the role of academic failure in the development of adjustment problems and deviant behavior. While I am in strong agreement with this general theme, I have come to emphasize the failure issue from a more interpersonal perspective. I might add at this point that the explanation for alcohol addiction proposed by the transactional analysis theorists (Berne, 1965; Steiner, 1971; Harris, 1969) fits quite well with a number of my ideas. When appropriate I shall attempt to point out these similarities.

I choose to use the concept of interpersonal failure to explain the basic rationale for alcohol addiction and problem drinking. In essence this concept refers to a life-style characterized by a very significant lack of learning of effective interpersonal skills. This process is initiated at birth if not before. It amounts to a form of complete interpersonal conditioning, which by the age of four or five, amounts to being potentially programmed for life. Let us explore some of the possible developmental specifics of this process of learning to be an interpersonal failure.

A good segment of any random sample of alcoholics simply were not wanted from birth. How potent a form of introduction into the role of interpersonal failure can this be? Being born into this form of emotional family constellation amounts to having failed prior to being given any chance for interpersonal success. Being raised by grandparents, relatives or foster parents and growing up in a basically institutional climate all initiate the reality of interpersonal failure for many eventual alcoholics and problem drinkers. In many respects this amounts to a priori interpersonal status of something less than a human being. While the degree of parental or surrogate rejection is usually something short of this, the general effect is essentially the same. This form of childhood experience precipitates the development of a self-concept devoid of basic good feelings and perceptions about oneself. This life script or life position has been referred to as the "I'm not OK" role by some theorists (Harris, 1969). This initial experience with the world, oneself and significant others sets the stage for an ongoing process of interpersonal failure. Feelings of inadequacy, inferiority and secondary citizen status can be the only result of such early interpersonal programming. It is also apparent how overcompensation mechanisms and counterdependent behavior emerge from such a conditioning paradigm. Initial learning to the effect of "People don't like or want me," "I'm no good," etc., initiates the groundwork for a perpetual self-fulfilling prophecy of final failure. Central to such learning and its life experience is people. For this very potent reason I refer to such an experience as one of learning interpersonally to be a failure. This same general process is very much a reality of the experiential situation of many children growing up in affluent, intellectually oriented, seemingly well-adjusted family constellations. In effect this accounts for the segment of alcoholics who purportedly "have had everything," and there seemingly is a lack of deprivation-oriented explanation for their addiction. While all may seem well on the surface, such is not at all the case on close interpersonal scrutiny. What is actually communicated to the individual via the process of interpersonal relations and what is correspondingly felt by that same individual becomes the crux of the issue. Double messages, distorted communication, learning to wear the mask and basic armoring often distort our ability to ferret out the reality of one's experiential being.

Once this basic course has been established it becomes an ongoing process, continually reinforced by the individual as well as the phenomenal field. It is apparent how such feelings about oneself, initially structured during the first few years of life, begin to establish an operant relationship with the world that only serves to reinforce the failure identity. This global process accounts for what I refer to as the development of "secondary failure identity" transactions with the phenomenal world. This simply amounts to the later developmental sequel of failure which the alcoholic experiences. Perhaps foremost in this regard is academic failure. If we evaluate the academic record of the majority of alcoholics and problem drinkers we will find that as early as the second and third grade these particular individuals began to experience significant academic difficulty. Often this is the case in spite of average or above average intelligence. The segment of this same group which eventually terminates all academic experience by the tenth or eleventh grade is appalling. Realizing the premium which our society places upon education and advanced training one can readily appreciate the potency of this additional stamp of failure. In a very real sense this amounts to a form of validation with the world that one is truly a failure. Eventually this process includes job losses, marital failures, failure as a parent, etc. In short, the alcoholic actively constructs through this process a basic identity which increasingly has failure at its core. Genetic to this process is the growing and continual feedback from significant others that one, in fact, is a failure. Whereas the rudiments of the failure identity initially stem from the immediate family constellation, the reinforcement and input essential to the maintenance of this identity increasingly take on a more worldly or generalized basis. As this becomes more and more the case, the potential for transcending or breaking out of this failure identity becomes increasingly difficult. Having three or four significant others perceive and interact with one in such a fashion as to convey the message "You are a failure," is certainly less potent than interacting with an almost total phenomenal world which conveys this same basic message.

Relating alcohol addiction and problem drinking in a causative fashion to the failure identity is certainly no hard task. The individual with this type of identity and its concomitant emotional correlates learns rather quickly that this morass of unpleasantness can be partially extinguished through the consumption of alcohol. Indeed, much of the overt behavior of any alcoholic or problem drinker while intoxicated is clearly an attempt to demonstrate to the world that he is "somebody," something other than a failure. Aggressive outbursts, buying a round for the bar, fast driving and rumination over past conquests and escapades can all be interpreted as ineffective or neurotic attempts at communicating one's manliness or adequacy to the world. This amounts to an attempted dialogue with significant others and the world which will convey that the alcoholic is both potent and successful — quite the antithesis of a failure.

Often the basic dislike for oneself which becomes a crucial aspect of the failure identity is manifest via the body somatotype. Certainly this is most evident during the latter stages of addiction. Remaining drunk and not eating, developing a protruding stomach, overaging and all the other bodily aspects of prolonged drinking thus become a means of validating this basic failure identity to oneself and others. How we feel about ourselves, our personal respect and indeed the extent to which we basically like ourselves is very much a part of how we maintain our physical self. Other nonperson extensions of the self, such as clothes, car, house, etc., become a part of this same identity process. What kind of an identity is possible for a drunk, unshaven and unkempt, unemployed person? I maintain that such an individual, for the most part, can only perceive himself and be perceived by others as a failure or loser. It becomes increasingly apparent that knowing himself to be a failure and continually making himself and the world aware of this identity becomes the *modus vivendi* of the alcoholic. In many cases, this amounts to a perpetual form of total reinforcement which amounts to nothing more than a trap.

In this chapter I have presented a number of explanations which have been explored as causative or etiological determinants of alcoholism and problem drinking. It is my feeling that interpersonal failure is perhaps the most important single variable in the explanation of alcohol addiction. Hopefully the reader can appreciate the total impact of this particular dynamic. Learning the failure identity accounts for the life script of alcoholics. As the individual experiences and interacts interpersonally to the tune of "You are essentially worthless, you are a failure," he progressively negates potentially more healthy and adaptive interpersonal roles. This experiential reality entails a rather predictable outcome for many individuals so programmed interpersonally. In this sense alcohol addiction might be theoretically perceived as a relatively healthy adjustment choice. I suspect that in retrospect it is rather apparent to the reader that I have in essence constructed a number of ways to facilitate the development of a success identity in the context of the treatment-oriented chapters. This has surely been one of my primary objectives, as I have consistently found that when people can be successful at something they begin to like themselves and correspondingly begin to feel and behave in more appropriate and socially acceptable ways. Building a success identity can be accomplished in any number of ways, psychotherapy being only one method. Whether in the context of individual or group therapy, couples' therapy, Alcoholics Anonymous or whatever other interpersonal encounters we provide under the rubric of "rehabilitation" we must endeavor to help the alcoholic construct a success identity. Communicating that we care, being warm and personal and sharing our own feelings and basic humanness with the alcoholic is essential to this process. Dealing with reality issues, focusing upon concrete behavior in the here-and-now, eliminating punishment and requiring commitment in the fashion described in the preceding treatment chapters facilitate the successful rehabilitation of alcoholic and problem-drinking individuals. While I would not advocate these specific treatment strategies for all people experiencing emotional and interpersonal difficulty, I do feel that these core conditions do account for a great deal of what happens in any therapeutic milieu.

SECTION THREE

CLINICAL READINGS IN THE TREATMENT OF ALCOHOLISM

Chapter 14

ALCOHOLISM AND SELF-DISCLOSURE

SELF-DISCLOSURE or transparency has long been a topic of relevance and interest to those of us in the helping professions of counseling and psychotherapy. Indeed, we have been actively theorizing and conducting research relative to self-disclosure and the therapeutic enterprise for at least fifteen years. These theoretical and research efforts have focused upon a diversity of issues. Patient level or amount of self-disclosure, therapist disclosing behavior, adjustment and self-disclosure and ethnic background and patterns of disclosing behavior are but a few of the many areas we have thus far investigated. As I attempt to evaluate and assimilate the results of our arduous efforts in this specific niche of the psychotherapy profession I am frankly a bit confused. As counselors and psychotherapists we seem to have globally shared the basic belief that self-disclosure is a core ingredient in successful psychotherapy of a diversity of "schools" or theoretical orientations. This seems to be particularly true with regard to client or patient self-disclosing behavior. Patient self-disclosure has been perceived as a basic prerequisite to any form of therapeutic relationship. Therapist self-disclosure seems to be a somewhat more controversial issue. While counselors and therapists of a more existential, Rogerian or humanistic orientation have advocated self-disclosure, openness and genuineness upon the part of the helper, the behavior therapists, psychoanalysts, and psychoanalytically oriented psychotherapists have tended to question therapist behaviors of this type, if not outrightly rejecting them as antitherapeutic. Much of this debate has been clinically based and has remained the subject for theoretical and esoteric discussions. Research findings relative to self-disclosure and the process and outcome of psychotherapy have been even more difficult from which to interpret and generalize. One very plausible explanation for inconsistent research findings has had to do with the various measures of self-disclosure which we have employed in our investigations. Taped vignettes, rating scales and various questionnaires and psychometric procedures have been employed as methods of assessing numerous aspects of the relevance of the self-disclosure variable to the psychotherapeutic enterprise. In contrast to this position some might argue that employing such a diversity of measures of self-disclosure should enhance the probability of identifying and substantiating common elements in this area of investigation.

For the most part, it is my feeling that those of us with a particular interest in this area of psychotherapy, theory and research continue to maintain a strong belief in the relevance of the self-disclosure variable as a basic ingredient in successful psychotherapy. Rather sporadically I find myself becoming excited about this issue and from time to time initiate some form of research designed to perhaps answer some of the self-disclosure-oriented questions that I have at that particular moment. I must confess that living with this process for some five years has had its frustrating moments. I suspect that I could empathize with those who have had similar feelings for perhaps as long as fifteen or twenty years. What I would like to share in this brief manuscript are some of my clinically based feelings and perceptions about the relevance of self-disclosure or transparency to the problem of alcohol addiction and problem drinking. As an advocate of both therapist and patient self-disclosure within the therapeutic context, the experience I have had with this particular clinical population during the past seven years has been most rewarding. This personal experience has validated for me the very real relationship between self-disclosure, personal growth and personality change. My earlier academic interests in self-disclosure as a curative interpersonal process via practicum supervision, the "teaching" of psychotherapy research within a medical school department of psychiatry and community mental health work simply did not "bring home" to me the very real healing nature of transparent interpersonal behaviors. I liked what I read about self-disclosure and adjustment, but somehow these clinical settings failed to meaningfully validate for me just how very real and observable this relationship between self-disclosure and personal growth is. Somehow it was as if I was always a step removed from really feeling and understanding this relationship, in spite of my academic and cognitive belief. Perhaps this total situation was the product of my personal lack of experience and relative neophyte status as a psychotherapist. At any rate, my involvement with alcoholics and problem drinkers in group and individual therapy, Alcoholics Anonymous, marital couples' therapy and other treatment modalities within an alcoholic rehabilitation center setting has provided the experiential framework essential to a growing personal understanding and appreciation of the relationship between self-disclosure and behavior change. It is this relationship between self-disclosure, alcoholic behavior and "recovery" which I now wish to discuss.

Very early in my therapeutic work with alcoholics and problem drinkers I observed two primary characteristics which seemed to apply to those individuals as a group almost without exception. When sober, in this particular case when engaged in a rehabilitation process, these individuals first of all appeared to be noticeably uncomfortable in the most casual of interpersonal relations. Indeed, it seemed as if the most superficial forms of person-to-person relating presented an extremely stressful endeavor for the sober alcoholic. Certainly this would appear antithetical to the "life of the party" drunk or the typical barroom behavior of most heavy drinkers. The second characteristic which I consistently observed was simply an almost total lack of self-disclosure upon the part of these individuals. Needless to say, my personal interest and bias relative to the self-disclosure variable helped set me up for this observation. I should also point out that these two characteristics were a part of the behavior of alcohol-addicted individuals with a few days or perhaps only hours of sobriety. A good deal of this non-person-oriented behavior, as well as the lack of self-disclosing behavior, could be related to physical and psychological variables specific to the condition of the patient at that particular time. However, group therapy experience continued to personally validate the reality of these two characteristics of alcoholic patients with more extended periods of sobriety — perhaps with as long as three or four months of total sobriety. In the absence of booze it appeared as if these seemingly gregarious individuals suddenly became withdrawn and apprehensive when faced with interpersonal encounters, and perhaps more importantly they were clearly nondisclosing in their relationships with others. As I began to interact and have significant experience with "recovered" alcoholics — people with perhaps as much as ten or more years of total sobriety — I soon found these individuals to be some of the most disclosing that I had ever met. Indeed, at times it seemed as though all these sober individuals ever did was self-disclose! Interacting as well as observing these "recovered" alcoholics personally validated their interpersonal style of total self-disclosure. As I continued my individual and group therapy work with this population I eventually found that those individuals who failed to make the transition from very little disclosing behavior to a pattern of diffuse self-disclosure were unable to maintain their sobriety. While I have only been involved in this area professionally for seven years, I have yet to see a patient maintain his or her sobriety for over six or seven months in the absence of a marked increase in self-disclosing behaviors. As every "recovered" alcoholic knows, sobriety alone is not enough. All of us could clinically hypothesize any number of changes which must occur both with and after the achievement of initial sobriety in order to enhance the probablity of maintaining sobriety. Specifically I am suggesting that long-term sobriety is contingent upon learning and engaging in an interpersonal mode which is highly self-disclosing in nature. Assessing the amount of self-disclosure essential to the maintenance of sobriety is another issue. This appears to be a somewhat individual matter. Perhaps if we could videotape a certain alcoholic twenty-four hours a day for X length of time we could establish a baseline of disclosing behavior essential to his or her sobriety. Falling below a given level of self-disclosure might predictably result in resuming drinking for this particular individual. Needless to say this is an impossibility, and furthermore, I have serious doubts about even the theoretical basis of such an undertaking. What I am attempting to convey is simply that self-disclosure is an essential ingredient in sobriety.

Initially I pointed out that a primary characteristic of the "practicing" alcoholic was that of interpersonal anxiety. Being uncomfortable around others, withdrawal and "loner" behaviors are much a part of this pattern of interpersonal anxiety. Certainly self-disclosing behaviors would predictably not be a part of the alcoholic's behavioral repertoire under such interpersonal circumstances. I have found this to be the exact case. Alcoholics and problem drinkers are not capable of self-disclosing behavior at this point, unless they are intoxicated, which only serves to invalidate the meaningful nature of such disclosures. It must be remembered that surface or apparent self-disclosing behavior may well be a part of general barroom or drinking behavior. This behavior is alcohol facilitated and as such it is in the end not real. This applies to the apparent jovial nature of the alcoholic, his vast wealth of friends while drinking, etc. While Joe may appear to be happy-go-lucky while drinking, certainly anything but interpersonally anxious on the surface, take his booze away from him for a few weeks and observe him interpersonally. Spouse, family and friends as well as professionals will attest to the process of movement away from people which Joe typically initiates upon his termination of drinking. In the absence of learning self-disclosing behaviors during this period of sobriety Joe will in my experience eventually resume his drinking. In this respect, learning self-disclosing behaviors facilitates movement toward others which is another essential ingredient in the process of long-term sobriety. This movement toward others must be initiated while the individual is sober and must be of significant duration and intensity. In the absence of a prolonged sober (at minimum six to eight months) experiential engagement with significant others, which encompasses a growing capacity for self-disclosure, the alcoholic is subject to undergoing diffuse regressive phenomena. Typically such a regression is alcohol oriented.

Many of us have had opportunity to observe the relationship which develop between the therapeutic bartender and the patron who "unloads" his woes on this listening ear. This process is essentially one of self-disclosure upon the part of at least one of the parties involved, if not both. In many respects this dialogue often takes on the essential characteristics of a helping relationship. I suspect that the confessional and cathartic nature of such an exchange often allows both parties to go away feeling somewhat better. However, this form of interpersonal dialogue, while partially effective as a means of dealing with emotional turmoil, is nonetheless essentially neurotic. The suffering parties reap enough gain from such interactions to continue functioning interpersonally, but the core factors essential to their respective conflicts are never resolved. This situation is the exact *sine qua non* of all neurotic behavior. I suggest that if such dialogue were to occur on an ongoing basis for the parties involved, in the absence of alcohol as a facilitative ingredient of such dialogue, significant interpersonal growth would be a natural by-product of the process. As mentioned earlier, alcohol-based relating is not real. Meaningful involvement and relating are what the alcoholic and problem drinker needs most. Indeed, it may well be something that he or she has never before experienced on an ongoing basis. These badly needed behaviors are what the alcoholic has never learned, but yet has constantly struggled to achieve in a neurotic or ineffective manner.

To date Alcoholics Anonymous has been one of the most effective organizations to "heal" alcoholics and problem drinkers. I maintain that the success of this organization is predicated upon teaching the alcoholic self-disclosing behavior as well as simply relating types of behavior. The essence of most A.A. meetings has to do with telling others about one's self. This disclosure is very total, and it is done in the absence of alcohol. Engaging in this form of behavior becomes the basis for relating to others in a rewarding and meaningful way. Within the confines of A.A. the individual learns that he can unload the emotional crap he has been carrying inside himself for all those years, be valued and loved in spite of all these inadequacies and indeed make friends and be accepted as a human being in the process. Once this process is initiated it accounts for a radically changed life-style for the alcoholic. Movement toward others and self-disclosure suddenly become his or her *modus operandi*. The spiraling or generalization of this process accounts for the success of Alcoholics Anonymous. Twelve-stepping, helping others and community service often become the hallmark of the recovered alcoholic. At times it is somewhat amusing to watch the neophyte at sobriety attempting to sober up the world. I view this as a natural process. This process involves telling other alcoholics about one's self, as well as direct involvement with these individuals in a helping manner. Knowing how hard he has sought what he now has found and how painful all those years of seeking were can only result in the recovered alcoholics wanting to give or share what he now has with all those still caught in the dilemma or trap. Paradoxically it is so simple and yet so difficult to learn this process of self-disclosure and movement toward others.

Those familiar with the format or philosophical basis of A.A. will understand and appreciate the relevance of self-disclosure to the success of this organization. Being honest with oneself, developing a manner of living which demands rigorous honesty, admitting to being powerless over alcohol, making a searching and fearless moral inventory of oneself, and admitting to God, to oneself and to another human being the exact nature of his or her wrongs are all essentials of self-disclosure. The more one evaluates the basis of this organization the clearer it becomes that self-disclosure is indeed a cornerstone of the program of recovery. Fellowship, relating and moving toward people become possible through the medium of self-disclosure. Very often, admitting that one does in fact have a problem with alcohol and that one is an alcoholic is the first step in this process of learning more effective self-disclosing behaviors. For many this initial self-disclosure opens the door for successive disclosures which pave the road to interpersonal growth and development. The very real and spontaneous nature of these disclosures is readily apparent to long-term A.A. members as well as the casual observer of an A.A. meeting. Being real in these transactions and being comfortable with personal disclosures and interpersonal relations can only result in an inner tranquility for the alcoholic. It is my feeling that engagement with A.A. means involvement in a particular environment which both teaches and reinforces self-disclosing types of behavior. This environment is in essence made up of models (recovered alcoholics) who actively shape and reinforce patterns of interpersonal behavior which are both self-disclosing in nature and oriented toward engagement with others.

The implications for rehabilitation personnel and therapists involved in the treatment of the alcoholic patient relative to self-disclosing behavior are clear cut. It is imperative that therapists and rehabilitation facilities first of all provide an environmental climate in which patients feel free to engage in self-disclosing behavior. While it seems to be a natural assumption that we do provide this type of environmental press, I would point out that this is not necessarily the case. In fact, I am convinced that all too frequently our rehabilitation milieus have failed to provide the conditions essential to learning self-disclosure and more person-oriented behaviors. In this capacity we as behavioral engineers may have helped facilitate an iatrogenic process. All too often we have failed to appreciate our role as models to the patient. If we relate in a nonpersonal, detached manner how can we expect patients to move toward others? This exact situation may partially explain the superior success which "recovered" alcoholics often seem to have in treating and reaching other practicing alcoholics. Recovered alcoholics who function as counselors are, for the most part, very disclosing. They are also action oriented with regard to initiating patient involvement and patient participation in the rehabilitation process. I would suggest that professionals try out some of these self-disclosing behaviors as they interact with their alcoholic or problem drinking patients. Humanizing seems to open the door to growth potential for all of us. In the absence of self-disclosure, humanizing or simple relating become parataxic at best.

In this chapter I have for the most part discussed my clinical observations of the relationship between self-disclosure and alcoholism. Simply stated, alcoholic patients who "recover" seem to be those who progressively engage in more disclosing types of interpersonal behavior. The process of learning to be more open concomitantly involves progressive movement toward others. A life-style increasingly characterized by self-disclosure and people-oriented behavior enables the alcoholic to terminate his or her substance dependency. Perhaps more importantly, these newly acquired interpersonal skills provide the initial prerequisites essential to growth potential of a more global nature.

Chapter 15

ALCOHOLISM, DEATH AND REBIRTH

ALCOHOL-RELATED literature has historically focused upon the destructive aspects of problem drinking and chronic alcoholism. Destructive behavior facilitated by alcohol ingestion has been depicted via such phenomena as suicide, gastrointestinal and other medical problems specific to prolonged alcohol consumption, automobile accidents and homicide. In fact, 85,000 annual deaths can be attributed to problem drinking or chronic alcoholism. One must seemingly acknowledge the destructive potential of alcohol ingestion in the face of such staggering statistics. In spite of such information, thousands of new individuals yearly enter the ranks of the "known" alcoholic or problem drinker population, thousands of people continue to die annually on the highways as a result of intoxication, and in numerous other ways we collectively continue to attempt to deny the reality of what destructive drinking precipitates. While this global process is very relevant to all of us, it is of particular significance to those individuals who eventually become caught in the trap of chronic alcoholism or alcohol dependency. Individuals comprising this group, presently involving at least some nine million, although frequently noncognizant of the process of self-destruction which alcoholism involves, are the ones who comprise the destructive statistics. This select group annually destroys itself and others at a rate which far exceeds that of the general population. A growing societal realization of the pathology of this process has recently stimulated interest in the individual problem drinker, as well as helped facilitate rehabilitation measures aimed at this overall segment of society.

It is the purpose of this manuscript to discuss some of the destructive aspects of alcohol addiction as they apply to those individuals becoming addicted who eventually "recover."

Retrospective evaluation of the process of becoming an alcoholic and subsequent termination of drinking pathology is perhaps the only method available for developing a meaningful understanding of the truly destructive nature of chronic alcoholism. Being able to participate as an active, involved significant other in the addicted person's life space is essential to this understanding. It is from this type of experiential relationship that alcoholism can be viewed as a developmental process resulting in the eventual psychic death and rebirth of the addicted individual.

Configurationally alcohol addiction and subsequent "recovery" can be viewed as a developmental process involving three essential stages. Initially, one must become labeled "alcoholic" or identified as a problem drinker. This first stage encompasses the individual's total drinking history prior to being labeled. As such, this process may encompass any number of years; typically in our society the individual has reached the middle thirties or early forties prior to effectively becoming labeled. Although the individual labeled "alcoholic" may continue to deny that he has a problem with alcohol, at some given point the totality of his social transactions, including pathological alcohol consumption, result in his being identified by the immediate phenomenal field as an alcoholic. At this point the probability of the addicted individual's symptomatic behavior changing is significantly enhanced. External pressure may dictate behavioral change. A review of any given alcoholic's life history taken at this point (the point of becoming publicly labeled as an "alcoholic") will reveal a lifelong case history of self destruction. The frequency of automobile accidents, arrests, beatings and job losses attests to a blatant need for punishment. Indeed, these are but a few of the self-destructive indices. Suicidal attempts, depressive episodes and generalized patterns of interpersonal behavior are perhaps even more direct examples of the alcoholic's self-destructive behavior. This overall process of self-destructive behavior can be viewed as a life-style of continued suicidal intent. During infancy, childhood, adolescence and adulthood the alcoholic has experienced a chronic emotional inequality which demands punishment. A self-concept devoid of basic positive self-esteem demands societal and self assurance. In the absence of good feelings about the self, one must of necessity question one's self-worth. If significant others consistently communicate to the individual a sense of nonconcern, unworth, unlove and other essentially negative feelings, this individual is "set up" for a self-punitive life-style. The unconscious or preconscious equation becomes "If I am unwanted and unloved, something is wrong with me, and therefore I *deserve* to be punished." Needless to say, other neurotic manifestations of this basic equation become possible. In order to neurotically punish others the individual becomes caught in the trap of self-destruction, etc. Within this system the alcoholic person becomes committed to a total life-style of self-destruction. At some undetermined point in the individual's life space, the only possible escape from this punishment paradigm becomes death. While death becomes a concrete reality for thousands of alcoholics annually, the dying phenomenon more typically is expressed in a symbolic fashion. In fact, any drinking episode which terminates by virtue of "passing out" may be equated with self-destruction and symbolic death. Individuals suffering from alcohol addiction may have experienced this symbolic form of death on a daily basis for many years. However, in order to become totally abstinent, the alcohol-addicted individual must symbolically die on a number of additional levels. This second developmental stage is extremely complex and all-encompassing. In certain respects this process of dying may be akin to the process of "surrendering." Death in essence means the end or termination. As such, the death process for the alcohol-addicted individual must encompass a significant number of those previous variables which served to maintain the individual's alcohol pathology. At this juncture, death and the third developmental stage, rebirth, become fused. This process of dying frequently means the termination of interpersonal and social relationships, to include possible close friends and spouse. This is particularly the case when interpersonal relationships are based upon the common denominator of drinking, which is rather standard for many alcohol-addicted individuals. Death may mean the termination of a vocation of ten to twenty years duration. In short, the process of symbolic death is, in many respects, traumatic and total. It is my feeling that anything short of this is incapable of producing long-term sobriety. In order to remain sober, the alcohol-addicted individual must terminate all those significant behaviors and interpersonal transactions which have served to maintain and enhance his alcoholism. This process results in the death of the alcoholic self.

In order to be reborn one must first die. The alcohol-addicted individual incapable of terminating those aspects of his self-system which maintain his alcoholism, hence unable to symbolically die, can only remain intoxicated. The third developmental stage in the process of the alcohol addiction and "recovery" is totally contingent upon the death process. This process of rebirth is widely acknowledged within the confines of Alcoholics Anonymous. Over and over "recovered" alcoholics refer to their being able to achieve prolonged sobriety as a "rebirth." Becoming sober on a long-term basis involves basic life-style changes which are the equivalent of rebirth. The establishment of new friendships, new social behaviors and a generalized modification of interpersonal behaviors contributes to the development of a radically different self-system. Being able to accept the simple responsibility of paying bills, becoming vocationally functional and learning to give and receive love in a more healthy manner are but a part of the rebirth. It is of significance to note that a religious flavor often accompanies this process of rebirth. Indeed, being able to rationally evaluate twenty years of continued intoxication can understandably give one something for which to be thankful. The simple fact that one has been sober for a year or more and has become capable of evaluating self from this perspective, as opposed to the former intoxicated self, is of major importance. At this point the "crazy self" has died, and a new or modified self has evolved. Assuming responsibility, making decisions, learning to drive a car and thousands of other new behaviors are a potential part of the rebirth process. It is truly amazing how much a "recovered" alcoholic may anticipate and enjoy each new day; in many respects, this rebirth makes such individuals more appreciative of what they have found than the average person. Certainly a part of this is the self-doing nature of the rebirth. Being able to experience the rebirth process is very much contingent upon the alcoholic himself; while spouse, family, friends and change agents may help facilitate the process of sobriety and rebirth, it is the alcoholic himself who must in the end be responsible for his sobriety. As such, only he can fully appreciate and enjoy his new-found life of sobriety.

It is equally important to note how family and friends relate to the "recovered" or recovering alcoholic. These significant others are readily cognizant of behavioral change on the part of the recovering alcoholic. Statements such as "John sure has changed," "You wouldn't believe what he used to be like," etc. are standard expressions of this acknowledged change. It is the experience of those involved in alcoholic rehabilitation work to similarly be amazed at "before and after" case histories.

In summary, alcoholism is viewed as a developmental process in which the addicted individual progressively engages in self-destructive behavior. Unconscious and preconscious self-destructive trends precipitate an eventual intolerable life-style. Individuals who eventually "recover" from alcoholism must in essence die in order to achieve prolonged sobriety. Although a symbolic death on many levels, this death or termination of specific behaviors must be a rather concrete process on several behavioral levels. Death, via termination of interpersonal relationships and other dynamics serving to maintain the alcoholic life-style, eventually facilitates the process of rebirth. Rebirth is a total experience. New friendships, new jobs, new feelings and new behaviors are very much a part of the recovered alcoholic's modified self-system.

Chapter 16

ALCOHOLISM:
THE EMOTIONAL PLAGUE REVISITED

SOME twenty years ago Wilhelm Reich postulated mankind to be the victim of a cancerous emotional process which he referred to as "the emotional plague." "Man is born free, and everywhere he is in chains. One thinks himself the master of others, and still remains a greater slave than they" (Reich, 1953). Reich noted that the answer to this dilemma of living had historically remained unsolved, stating that "all human philosophy is riddled with the nightmare of searching in vain." For Reich the answer rested in the concept of the emotional plague of mankind. In essence Reich's concept of the emotional plague relates to man's emotional structure, his character structure. Armored man becomes caught in the trap of the personal pathology of his emotional being. While advocating the initial solution to the emotional trap as being one of first finding the exit out of the trap, Reich paradoxically states that finding the exit is the greatest riddle of all.

> The most ridiculous as well as tragic thing is this: The exit is clearly visible to all trapped in the hole. Yet nobody seems to see it. Everybody knows where the exit is. Yet nobody seems to make a move toward it. More: Whoever moves toward the exit, or whoever points toward it is declared crazy or a criminal or a sinner to burn in hell. It turns out that the trouble is not with the trap or even with finding the exit. The trouble is within the trapped ones (Reich, 1953).

An in-depth exploration and understanding of the Reichian concept of the emotional plague as it relates to armored man is beyond the scope of this manuscript. What is essential to Reich's theoretical frame of reference is his belief that man's inner being is at core culturally neurotic. This fundamental point is essential to the present article. Reich supports this position of cultural neuroses (the emotional plague concept) via such collective acts of behavior as the murder of Christ. While this very situation, both with regard to interpersonal adjustment and collective pathology, can be viewed from a number of diagnostic perspectives, it is my feeling that the present social problem of alcohol addiction in certain respects lends itself well to conceptualization along the lines of the Reichian emotional plague model. It is just this viewpoint of alcoholism as an emotional plague phenomenon which I want to explore. In so doing I wish to focus upon three primary aspects of the Reichian concept of the emotional plague as applicable to the problem of alcohol addiction.

Let us begin with the actual plague concept. According to Reich, the masses of humanity are emotional plague victims. Escaping the trap has become an impossibility for the victims. It was his feeling that dreams, poems and great music and paintings were perhaps the only means of transient escape from the plague. While I personally suspect that Reich would view the problem of alcohol addiction as only one particular dyna- mism of the emotional plague concept *in toto,* I would rather suggest that the pervasive magnitude of this problem has be- come such as to render it susceptible to being labeled "plague." I should point out that I am fully cognizant of the many clin- ical issues surrounding pathological drinking. Aside from such issues as "alcoholism and problem drinking as symptoms," I am simply suggesting that the more global issues surrounding alcohol addiction are so interpersonally and culturally potent as to render this problem one of plague proportion. Let us consider some of the known dimensions surrounding problem drinking and alcoholism. In December, 1971 the U.S. Depart- ment of Health, Education and Welfare reported a number of staggering statistics in its first special report to the U.S. Con- gress on Alcohol and Health: alcohol is the most abused drug in the United States; among the more than ninety-five million drinkers in the nation there are some nine million known alco- holic men and women; 10 percent of the nation's work force is known to be either alcoholic or problem drinking; one half of all traffic fatalities (amounting to some 28,000 lives in one recent year) and one third of all homicide victims have significant amounts of alcohol in their bloodstreams at the time of autopsy; alcoholism costs the economy an estimated fifteen billion dollars a year, and public intoxication alone accounts for one third of all arrests reported annually. It was stated in the HEW report that among American Indians the incidence of alcoholism is at an epidemic level, the rate being at least two times the national average, amounting to 25 to 50 percent of the Indian population on some reservations; at least 85,000 annual deaths can be attributed to chronic alcoholism or problem drinking; the chronic progressive diseases of the central and peripheral nervous systems and of the liver, heart, muscles, gastrointestinal tracts and other bodily organs and tissues make alcoholism the fourth-ranked medical problem; one out of five persons surveyed reported that someone close to them — most often a family member — was either a problem drinker or alcoholic. These global statistics are only a part of the reported findings of the HEW task force. Other experts report alcohol-facilitated behavior problems to be at an epidemic level among early adolescents and teenagers. Similar, more staggering statistics surrounding the problem of alcohol addiction have more recently been reported (*Time*, 1974).

Based upon findings such as these, I conceptualize the problem of alcohol addiction to be singularly one of emotional plague dimensions. While the culture *in toto* may well be comprised of a mass of "armored" individuals, neurotic and parataxic in whatever individual or group ways, the pervasive symptomatic effect of alcoholism and problem drinking is so clearly evident that to view this individual and social pathology as anything less than "plague" is to clearly deny the many realities surrounding the singular problem of alcohol addiction. While Reich would view alcohol addiction as a symptom of armored man, as perhaps an attempt to break down the rigidities of the character armor and break through into the vegetative realm, it is my feeling that his emotional plague concept is quite congruous in scope with the problem of alcohol addiction. In both contexts the essential issue remains that of collective behavior which is pathological or symptomatic.

A second major point of similarity between the Reichian emotional plague concept and the problem of alcohol addiction has to do with the individual "caught in the trap." Viewed from this perspective the essential problem in both cases has to do with the emotional adjustment of the individual. Rather than being a social or cultural phenomenon, the "trap" becomes that of the internal psychodynamics or character structure of the alcoholic or emotional plague victim. The Reichian victim is a slave to his or her character armor, which in essence clinically becomes an obsessive-compulsive dynamism of virtually unlimited dimensions. Sexual inadequacy, phobias and fears and other essentially neurotic patterns of adjustment become the hallmark of the Reichian armored man. The alcoholic, in addition to manifesting these various neurotic symptoms, becomes caught in the explicit trap of his or her obsessive-compulsive substance dependency. Reich's armored man appears to be the victim of a more theoretical or less observable form of pathology. While symptoms and other indicators of a less than optional adjustment are central to the being of the Reichian emotional plague victim, to me these phenomena are clearly less observable and certainly more functional than the concrete and comparatively specific behaviors of the individual caught in the trap of alcohol addiction. Both the emotional plague victim and the alcoholic seem to share a number of clinical similarities. Just as an individual's character armor initiates and maintains a neurotically functional lifestyle, so does alcohol facilitate such a costly interpersonal mode of adjustment. Character armor and alcohol serve to block or distort real feelings and interpersonal being, both compensate for inadequacies as well as block out the multiplicity of realities surrounding interpersonal exchanges with the phenomenal world. Both alcoholism and character armor represent the example par excellence of an inflexible, rigid, obsessive-compulsive dynamism or life-style. Indeed, I view both the plague concept and alcohol addiction individually as attempts by the human organism to establish some sort of barrier, perhaps somewhat akin to the role and function of a semipermeable membrane, between the self and phenomenal world. Such a conceptualization provides for unlimited parameters relative to clinical speculation and theorizing. Certainly the clinical similarities between Reich's plague victim and the alcoholic, viewed from an intrapersonal perspective, extend far beyond those discussed thus far. An essential point of congruence between the emotional plague victim and the alcoholic is simply that of individual personality warp or faulty adjustment. Beyond this, it is my clinical impression that we may be dealing with essentially the same psychodynamics in the case of both Reich's armored man and the individual addicted to alcohol. Speculation of this form is not without a multiplicity of caveats.

A third major point of similarity between the Reichian emotional plague concept and the problem of alcohol addiction has to do with the "cancerous" nature of both processes. I purposely refer to both alcohol addiction and the emotional plague as processes, since both are essentially developmental in nature, both are systems oriented with regard to people as well as tissue and body organs, and in other ways these phenomena appear to lend themselves to a process description. Reich, while perhaps somewhat fragmented and paranoiac in so doing, viewed Western culture as a breeding ground for emotional plague victims. The cultural dimension of the emotional plague, as delineated earlier, becomes the basis for an ever-increasingly sick or neurotic society. As individual plague victims interact with others, as they raise children, etc., they can only serve as models which both teach and reinforce maladaptive plague behaviors. This appears to be the essence of Reich's rationale for the "cancerous" nature of the emotional plague phenomenon. This exact situation appears to prevail with regard to the global problem of alcohol addiction. Without going into an extensive review of the literature relative to the etiological determinants of alcoholism, hopefully it will suffice to note that we have consistently found that roughly 50 percent of the children having an alcoholic parent will eventually themselves become substance-addicted, this substance most frequently being alcohol. Needless to say, such findings can be interpreted as genetically oriented, as well as environmental or learning theory based. The point to be made with regard to the "cancerous" nature of alcoholism is that it in a very real sense can be viewed as spreading from individual to individual. Alcoholism as a process affecting the individual can be viewed as cancerous. The developmental process of alcohol addiction progressively incapacitates the "victim" in a very cancerous fashion. This sickening emotional process almost always spreads to include those closest to the primary victim. Moreover, recent data support the position that alcoholism and problem drinking are collectively on the rise. The growing awareness of the multiplicity of social and interpersonal problems surrounding alcohol addiction would similarly seem to validate the cancerous nature of alcoholism and problem drinking. Behavioral scientists have speculated that as modern technological society becomes increasingly complex, man must progressively rely upon various mood-altering substances as a means of coping with the spiraling emotional stresses and strains precipitated by this all-encompassing societal change and complexity. Theorization of this type would understandably provide a basic rationale for the present drug and alcohol crisis which we are attempting to resolve.

Certainly other meaningful analogies can be drawn between the Reichian emotional plague concept and the current problem with alcohol addiction and problem drinking with which our culture is confronted. The three essential similarities which I have chosen to briefly explore will hopefully prove meaningful to the reader. An in-depth exploration of the Reichian emotional plague concept is simply beyond the scope of this manuscript. It is significant to note that Reich advocated both massive educational efforts and therapy as methods for the resolution of the plague dilemma. It was his feeling that the ultimate hope for mankind, i.e. escape from the cancerous nature of the emotional plague, rested with our education and work with children. Presently alcoholic rehabilitation personnel are actively embarked upon an all-encompassing program of education relative to the problem of alcohol addiction and problem drinking. This educational effort is being conducted upon regional, state and national levels, and is very directly geared to the needs of both children and adolescents. At the core of this global attempt to more effectively deal with the multiplicity of issues and problems surrounding alcohol addiction we find various strategies of psychotherapy and rehabilitation, many of which are in essence Reichian.

Chapter 17

HIDDEN ALCOHOLICS
IN THE MILITARY

THE recent emphasis upon the identification and rehabilitation of the problem drinker and chronic alcoholic within the military environment suggests movement away from the more traditional methods of attempting to deal with the reality of this segment of the military population (Forrest, 1973). Indeed, the problem of "covering up," hiding and in other ways denying the existence of individuals suffering from alcohol pathology has remained an area of major concern among those involved in rehabilitation efforts directed at this particular population. Industry has long been cognizant of the process of hiding alcoholic employees (Trice, 1962; Workov, Bacon and Hawkins, 1965). Those involved in law enforcement are aware of the press to maintain the anonymity of higher status individuals within the community who periodically engage in socially deviant behavior precipitated by alcohol consumption. Cursory examination of the definition and enforcement of social rules on alcoholism indicates a history of rather marked flux. It would appear that the American collective has long been aware of the problems surrounding alcohol consumption, but has nonetheless historically attempted to deny the magnitude of these problems. Within our culture the reality of the magnitude of alcohol-related problems is moreover confused by the multiplicity of alcohol behavioral expectancies manifested by the numerous groups which make up our overall collective. Behavioral expectancies surrounding alcohol consumption vary a great deal; while Negro Americans prescribe drinking on convivial grounds and prescribe or permit intoxication and tolerate alcoholism, Orthodox Jews by contrast prescribe drinking on religious grounds and in moderation and proscribe both intoxication and alcoholism. This example of confusion could be extended to numerous other manifestations of our society which serve to both enhance this process and simultaneously render it nearly impossible to empirically investigate.

What I want to explore in this paper are some of the interactional processes of "hide the alcoholic" within the particular context of the military. It is my opinion that those familiar with alcoholic rehabilitation are well aware of the problem of hidden alcoholism. Certainly this applies to the totality of our collective, the military being no exception. As such I would like to share some of my observations of "hide the alcoholic" within the military context.

Let me begin by suggesting that at this time the military environment has apparently consolidated an opinion as to what alcoholism is and has for the most part rather explicitly developed guidelines for the management of this problem. In this respect "flux" is currently not in vogue. While a similar attitude continues to become more prevalent within society at large, it is my opinion that the military complex has far surpassed community movement with respect to both education and efforts at rehabilitation per se. As such, in the military problem drinkers and alcoholics are to be identified and treated. After some three and one-half years as a clinical psychologist within a military alcoholic and drug addict rehabilitation center, I have become increasingly concerned with the problem of hidden alcoholism within this particular environmental press.

Alcoholic "hiding" has been described as an interactional process quite akin to the game of hide-and-seek (Rubington, 1972). I have found this to be an amusingly accurate paradigm within the military treatment context. As a side effect of the establishment of limits defining alcoholism and management procedures appropriate to dealing with this problem the military has, in effect, set up global behavioral expectancies for the problem drinker and chronic alcoholic. While this process in no way initiated a "witch hunt," it has facilitated a good deal of positive change regarding the overall management of alcoholic personnel. Perhaps now, more than ever, individuals within the military system are being confronted with the pathology of their alcohol-related life-styles.

In spite of all the enlightenment, hiding as a process continues to be a major obstacle to the treatment of the vast majority of the problem drinkers within this system. Such is the case with society at large, with as many as 70 percent of the alcoholic population being labeled as "hidden" (Rubington, 1972). As social pressure is exerted in the direction of identifying and treating individuals labeled alcoholic, a counter social pressure is exerted in the direction of avoiding the "seekers." Within such a phenomenological field those labeled alcoholic are in essence "it" in the game of hide-and-seek. Needless to say being "it" is to be avoided at all costs. While individuals labeled alcoholic are similarly "it" in society at large, it is my impression that they are comparatively exempt from a good deal of the pressure to terminate their deviant alcohol pathology. Within the military system being "it" very often means having one's total life monitored. Job status, marital relationships, financial matters, promotion and unit transfer are just a few areas which become open to public scrutiny. Clinically I feel this process has been positively related to behavioral change. The particular structure of this environment dictates movement in the direction of sobriety once one has been labeled "it"; failure to progress in the resolution of one's alcohol pathology may very well mean the loss of fifteen to twenty years of career. Understanding this, it becomes intelligible how important not becoming "it" may be!

This being the case, I have come to understand some of the sociological dynamics underlying the process of becoming "it." It should be noted at this point that my observations apply to civilian employees as well, as they are subject to many of the same basic environmental presses as active duty military personnel. Within this system, as with the industrial setting (Trice, 1962), the least skilled workers (lower ranks: E-1 — E-7) are the most rapidly identified as alcoholic. These individuals are labeled alcoholic, thus becoming "it," by both supervisors and co-workers. In contrast to the rapidity with which these individuals are identified, one is impressed with supervisory hesitancy to refer such individuals for treatment. The marked exception to this is the case of the openly falling-down drunk, who publicly engages in rather bizarre behavior. These individuals are quickly referred for "treatment." It is as if perpetual intoxication is to be tolerated as long as a limited number of fellow workers and supervisory personnel are the sole possessors of such knowledge. At this point hiding involves the alcoholic and those within the immediate field. Indeed, hiding may well become one of the primary modes of behavioral interaction for all involved. The process of hiding may involve any number of types of social interaction and may exist on a concrete level for several or all parties involved in the transaction. The crucial issue becomes that of public or growing awareness of the individual's alcoholism on the part of more peripheral workers and supervisors. When the alcoholic deteriorates to the point of becoming publically acknowledged as "it," he most assuredly will be referred for treatment. At this point alcohol ingestion is explicitly discouraged and the penalties imposed for continued intoxication become extremely severe. Unfortunately, a sizeable portion of the population eventually to become labeled alcoholic can persist in this pattern of self-destruction for fifteen to twenty-five years before they are labeled "it" and are thus affected by any rehabilitation efforts.

Higher ranking officers and civilian employees are the slowest individuals to be tagged "it." It seems as though the higher the social status of the individual, the longer it takes to be labeled alcoholic. In a similar line, high ranking officers (major and above) and civilian employees (GS-9 and above) tend to be involved in a process of hiding interaction which involves only a few individuals. This is very much in contrast to the hiding process of lower ranking enlisted men and civilian workers and supervisors. It would seem that the limited number of people involved in the game of hide-and-seek at higher organizational levels is determined by the amount of control these particular individuals manifest within the organization. Higher ranking officers and civilian employees can often directly control who does and who does not have access to monitoring their behavior. I would suspect that as a given higher ranking individual's alcoholic pathology progresses he must simultaneously receive growing social support, thus increasing the number of people involved in the game of hide-and-seek. Although individual alcoholics respond differently to the process of hide-and-seek, it is my impression that the vast majority of those eventually labeled "it" have participated in this game for extended periods of time; perhaps as long as twenty-five or thirty years.

As one might imagine, this game often takes on a rather amusing flavor within any organizational structure. Realizing that the gamesmanship presently in existence within the military requires referral of those who are "it" to an alcoholic rehabilitation facility, one might speculate on the possibilities of such an organizational climate operating with a number of hidden alcoholics within status positions of that organization. Certainly this same situation has historical roots within the totality of the American community. As this situation is anything but new, so are the means of dealing with it anything but novel. Presently the method of handling higher status alcoholics within the military environment is essentially a clandestine hiding process. A method which has been practiced in the past was that of hospitalization for the treatment of pneumonia or some similar medical problem. Reportedly detoxification and other medical procedures appropriate to the treatment of the chronic alcoholic have been carried out under the auspices of some "justifiable" medical diagnosis. Although this process has involved enlisted men and lower status individuals, it was a much less frequently practiced procedure for these individuals.

As the military system has modified its position regarding alcoholism and the treatment of the alcoholic, this procedure has come under increased scrutiny. It appears that today this methodology for treating higher ranking personnel has been for the most part terminated. However, it is quite clear to me that these higher status individuals continue to be treated (if they are treated) by facilities other than the rehabilitation centers provided by the military system itself. Within the confines of the Fort Gordon Alcohol and Drug Rehabilitation Center, we (staff and patients) are well aware of high-ranking military and civilian personnel who are currently "practicing" long-term alcoholics. On more than one occasion patients active in our program have participated as A.A. speakers for the local VA hospital and other local psychiatric inpatient facilities providing treatment for the alcoholic, only to meet their supervisors as inpatients on a locked ward for alcoholism treatment! While the organizational structure must be relatively aware of the absence of these higher status individuals, they have nonetheless avoided officially being tagged "it." I suggest that the majority of these individuals never experience a significant contact with the most elementary forms of "alcoholic rehabilitation" prior to reaching the late forties or early fifties. At that point rehabilitation efforts typically involve significant medical intervention.

I hope I have been able to impress upon the reader the reality of the existence of a large population of "hidden" alcoholics within the military system. Although virtually nothing has been written about this segment of the military population. Hidden alcoholism has been an area of major concern for those involved in alcohol rehabilitation efforts within industry and other organizational structures. This is certainly a major problem confronting the totality of American society. Hiding is an interactional process which actively involves any number of individuals plus the actual alcoholic. It is my observation that within the military context those who are first labeled alcoholic or tagged "it" in the game of hide-and-seek are lower status or lower ranking personnel. Once these individuals become "it" they are rather quickly referred to a military alcoholic rehabilitation center. Becoming "it" usually requires deviant social behavior; those individuals who are able to remain vocationally functional and remain short of "falling-down drunk" have an excellent probability of retaining the anonymity of their alcoholic pathology. Once labeled, these individuals are very clearly made aware that they have in fact been labeled alcoholic, or are "it," and are at this point very explicitly made aware of the consequences of further intoxication. Quite to the contrary, higher status or higher ranking personnel are the slowest to be labeled alcoholic. Although a similar hiding process becomes operational with regard to higher status alcoholic individuals, this process typically involves significantly fewer other people than that process employed with lower status personnel. Fewer people have actual access to the behavioral evaluation of high status individuals, and as such higher status individuals tend not to be as readily confronted with the deviance of their behavior. Within this system a sergeant simply does not confront a major with the fact that the latter is an alcoholic or drinking to excess! As the higher status person progressively deteriorates, his alcoholism becomes increasingly well known to a growing number of peripheral individuals, which eventually precipitates contact with some type of "treatment" facility. Unfortunately, in my experience this process is often delayed until the later stages of chronic alcoholism have already been reached.

One could predict that hidden alcoholism will continue to be a major problem confronting those involved in the process of alcohol education and rehabilitation. The answer to this dilemma lies in the realm of increased honesty and openness on the part of all involved in the process of hide-and-seek. Until the general public can become well enough informed to realize that alcoholism is a form of social disease requiring some type of other-person-oriented intervention, the problem of hidden alcoholism will continue to remain a paramount issue. Unfortunately those who continue to hide and cover for the alcoholic have failed to realize their role in the propagation of sickness. Indeed, those who hide the alcoholic paradoxically contribute to the eventual death of the same individual they have attempted to help. Hiding is frequently rationalized as helping the alcoholic; it is imperative that through educational media we extinguish this fantasy. Honesty, openness and self-disclosure have been rather threatening modes of interpersonal behavior within our culture. Allowing individuals the freedom to be able to say "I have a problem," "I am an alcoholic," or other such help-oriented requests is essential. Personal involvement and concern on the part of those who interact on a daily basis with suffering individuals is imperative. Those who have contact, on even a more superficial basis with individuals suffering from the disease of alcoholism, must begin to take the risk of confronting these disturbed people with the fact that something is wrong, and secondly must emphasize that they can change through the medium of change agent facilities. Saying that we have treatment facilities available is simply not enough. The detrimental statistics surrounding problem drinking and alcoholism within our social system dictate a growing involvement upon the part of all. Alcoholism can be successfully treated. Realizing that alternatives to the experiential hell which most alcoholics attempt to cope with are very real possibilities is a major step. Understanding that punishment models have been notoriously unsuccessful in the management of alcoholic individuals is another point to be emphasized.

Hopefully this paper might stimulate more positive modes of approaching the alcoholic patient. Certainly the content is anything but new to those involved in alcoholic rehabilitation. What is new is simply the acknowledgment of the existence of this significant problem. Realization of the detrimental role of hiding is certainly an important means of attempting to deal more effectively with this problem. From the perspective of hiding, alcoholism within the military is essentially similar to alcoholism within our total collective. It is my feeling that acknowledgment of the hiding transaction is an understandably threatening issue for many involved. However, it is my feeling that confronting and dealing with this issue in a reality-oriented manner is the only possible method of solution.

Chapter 18

RESOLUTION OF THE ALCOHOLIC
POWER FANTASY

IN the process of spending three and a half years as a clinical psychologist within an alcoholic rehabilitation center, including some twenty hours per week of individual and group psychotherapy, I have time and again been confronted with the most grandiose of what I term patient "power fantasies." Indeed, it has often been my experience that patients frequently make very little progress in the resolution of their symptomatic drinking behavior until such power fantasy material can be verbalized and eventually worked through. Although this particular type of thought process may be of a more generalized or diffuse type, it often takes the form of a specific event or sequel of behaviors.

In some cases it is apparent that the specific event or particular sequel of behavior is merely an extension of the patient's overall personality configuration, which frequently manifests a good deal of generalized grandiosity. This certainly is a step away from the depressive, anxious and inadequate self seen initially at any alcoholic treatment center. In fact, the grandiosity and power-oriented fantasy material I am acknowledging is the antithesis of the inadequate, ineffectual and overwhelmed individual with whom we are often initially confronted. Surely the concept of bipolarity seems appropriate to this particular dynamic of the alcoholic personality. It should be noted at this point that the "power fantasy" material to which I am referring is not typically an ideational constituent seen in the early stages of the therapeutic encounter with the alcoholic patient. While this type of material may be initially detected in the patient's manifest behavior and lifestyle, power-oriented fantasy content is usually not verbalized. Quite to the contrary, the patient typically represses and denies this element of his self-system until the later stages of the therapy process. In some successfully rehabilitated patients this material may never be explicitly dealt with; however, it is my impression that even in these cases the patient has preconsciously become aware of the existence of his power fantasy content, accepted and somehow resolved the irrational nature of this fantasy material.

For purposes of definition I shall describe two primary forms of the alcoholic power fantasy. I should point out that there may be other forms and varieties of this type of thought process and behavior; on the contrary, some experienced clinicians may feel that a singular red thread describes the totality of this particular aspect of the alcoholic's behavior and life-style. The two forms of alcoholic power fantasy described here are based completely upon my personal therapeutic work with alcohol-addicted individuals.

TYPE I ALCOHOLIC POWER FANTASY. This form of thought process I refer to as the specific power fantasy, and it is most clearly apparent in Case History 1. While patients manifesting the Type I form of power may verbally and behaviorally radiate an "I know it all" attitude, perhaps clearly counterdependent in life-style, prolonged individual therapy with these patients results in the exploration of one (or at the most two) episodes of grossly non-reality-oriented behavior in which the patient is firmly convinced that he or she carried out some totally impossible sequel of behavior. This specific type of issue has been central to the therapy of five of seventeen patients in which I felt power fantasy material essential to the therapy process. The specific issues included a plane hijacking, a plot to overthrow a foreign government and the prevention of a natural disaster. Central to all of these specific power fantasies were the following: the belief that one had carried out an "impossible" feat involving the control of many others; the total nonreality of such a feat in spite of the patient's conviction to the contrary; the "oneness" of such an event; and the extreme reluctance upon the part of the patient to divulge this ordeal to the therapist. "You won't believe this," or "I know you're going to think I'm nuts now, Doc," usually prefaced this type of disclosure.

TYPE II ALCOHOLIC POWER FANTASY. This form of power

fantasy constitutes a perpetual behavioral exchange with the world which amounts to "I can handle anything." I sometimes refer to this as nothing more than diffuse meglomania. This type of power fantasy usually incorporates a total life-style. Essential to this form of power fantasy is the fact that in reality the patient is not at all competent to the extent he feels himself to be, in the multiplicity of areas he believes himself to be. Nevertheless, he believes himself to be and readily communicates this belief to the world. Indeed, it is superficially hard to conceive of how most of these individuals can persist in this life-style in the face of the ongoing environmental feedback they receive to the contrary. This generalized power fantasy is as behavioral as it is verbal. It is my clinical impression that the therapeutic working through of this generalized power fantasy material is a crucial issue with at least 70 percent of any given alcoholic population.

Let me cite a few brief case history examples of what I term "power fantasy" through content, both the specific and generalized elements mentioned earlier, and then discuss some of the basic psychodynamic and psychotherapy considerations essential to understanding and resolving these fantasies.

Case 1. A thirty-nine-year-old white married male with a ten-year history of problem drinking, including the diagnosis of "chronic alcoholism with Wernicke's syndrome" was referred to the Alcoholic Rehabilitation Center, where he remained in outpatient treatment for some months. Treatment involved individual and group psychotherapy, A.A., psychotropic maintenance (anti-anxiety agents), marital therapy and the use of Antabuse. The patient was the oldest of three children. Growing up in a small rural north central community reportedly entailed no significant difficulties. However, the patient's mother divorced his father and remarried when he was seven. Problem drinking was allegedly related to the divorce. The patient related a family constellation in which the mother was clearly controlling and domineering, while the stepfather was passive and detached. All three children were reportedly emotionally "close." Upon graduation from high school the patient joined the Army. At this time the patient reported that he felt like somewhat of a "loner" and found it generally hard to relate to his peers. It was at this point that he first began to get "drunk." At the age of twenty-four the patient married his present wife who is five years his elder. His wife was from a similar rural background, although she had attended two years of college prior to marriage. The family presently includes two boys, ages seventeen and sixteen, and an eleven-year-old daughter. While the family had experienced numerous "ups and downs" as a result of the patient's drinking behavior, it had nevertheless remained surprisingly intact. The first ten years of military life and marriage involved a good deal of "controlled" drinking. The patient was first hospitalized as a result of prolonged intoxication at the age of thirty-four. From that time on the patient experienced a progressive global deterioration to include arrests, marital separation, job loss and further medical complications. The patient was hospitalized at least seven times between 1969 and 1971 for "drying out." It was at this point that the patient was referred to our rehabilitation center for treatment.

Being a bright, outspoken and aggressive individual, the patient initially stirred up feelings of resentment and hostility on the part of the staff and fellow patients as well. Psychological assessment at the time of treatment engagement with the Minnesota Multiphasic Personality Inventory (MMPI) indicated a basic 4-9 type of profile (Gilberstadt and Duker, 1965), which includes a predominance of acting-out, impulsive, immature and egocentric types of behavior. Indeed, this was the clinical picture. The patient was diagnosed as a passive-aggressive personality. There was no indication of disturbed or psychotic thought process. The patient radiated "I know it all," "I can handle any situation," to all involved with him. It certainly seemed as if he would do anything short of remaining sober! Very little progress was seen during the first three months of treatment. After three months of individual and group psychotherapy, A.A., and psychotropic maintenance, the patient and his wife entered marital therapy. Marital therapy was initiated by the patient and his wife rather than the treatment staff. It was during the third session with the patient and wife that things such as "I could have and should have been a doctor or lawyer, etc.," began to be verbalized; the striking thing about all these feelings and verbalizations was the patient's global feeling of being as competent in these areas as any trained professional with extensive experience. In spite of the patient's bright level of intellectual functioning. With the exception of these "power fantasies" the patient was completely reality oriented. It was two sessions later that the patient reported that he had something to tell me, but felt that it was so "far out" that perhaps his wife had best relate the entire episode. At that point the wife proceeded to explain how some three years earlier the patient claimed to have hijacked a jet to Cuba. Although she had never believed this "story" it had remained a secret between the two of them. The patient had allegedly hijacked the jet during one of his periods of extended intoxication. He had in fact flown to California (from Georgia) during the drinking episode, but reported remembering having directed the stewardess and crew to fly to Cuba, landing in Havana and seeing Castro and subsequently deciding that he wanted to go back to the United States. Needless to say, investigation rendered this entire incident fantasy. It was at this point that the patient terminated all drinking behaviors. He has been sober twenty months to date.

Case 2. A thirty-four-year-old white single male with a six-year history of problem drinking was referred to the alcoholic rehabilitation center as a result of missing work and drinking on the job. This patient had grown up in a quasi-slum district of a large eastern city. His only brother, seven years his elder, had long been a source of frustration for him. This brother had been athletic, was quite bright and completed medical school. The patient's father, a mill worker, was both a "heavy" drinker and well known carouser in the community. Marital discord, including outright physical assault, was genetic to the parental relationship. Engagement with the academia had been a prolonged trauma for the patient; he was no more than a C student at best (compared to his bright brother), he was markedly overweight, was a severe stutterer, etc. The patient reportedly had no friends, felt isolated and generally found life to be a painful experience. Immediately upon completion of high school the patient was drafted into the Armed Services. While he had experimented with alcohol on three or four occasions while in high school, he actually knew very little about the effects of alcohol. Once a part of the military, he found very quickly that he liked what alcohol did to him. He began to drink beer continually. Once under the influence of a "few beers" he no longer felt inadequate and ugly and became less aware of his speech defect. His drinking simply progressed to the point of needing a constant block against these painful feelings about himself. Needless to say, dating and courtship behavior were an impossibility for him. He had experienced no significant legal or medical intervention as a result of his drinking behavior. However, at the point of contact with our rehabilitation center, the patient was experiencing job difficulties. While being acknowledged as a good cook, he had reached the point of becoming vocationally dysfunctional. The patient entered individual and group psychotherapy and became active in the A.A. program.

Psychological evaluation with the MMPI resulted in a diagnosis of depressive reaction in a schizoid personality. Primary elevations were indicated on the 2-7 and 8 scales (Gilberstadt and Duker, 1965). Clinically the patient did appear moderately depressed, but evidenced no marked though disturbance. Certainly he appeared to have led a rather schizoid life-style. Individual sessions initially focused upon the patient's physical appearance and social behaviors. Being somewhat overweight and unattractive, the patient had always experienced a good deal of anxiety in social situations, had developed marked feelings of inferiority and was generally ill-equipped interpersonally. Moreover, the patient manifested a facial tic and was a severely handicapped stutterer. During the first two months of treatment the patient experienced numerous "slips." As the patient became increasingly able to discuss his feelings of inadequacy and inferiority he simultaneously became more open to expressing his fantasy life. Very rapidly our sessions turned into a dialogue in which the patient assumed the role of a handsome playboy completely surrounded with beautiful women, a secret agent, a philanthropist serving the needy, etc. Although operational to a limited extent during sobriety, these "power fantasies" assumed the major proportion of the patient's fantasy life while intoxicated. It was as if he was able to become all these ego ideals once intoxicated. Again, as this particular thought process became expressed and experienced in the therapy sessions, the patient was able to extinguish his problem drinking. The patient has been sober thirteen months to date.

Case 3. A thirty-six-year-old Negro married female, the mother of four, with a nine-year history of alcoholic behavior was referred to the Alcoholic Rehabilitation Center by a psychiatric service which had attempted to treat her for some five years. During that time the patient had been hospitalized on numerous occasions, received outpatient therapy and somatic treatment. Although partially intoxicated at the time of initial contact with our facility, she was a most cooperative, likeable person. This patient had grown up on an isolated farm in south Georgia and had eleven brothers and sisters. Reportedly she was in the "middle" of the sibling age range. Her father was cotton sharecropper. The overall picture of the family constellation was that of a rather primitive (neither of the parents could write) group which continually struggled simply to exist. Indeed starvation and hunger were an ever-present reality. The patient sporadically attended a rural school through the seventh grade and recalled having actually liked this experience — "It was a good chance to get away from it all." At age fifteen she left home and moved to a large city in central Georgia to live with an aunt. This amounted to entering a black poverty ghetto. It was at this point that the patient initiated a good deal of heavy drinking and sexual acting-out. At the age of seventeen she became involved with a soldier stationed at a nearby Army post, became pregnant and subsequently married. This relationship involved perpetual arguing and fighting, continual extramarital affairs primarily upon the part of the husband and an ever-growing need to be intoxicated. By the age of twenty-four the patient was reportedly drinking nearly a fifth of whiskey per day. This resulted in numerous hospitalizations of a psychiatric nature. Her medical care history included at least fifty ECT treatments. All of this eventually resulted in her referral to our alcoholic rehabilitation center. Shortly thereafter she entered the group therapy program, A.A. and individual counseling with a staff social work technician. Psychological assessment of this patient at the point of entry into the rehabilitation program with the MMPI indicated a markedly depressed personality configuration, with concurrent thought disorder (2, 7, 8, 6) (Gilberstadt and Duker, 1965). Clinically she appeared to be a chronically depressed individual, in addition to being somewhat confused and preoccupied. Prior psychiatric hospitalizations had included the diagnosis of psychotic depression. This particular woman became one of the most actively involved patients in our total program. It was apparent that in the past, treatment had been conducted "on" her, rather than any active involvement and commitment to the treatment effort upon her part. It was truly amazing how little she had learned from previous rehabilitation efforts. After having been a speaker in the A.A. program, approximately one month after entry into our rehabilitation program, she began an individual session by casually noting that as early as the seventh grade she had envisioned herself as a messianic person. Being black she had felt that it was her role in life to lead the black people "out of bondage." For a month thereafter therapy sessions were simply a deluge of thought process related to grandiosity and power. Feelings of superior intellectual functioning, of being a charismatic person, and of her being able to "cure" any alcoholic constituted the entire therapy sessions. It was at this time that the patient was able to terminate her drinking behavior. After five months of total sobriety the patient's husband moved in with another woman whom he had impregnated. Shortly thereafter the patient became markedly depressed and was hospitalized. At this point she was placed on a heavy dosage of Mellaril, treated on an inpatient basis for five weeks and released. Limited contact (she attended A.A. twice within a two-month interval) suggested she might possibly have become as addicted to her prescribed medication as she had originally been to alcohol. This patient committed suicide via a gunshot wound some three months after being released from the inpatient treatment. The primacy of external reinforcement or environmental press factors upon internal feelings and behavior is clearly indicated in this case. I suggest that the partial therapeutic resolution of this patient's power fantasy material was essential to her five months of sobriety; however, this alone was obviously not enough.

Let me emphasize that these case histories are not atypical. I have often been therapeutically confronted with this type of power fantasy thought process.

Certainly the concept of "power fantasy" is not a revelation to the alcohol-related literature. Cutter et al. (1970; 1973),

McClelland (1971), McClelland et al. (1972; 1966) and Davis (1972) have all experimentally attempted to study the relationship of alcohol use to the need for power and power imagery. While these authors have attempted to experimentally validate the relevance of the power variable to alcoholism via the use of college students and "blue-collar workers," studied in such "natural" settings as bars and fraternity houses, in contrast I am reporting the relevance of this similar power concept experienced within the confines of prolonged, intensive psychotherapeutic work with alcohol-addicted persons. Moreover, McClelland (1971), McClelland et al. (1966; 1971; 1972) and Cutter et al. (1970; 1973) have largely relied upon projective (Thematic Apperception Test) psychological testing in their reports on the relationship between alcohol, power and inhibition. Hopefully the present clinical approach to this area of controversy might provide useful data for those involved in the actual treatment of alcohol-addicted patients, as well as prove heuristic in a more general sense.

Of some twenty-four alcohol-addicted patients I have seen in individual psychotherapy for more than thirty hours, power-oriented issues of the type presented in the earlier case histories were of major importance therapeutically in at least seventeen of the cases. Needless to say, this assessment is a product of my personal clinical experience and as such is biased. However, I might add, it is my feeling that power fantasy issues represented an area of significant therapuetic engagement for all the people I have worked with experiencing difficulty as a result of their drinking behavior. In some cases the power-oriented material was certainly less important strategically, as far as drinking behavior was concerned, and could have been classified as a problem relating to manipulation.

Psychodynamic Considerations

Realizing that most alcoholics have led a life-style which is outwardly antithetical to the power fantasy thought process delineated herein, one is confronted with the task of making sense out of this apparent disparity.

The power fantasy has its roots in early childhood. The

frequency of broken homes, unhappy marriages, illegitimacy and other similar disconcerting influences with which many alcoholics have been subject to coping facilitates the development of power fantasy thought process. All of those factors which contribute to the development of a self-concept devoid of feelings of positive self-worth contribute to the establishment of the power fantasy thought process. The alcoholic has not been able to incorporate into the self-system real experiences and feelings to the effect of "I am good and capable of successfully operating upon the environment." If, in fact, the individual's total experience with reality is in direct opposition to the development of positive self-esteem, it becomes imperative that these interpersonal needs be met somehow. This becomes a major function of fantasy. At a very early age the individual "learns" that he can feel good about all those things he imagines about himself and his capabilities. In realizing how painful reality has been developmentally for many alcoholics it becomes understandable how the fantasy function becomes increasingly essential to the maintenance of interpersonal relations. If the individual is totally unable to secure good feelings about himself, he is completely overwhelmed. It seems as though this entire process is continually relived by the alcoholic. Academic difficulty in grade school and high school, interpersonal difficulties, loss of jobs and legal complications continually confirm childhood feelings of being somehow inadequate, unwanted and unloved. Very often this amounts to being a perpetual nobody. A reality as unpleasant as this may precipitate psychoses for certain individuals. The adaptive nature of fantasy is operational here. As long as the alcoholic can be "potent" in his fantasy life, he can continue to function. The immediacy of escape from unpleasant reality compounded by the reinforcement of a fantasy experience of being actually human, if not something more than human, makes the alcoholic power fantasy comprehensible. This is particularly true if one has never been fully human.

It is generally accepted that the less an individual has going for him, the greater the potential for developing a fantasy life as a compensation mechanism. This is the exact case with the alcoholic and the development of power fantasy ideation. This overall process is evident in many psychiatric disorders, perhaps most clearly in the schizophrenic disorders and allied states. Viewed from this perspective, the essential problem becomes that of identity distortion. It is my opinion that identity distortion is central to the alcoholic's development and use of power fantasy material. In my experience the alcoholic and problem drinker have developmentally failed to establish ego boundaries capable of clearly distinguishing between real, ideal and fantasy states. Often this is the result of inadequate parental models. Certainly individual character structure, family dynamics and environmental variables help facilitate this identity confusion. When people learn to basically dislike themselves and when they experience difficulty differentiating between real, ideal and false systems of personal identity, they frequently move in the direction of becoming alcohol addicted. In my experience this global process incorporates the development of a power fantasy oriented thought process, the resolution of which becomes essential to sobriety. Let us now turn to the problem of therapeutic management of the alcoholic power fantasy.

Psychotherapeutic Considerations

In discussing therapeutic strategies of intervention with any patient population, to include those who are alcohol-addicted or experiencing difficulty as a result of drinking behavior, we often tend to become "boggled" down with theoretical and esoteric matters which convey little to the rehabilitation personnel involved in actual patient care and treatment. I wish to avoid this pitfall in the present context. Let me initially state that the therapeutic mode of operation discussed in this section globally represents that which "works" for me personally as a therapist. It will be apparent to those versed in theories of counseling and psychotherapy that I lean heavily toward the existential school of therapy. Stressing human relatedness, being and defining the therapeutic relationship as an encounter depict this model. Stressing the "now," dealing with such issues as "Who am I?" and accepting oneself are also part of this general theoretical orientation. In addition, I lean heavily toward the Reality Therapy (1965) approach as advocated by Glasser. The primacy of dealing with reality issues therapeutically, the emphasis upon personal responsibility for one's behavior, choosing behavioral alternatives and, again the role of the "now" are all clearly reality therapy techniques. Freudian theory could well be related to the repression of such power fantasy thought process, as well as oedipal considerations specific to the identity and oral issues relative to alcoholism. What I am most desirous of conveying to the reader in this section is an understanding of a particular personal treatment strategy for individual psychotherapy with the alcoholic patient.

This in essence amounts to a "nuts and bolts" approach to the resolution of the alcoholic power fantasy, which in my experience significantly relates to the establishment of long-term sobriety.

One of the initial goals in the therapeutic process with the alcoholic patient must be the establishment of a basic identity. Identity distortion is genetic to the alcoholic personality. The alcoholic seen in most rehabilitation settings is attempting to deal with acute identity crises related to vocational adjustment, marital and family roles and very often basic "humanness." Although the question of "Who am I?" has never been satisfactorily resolved by the majority of alcoholics, it becomes a crucial issue when the individual can no longer struggle with his alcohol-related behaviors and must seek help.

Once sober, the patient is confronted with the reality of his total being. We see the same old denial and distortion defense mechanisms in operation during the initial stages of sobriety; in my experience, prolonged periods of sobriety are accompanied by a growing reality orientation. In spite of all the tragedy and emotional pain, the patient is able, perhaps for the first time in years, to accurately take stock of himself and say "this is me." Once this point is reached, the A.A. dictum of being able to "accent myself as I am" becomes paramount. This is no simple task, as very often the reality of "me" is in itself rather traumatic. Accepting the self one has attempted to deny for ten or twenty years may be similar to awakening one morning to find that one had changed colors during the interval of sleep!

A strategy which I find myself employing, quite honestly I think, could be characterized as "so that's you." Once the patient begins to establish an identity, which may be filled with a lot of "bad me," I attempt to validate his self-references in a manner which conveys that I simply accept him as another human being. In reality, that other human being may have engaged in socially unacceptable behavior or in other ways may have been somewhat less than a good samaritan; nonetheless he is human. In fact, I really don't give a damn about all those "holes" in his background. However, I am at the same time very much concerned about the "now" in the patient's life space. When the patient and I can reach the point of agreeing on who he is, establishing an identity as it were, when he can integrate the fact that I do care about him and his behavior as a human being, he has reached the point of beginning to assume some responsibility in the "now" of his behavior. Assuming responsibility means, in effect, terminating his alcoholic behavior and the craziness that goes with it. In this process the patient is more and more able to be himself within our encounters. With this increased reality input comes the power fantasy material.

Simply being sober is a new reality experience of major significance for most long-term alcoholics. The patient's power fantasy material and his growing ability to be reality oriented must eventually become mutually exclusive. This process of defining oneself realistically, to the point of integrating the irrationality of the power fantasy, becomes the essence of therapy in many cases. This is very much the process of learning to accept oneself. The patient surrenders as it were, behaviorally saying "This is me," "These fantasies simply aren't real," and "I can now somehow accept what I see in the mirror." An excellent sample of this process was an alcoholic at an A.A. meeting I recently attended who noted that he was "pretty ugly" (which in reality he was), that he nonetheless knew this and was glad to be what he was, jokingly adding that he now realized why all the females in the bars hadn't been particularly attracted to him in his drinking days. During his "practicing days" he had always felt himself to be quite the ladies man but now realized how they actually perceived him. As the patient begins to acknowledge the irrational nature of his fantasy life within the therapy sessions, he may well demonstrate a good deal of insight into the functional nature of his power fantasy material. Indeed, this has been my experience. Sometime later the most bizarre of these fantasies may be verbalized in group sessions, A.A. or in similar interpersonal encounters. Once the patient is able to openly express these fantasies and can partially understand and deal with the developmental functionality of such material, the probability for remaining sober is excellent.

From the therapeutic standpoint we must first allow the patient to discover who he is. Being sober, the first step in this process, is essential to the patient's development of an accurate identity. Identity becomes accurate as the alcoholic distortions become less and less essential to the maintenance of the alcoholic's self-system. He is more and more able to accept himself as he is. Movement from "This is me" to "I accept me" is essentially a process of growing reality orientation. The alcoholic power fantasy thought process, the product of years of constant interpersonal reinforcement along the lines of "I am a nobody," becomes juxtaposed to the patient's progressive reality orientation. As the patient can increasingly accept himself, accept the reality of his life experience and can accept the responsibility of now, he becomes less dependent upon his fantasy life as a means of maintaining a functional level of self-esteem. Frequently the patient can integrate the unreality of his power fantasy thought process to the point of becoming verbally able to express the actual fantasy. Experience indicates this to be a turning point in the alcoholic's life-style; sporadic sobriety may well become long-term at this juncture.

In summary, clinical experience indicates the existence of a power fantasy type of thought process relative to a significant number of alcoholic patients. Frequently this type of thought process is genetically related to a life-style devoid of positive feelings about the self. In the absence of a positive identity the patient is forced to take refuge in fantasy. Alcoholic dependence, another neurotic attempt to maintain the self-system, only reinforces the patient's non-reality-oriented life-style. Engagement in the psychotherapeutic encounter facilitates the patient's establishment of an identity, an acceptance of the reality of his being and growing personal responsibility for his behaviors. Within the therapeutic encounter the patient can experience the power fantasy with another significant human being, come to understand the basic unreality of this particular segment of his experiential self and begin to work at the process of remaining sober. Establishing a therapist-patient relationship conducive to the working through of power fantasy material is crucial in the establishment of long-term sobriety.

Chapter 19

ALCOHOLISM:
AN EROTIC EXPERIENCE

ATTEMPTING to determine why particular individuals become addicted to or abuse alcohol has proven a most difficult task. Indeed, it appears that historically mankind has been perplexed by this matter. A diversity of explanations have been proposed as causative models of alcohol abuse and addiction. Moral deterioration, insanity, learning and conditioning models, the "disease" concept and genetic factors are but a few of the many explanations and paradigms which have been associated with the problem of alcohol addiction in a cause-and-effect fashion. Needless to say, such singular explanations of why people become alcoholics or problem drinkers have for the most part proven inadequate and rather fragmented. In reality I suspect that the interaction effect of a multiplicity of variables such as those noted account for the development and maintenance of the addiction process. Perhaps at some future point we may possess the technological and research sophistication essential to ferret out more precisely the exact nature of the many cause-and-effect variables and interaction effects as they relate to the development and maintenance of pathological drinking behavior. A neglected and significant variable related to the causative aspect of alcohol addiction is that of sexuality or erotica. This dimension of drinking behavior has received relatively little clinical and research consideration. It is this erotic component of alcoholism and pathological drinking which I wish to discuss in the present chapter. Quite simply, it is my contention that the association between drinking behavior and human sexuality in part relates to why in fact certain individuals become addicted to alcohol.

Alcoholic beverages have been a part of virtually every cul-

277

ture. While it is assumed that alcoholic beverages were discovered rather than invented in prehistoric times, the actual presence of wine and beer is rather well documented in the archaeological records of the oldest civilizations and in the diets of most preliterate peoples. It would seem logical to assume that prehistoric man appreciated the mood-changing effect of these substances. This assumption is clearly supported via the various religious rituals of many cultures which incorporated the use of alcoholic beverages as a means of manipulating divine or magical powers. Rather obviously, alcoholic substances are more suitable than others for facilitating affective change, mystification and similar variation in experiential being. Of particular significance to the present chapter is the fact that alcoholic beverages facilitated the rites of orgiastic communicants. It is not in the least surprising tht Dionysus-Bacchus became the most popular of the gods among the Greeks and Romans! The best documented early civilizations, such as the Sumerian-Akkadian, the Babylonian-Chaldean, and the Egyptian as well as the classical peoples — Greeks, Hebrews, and Romans — combined sexual behavior with the use of alcoholic beverages. In addition these cultures celebrated births, puberty initiations and marriage with a good deal of alcohol consumption. As the use of alcoholic substances spread from religious and magical purposes to include medical and more global utility, the element of sexuality persisted.

It is of significance that along with the recorded history of alcoholic beverages one finds a corresponding diary of alcoholism and the many social and interpersonal difficulties experienced by certain individuals as a result of their inability to control various behaviors once under the influence of alcohol. Drunkenness and undoubtedly what we know as alcoholism today were well-known problems among the ancient Chinese, Greeks, Jews and other major cultures. Governments as well as individuals have historically attempted to reform or control the consumption of alcoholic beverages and the associated resultant behaviors. To assert that problem drinking and alcoholism are problems of the twentieth century, associated with industrialization and technology, affluence or poverty, is to deny the historicity of mankind. An ever-present red thread in this history of alcoholism per se is that of an association with erotica and frank sexual behavior. A major element in the general historic disapproval of the alcoholic and problem drinker has centered around the explicit sexual behavior of the intoxicant. Without going into a detailed historical account of this relationship between alcohol consumption and the subsequent sexual behaviors of the intoxicant or the group, suffice it to say that the inference that this particular combination could best be characterized as highly ambivalent from any number of perspectives is rather elementary. When individuals become intoxicated they frequently act-out sexually, as individuals or as a group, and although this behavior is enjoyed and tends to be repeated upon subsequent occasions by certain individuals, it is at the same time disdained and abhored by other individuals who act in ways which serve to both repress and deter the occurrence of further behaviors of this type. Moreover, many individuals who act-out sexually under the influence of alcoholic beverages find their own alcohol-facilitated behavior unacceptable and to various degrees attempt to control or modify their pattern of consumption. This matter indeed becomes most confusing. Thus far I have attempted to provide the reader with a brief overview of the historical relationship between alcoholism and sexuality. An in-depth examination of the alcoholism or problem drinking behaviors of particular individuals or cultural groups at some point in history is beyond the scope of this chapter. Moving on from this truncated historical account of alcohol abuse and sexuality, I would now like to focus rather directly upon more recent clinical observation and speculation in this realm. A good deal of this material is based upon my personal clinical experience, and for the most part the emphasis throughout the remainder of the chapter will be upon individual psychodynamics as they encompass the alcoholism-erotica paradigm. It should be apparent at this point that there are in fact a good deal of historical data to support the position that drinking behavior, and more precisely alcoholism, can be concretely associated with sexual behavior and the erotic dimension of human "being" in a variety of ways.

Perhaps it would be well to emphasize my initial point that in part individuals become addicted to alcohol as a result of the association between drinking behavior and sexuality. This basic association is multifaceted and virtually limitless with regard to the individual and his or her interpersonal parameters. Freud was certainly one of the most astute observers of human behavior. Although not particularly interested and clinically experienced in the treatment of alcoholism, it was his essential position (Freud, 1933) that the alcoholic suffers from pregenital fixation and possible latent homosexuality. Freudian psychoanalytic theory views the alcoholic as an orally fixated individual, with concomitant passive-dependent, narcissistic, oedipal and anally oriented conflicts. The clinical relevance and validity of these constructs as they apply to the behavior and psychodynamics of the individual addicted to or abusing alcohol remain very much in question today.

While a number of clinicians and psychotherapists strictly adhere to these basic constructs and tenants in their therapeutic work with alcoholic patients, many totally or partially reject this fundamental stance of the Freudians as it relates to the understanding and treatment of the addicted patient. What is of significance to me in this regard is simply the very primary link between human sexuality and alcoholic behavior genetic to Freudian personality theory. This in essence seems to mean that people in part become addicted or dependent upon alcohol as a result of sexual and identity conflicts. Alcohol addiction in this sense can be viewed as a neurotic solution to these particular intrapersonal difficulties. This is indeed a conflict-oriented solution. Escaping, repressing or denying and avoiding these basic sexual conflicts becomes the source of gain or motivation behind the addictive behavior. Chronic alcohol addiction viewed through eyes of the Freudian thus incorporates the position that the addiction process is both caused and maintained via unresolved sexual conflicts. As such, that interval of time between the inception and termination of pathological drinking behaviors can be viewed as sexually determined and maintained, for perhaps as long as forty years or more. For better or worse, is this not the example par excellence of an erotic experience? Rather unfortunately, this alcohol-oriented sexual and identity adjustment is chronically uncomfortable at best for most individuals so affected. As a matter of fact, this situation somewhat paradoxically dictates continued intoxication upon the part of the individual caught in this particular trap. It is my contention that in the absence of establishing and maintaining sobriety, the alcoholic individual who drinks as a result of this form of pathological erotic pattern can only hope to remain intoxicated. While sobriety precipitates an acute identity crisis, in which the addicted individual is confronted with issues related to orality, homosexuality and other more frank sexual dynamics, as well as more socially oriented identity issues (job and career, marital and parental roles, and more basically "Who am I? and Where am I going?"), it is only through the sober confrontation and resolution of sexual matters such as these that long-term sobriety and more effective interpersonal adjustment become possible for the alcoholic. In the absence of learning to successfully deal with these sexual and identity conflicts, in failing to effectively work through or resolve these conflicts developmentally, it is apparent that the alcoholic and problem drinker are fated to neurotically cope with these issues through the medium of alcohol for perhaps the duration of their lives.

It would appear that viewing alcoholic behavior from this viewpoint, as it relates to erotic or sexual dynamics, is in essence an intrapersonal account of why given individuals become and remain engaged in the addiction process. This becomes a most recondite issue. It is my impression that the erotic component of pathological drinking behavior is more often clinically associated with the interpersonal transactions of the individual becoming caught in the trap of addiction. While perhaps 10 percent of any population of individuals engaged in psychotherapy or some program of rehabilitation designed to explicitly change or modify their drinking behaviors, manifest frank homosexual conflicts, pedophiliac trends, or other primary sexual deviations or pathology. It is my experience that the other 90 percent experience erotic difficulties of a more interpersonal nature which significantly reinforce their addiction. Certainly when an individual acts-out in a homosexual or other socially determined form of sexually deviant behavior such a transaction by definition becomes interpersonally oriented. Overt sexual deviation involves roughly 10 percent of any given population of alcoholic or problem drinking patients. This situation may very well be juxtaposed to the ideational and fantasy-oriented conflicts of this same group of individuals. No doubt such fantasy content can and does facilitate the addiction process for many alcoholics. As such, the therapeutic management of ideational material is essential to successful work with this clinical population. However, this element of the alcoholic's self-system remains most typically an intrapersonal matter. In this sense, it happens within the confines of his or her head! Rather obviously this is the case in spite of the profound impact such fantasy-oriented conflicts can effect within the interpersonal realm.

Let us move on to a consideration of the more obvious interpersonal dynamisms, which either directly or indirectly relate to the erotic component of alcoholic behavior, in a cause-and-effect fashion. Clinically I have found the vast majority of alcohol-addicted and problem drinking patients engaged in therapy to be extremely uncomfortable with the demands of interpersonal living (Forrest, 1974; Forrest, 1975). This situation is quite antithetical to the apparent interpersonal *modus operandi* of the intoxicated or partially intoxicated alcohol abuser. Human sexuality represents but one form of interpersonal behavior. In my experience alcohol abuse and addiction enable select individuals to function interpersonally; indeed in the absence of learning to become addicted or dependent upon alcohol it is my suspicion that a sizeable segment of this population might well acquire methods of coping with the many stresses of interpersonal living which would be significantly more disturbed or pathological. Alcohol addiction in this sense possibly represents a relatively healthy choice of symptomatology. Acting-out behaviors of a sexual or erotic type predominate the global pattern of daily living difficulties experienced by most alcoholics and problem drinkers. These interpersonal conflicts of a sexual nature differ in various ways from those of the more "acting-in" or intrapersonal variety noted earlier. Although the net result of these interpersonally oriented conflicts may be quite similar to those facilitated and maintained via the intrapersonal realm, and while sexual acting-out is in no way totally dichotomous from sexual acting-in, it is nevertheless tremendously important to first acknowledge that most alcoholic patients enter treatment as a result of their acting-out interpersonal behaviors. Quite typically this means that at the point of engagement in the treatment process the addicted individual has been effectively labeled an alcoholic. The interpersonal transactions of the addicted individual reaching this point have been so socially deviant as to render him or her inescapable of avoiding the labeling process. Not infrequently sexual acting-out is fused with the explicit drinking behavior precipitating labeling. As we are all relatively well aware, our culture is very conformity oriented; thus we are highly intolerant of the deviant, be he madman or "alcoholic." One method designed to modify or eliminate deviant alcoholic behavior is most assuredly psychotherapy or "rehabilitation." Socially we seem to demand rehabilitation and treatment when overt sexual acting-out becomes associated with the alcoholic behavior of a given individual.

Sexual approach oriented behaviors are perhaps of foremost relevance when we begin to consider the alcoholic's interpersonal behaviors which relate both to the addiction process in a cause-and-effect fashion and simultaneously cause the addicted individual significant difficulty. One of the historic "benefits" of the usage of alcoholic beverages has been that of a "social lubricant." Alcohol blocks interpersonal anxieties and other unpleasant affects, thus enabling people to relate to one another on a more comfortable level. Approach-oriented interpersonal behaviors, facilitated via the ingestion of alcoholic beverages, apply to people in general — not just the alcoholic or problem drinker. This exact situation applies to a gamut of interpersonal behaviors, sexuality very definitely being of particular significance in this realm. However, it becomes readily apparent that alcohol-facilitated, interpersonal behaviors of a sexual flavor become a source of eventual difficulty far more frequently for those individuals who for whatever reasons experience problems as a result of their explicit patterns of alcohol consumption. Foremost, it must be emphasized that sexual and erotic approach behaviors made possible in part by the ingestion of alcohol represent for the alcoholic and problem drinker, as well as for the so-called "normal" drinker, a very meaningful and significant source of pleasure and gain. Such a situation dictates repetition, learning and eventual overlearning to the possible extent of stamping in maladjustive neurological associations of the conditioned reflex order involving the alcohol-sexuality dynamic.

Most of the alcoholic and problem drinking patients that I have worked with clinically experienced a great deal of difficulty when it came to matters of dating, courtship and other sexually oriented approach behaviors. As a group these individuals do not possess the social skills prerequisite to effective and comfortable heterosexual interpersonal relating — this applies to interpersonal relations in general, but for the purposes of the present chapter I wish to stress this dynamic as it applies to sexual or erotically oriented approach behaviors. The individual who struggles with generalized feelings of inadequacy, inferiority, identity conflicts and interpersonal anxiety quite typically learns in a matter of a few trials that these painful and threatening feelings can rather effectively be controlled if not extinguished by the ingestion of alcohol. As such, intoxication or partial intoxication becomes a methodology by which the alcoholic or problem drinker becomes capable of approach or assertive sexual behaviors. It is understandable that drinking behaviors will persist in such a situation; approach behaviors represent a very real source of pleasure, meaning and good feelings for the anxious and inadequate person. Moreover, alcohol makes this pleasure possible while in a related fashion it very directly blocks various aspects and sources of intrapersonal and interpersonal anxiety and pain. This amounts to a learning theory oriented explanation of the relationship between problem drinking and alcoholism and human sexual and erotic behavior. It has consistently been my observation that even the most seemingly gregarious of alcoholic individuals, upon reaching the point of terminating their addictive behaviors, become socially and interpersonally anxious to the extent of assuming the role of an isolate or "loner" for perhaps as long as four or five months. This is particularly the case with patients involved in individual or group psychotherapy and not engaged in Alcoholics Anonymous. In my experience, patients consistently involved in A.A. on an active basis work through this interpersonal stance much earlier. In order to establish and maintain long-term sobriety, it is essential that the alcoholic learn more effective global interpersonal approach oriented behaviors, to include sexuality. The alcoholic must learn to feel comfortable asking for a date, initiating sexual intercourse and other more frank sexual behaviors in the absence of intoxication or partial intoxication. I feel very strongly that we have, as professionals and paraprofessionals engaged in the work of alcoholic rehabilitation, failed to recognize the very significant relationship between the neurotic use of alcohol as it relates to potentiating assertive sexual approach behaviors. I find it somewhat difficult to understand our relative lack of clinical exploration of this seemingly vociferous relationship between booze and sexual acting-out. We are confronted with this exact situation via the media on a daily basis; yet, we appear not to have fully appreciated the reinforcement or learning theory oriented basis of this paradigm.

Not infrequently the exact equation which serves to reinforce and maintain the addictive behavior, this being in part alcohol ingestion facilitating assertive sexual behaviors which in turn are rewarding, eventually contributes to the extinction of drinking behavior. This applies to both acting-out and acting-in oriented sexual behavior, as such behavior relates to alcohol abuse. This may come about in a number of ways. Certainly alcohol-facilitated sexual behaviors which become grossly overt and contribute to the labeling and identification of the alcoholic as a deviant came to the fore in this respect. The alcoholic or problem drinker who in an intoxicated state sexually molests a daughter or step-daughter, and is "caught" in the sense that the mother or some significant other learns of or observes this transaction and subsequently involves legal and professional parties, very definitely becomes the recipient of a multiplicity or reinforcement contingencies which in effect say "no more drinking." Prolonged incarceration may very well be one such contingency of reinforcement which is generally quite effective (during the period of incarceration) with such individuals. Another impetus toward extinguishing alcoholic behavior as this behavior relates to sexuality is the situation in which the alcoholic begins to find himself either impotent or partially impotent as a result of overindulgence. I suspect that this dilemma applies to the female alcoholic or problem drinker as well as it applies to the male, but as a result of the nature of the sexual apparatus of the male the reality of this experience is clearly more evident and usually more traumatic in scope for the latter gender. Finding out that one can in fact "cut the mustard" upon establishing some duration of sobriety amounts to a significant source of reinforcement to remain sober in many cases. Unfortunately it does not always work this way. Discovering that one is unable to experience an erection or perhaps that one cannot maintain an erection becomes a rationale for remaining intoxicated in all too many cases. Indeed such an awareness may well be so traumatic in nature as to dictate further intoxication as a method of coping with the reality of this matter. The individual who has become in part dependent upon alcohol as means of blocking homosexual fantasies and trends, as well as other inappropriate sexual object conflicts, may well act-out these intrapersonal struggles while in a state of acute intoxication. Case histories of male or female patients regaining consciousness and finding themselves in bed with a same sexed friend or acquaintance met in the course of an alcoholic debauch are not at all atypical. Quite frequently this is a very traumatic and ego-dysyntonic experience. The anxiety, guilt, confusion and depression facilitated by such an experience may help "push" the individual into some form of treatment aimed at curtailing further episodes of this nature.

The primary theme of this chapter has simply been that sexual factors, in a multiplicity of ways, quite frequently serve to facilitate and maintain the process of alcohol addiction.

Thus far we have explored some of the clinical explanations and observations relative to this specific interaction. At this point I would like to briefly comment upon our professional and paraprofessional denial and repression of the erotic or sexual component of pathological drinking behavior.

It has been my experience that even within the confines of long-term individual or group psychotherapy most alcoholic and problem drinking patients are extremely uncomfortable and reluctant to deal with their sexually oriented conflicts. This is the case with sexual matters per se, as well as with regard to the combination of sexuality and problem drinking or the addiction process. Quite frankly I am not at all surprised by this situation. It is only within the past twenty years that human sexuality within Western culture has become a topic of conversation and open discussion, let alone an area subject to investigation and research. Nonetheless, those trained and experienced in the intimacy of psychotherapy with other clinical populations can surely appreciate how relevant and very real sexually oriented content becomes within the confines of this particular type of relationship with most patients. I have not found this to be the case in my own therapeutic work with this population, nor have I found this to be the case in the therapeutic work of some twenty therapists primarily engaged in therapeutic work with the alcoholics and problem drinkers which I have supervised during the past six years. Certainly the "whys" and other factors contributing to this reality are open to clinical speculation. In a similar vein I have observed this same avoidance of sexual dynamics within clinical staffings and case conferences in which alcoholic patients engaged in psychotherapy, and other more comprehensive rehabilitation measures were being evaluated and discussed in depth. Invariably the focus seems to center upon job performance, legal matters, the family constellation — excluding frank exploration of the sexual dynamics pertaining to the husband and wife and quite possibly significant others. Rarely do we consider the relevance of the sexual conflicts of the patient, in a polymorphus sense, as they relate to the addiction process.

Moving away from the more formal or explicit alcoholic

rehabilitation and treatment setting and into the Alcoholics Anonymous, Al-Anon and Alateen milieu has provided me with a wealth of interpersonal data highly congruous with that just noted. In the course of attending A.A. weekly for over two years and Al-Anon weekly for some eighteen months I have observed an almost total avoidance of sexually oriented discussion, verbage and other content of this specific nature within these groups. This finding is perhaps even more significant if one accepts my personal position that this total community (Alcoholics Anonymous, Al-Anon and Alateen) is in fact highly therapeutic in nature and constructed around an almost total program of rehabilitation (Forrest, 1975). The basis for this program of rehabilitation rests upon the concepts of honesty, self-disclosure and openness — all of which are, in my opinion, conducive to dealing with sexual matters. While some A.A. or Al-Anon meetings may include or focus upon the former sexual escapades of either the alcoholic, spouse, or both, such accounts in my experience have been for the most part superficial, "other" oriented and not at all in-depth explorations of the identity conflicts and other sexually based reinforcers of pathological drinking and interpersonal difficulties experienced by the participating parties. In reference to the Alcoholics Anonymous and Al-Anon community, I might add that on many occasions I have been approached as a professional, usually in a somewhat confidential manner, about this matter of sexual dynamics contributing to a given individual's drinking behavior. Quite honestly I feel that the relationship between sexuality and alcoholism is rather well understood within the A.A. and Al-Anon community, certainly at a preconscious if not conscious level, but that it remains a topic that is simply not talked about for the most part. As in the case of counselors and therapists who seem not to deal with this relationship between booze and sexuality, we could speculate at length upon the "whys" of this matter within the A.A.-oriented community.

In the process of assimilating the material covered thus far, I would hope that the reader has been asking himself or herself just how relevant it is to focus upon the erotic or sexual component of pathological drinking behavior as this matter relates to effective psychotherapy and rehabilitation efforts with alcoholics and problem drinkers. I must confess that this is a question that I quite frequently ask myself, and as yet have not completely resolved. If I am accurate in my observation that the matter of sexuality as related to the causative and maintenance aspects of alcohol addiction is not a major or significant part of Alcoholics Anonymous, does this mean in effect that this particular treatment community would be more effective should it include a more pointed emphasis upon this dimension of interpersonal or intrapersonal behavior? Would counselors and psychotherapists involved in the work of alcoholic rehabilitation be more effective in their roles as change agents if they began to relate more fully to the sexual dynamics of their patients? At this point I am simply unable to respond to questions such as these in any definitive fashion. I do suspect that providing individuals with the opportunity to come to grips with this specific matter as it relates to their interpersonal and intrapersonal difficulties and struggles might well help them "raise their bottom" a bit. In other words the termination of the addiction process and the serenity so long sought for, in my opinion, potentially would occur more quickly once the patient began to work at these identity-oriented issues within the psychotherapeutic encounter or perhaps within the confines of A.A. and other helping-oriented milieus. I do feel we must more fully explore the clinical relationship between pathological drinking behavior and sexuality. It is my impression that we have yet to begin to understand many of the most basic and fundamental psychodynamic issues surrounding the alcohol-sexuality rubric. Certainly in our role as change agents we must focus upon alcoholism or drinking behavior per se; by the same token reality dictates that we work on numerous other factors related to drinking pathology, sexuality being only one of these more secondary avenues of therapeutic approach.

The essence of this chapter has been that alcoholism and pathological drinking, for better or worse, include highly eroticized experiences. Indeed, the history of alcohol use and abuse supports this position. I have stressed the point that people in part learn to become addicted to alcohol because this particular substance enables them to neurotically manage sexual and erotic conflicts and drives. I would hope that we might begin to investigate this aspect of alcohol addiction more fully.

Chapter 20

SUCCESSFUL REHABILITATION OF THE ALCOHOLIC PATIENT: A CASE HISTORY

THE case history of J.B. is presented as an example of the successfully rehabilitated alcoholic patient. Although the background, family constellation and psychodynamics of this case are specific to J.B., as are numerous other variables which facilitate and maintain any particular individual's alcoholic behavior, it is nonetheless felt that the overall case history of J.B. is representative of those individuals experiencing social and interpersonal difficulties as a result of their drinking behaviors. Unfortunately this case is atypical in that J.B. was able, through his efforts within an alcoholic rehabilitation center, to successfully terminate his drinking behaviors and once again enter society as a productive individual. Only recently have we begun to recognize that the alcoholic can be successfully rehabilitated and helped to return to a socially productive role. Our current emphasis, via federal and state expenditures, legal and medical attention, as well as public concern, on the alcohol and drug problem with which our society finds itself confronted attests to a growing consensus of opinion that these particular individuals can be helped to reestablish themselves as productive citizens. It is hoped that this case history will contribute to that growing consensus of opinion that the alcoholic personality can in fact be successfully rehabilitated.

Case History. J.B., age thirty-eight, is the oldest son of a family of five, including a younger half sister age thirty-one, a half brother age nineteen, a stepfather age sixty-two and mother age sixty. J.B. grew up in a small, rural, north central community. J.B.'s actual father was divorced by his mother when he was three and subsequently remarried when he was seven. J.B. recalled nothing of his actual father, but problem drinking was allegedly related to the divorce.

Although J.B. recalled little of his childhood, he did manifest rather specific feelings for his family constellation during his preadolescent and adolescent stages of development. The stepfather, a moderate drinker, was portrayed as a rather cool, detached individual. In spite of his physical presence he maintained a good deal of emotional distance from the other family members. J.B. rather consistently reported very limited emotional involvement with his stepfather. His mother, however, was recalled with a good deal more emotional flavor. J.B. reported her to be generally quite controlling, responsible for family decisions involving financial matters, discipline and virtually every other aspect of family living. The father responded to this by a means of passive withdrawal which established a fixed pattern of interpersonal relations for the duration of J.B.'s familial experience, which terminated shortly after J.B.'s seventeenth birthday.

The family did attend church and was to a limited extent involved in community activities throughout J.B.'s recalled adolescence. In addition to a good deal of physical disciplining, dealt primarily by his mother, J.B. was emotionally conditioned to the "I'll love you and value you as a person as long as you do what I want you to, when I want you to" paradigm. Anything short of complete obedience to this model resulted in almost total withdrawal of emotional support by both parents. J.B. reported a long-standing camaraderie with his sister. It seems as though they were always able to share feelings and generally got along quite well. This relationship has remained intact to the present. Due to the age discrepancy and his departure from home at seventeen, J.B. feels he has never really known his younger brother.

Within six months of graduation from high school, J.B. decided to join the Army. J.B. reported having progressed through elementary, junior high and high school with little academic difficulty. In fact, he was a somewhat above average student. His only complaint directed at this stage of his life was that he had very few friends. "It is as if I was always on the outside looking in — kinda a loner even then." His global recall of the pattern of interaction within the family constellation prior to enlistment seemed to be most bland. A rather emotionally cool, farming family, with the various family members going about their individual matters of living is the picture portrayed. J.B. felt no lack of physical or material providing, but pointed out time and again that his present feelings of being a "loner" must have surely been related to this extended pattern of familial interaction.

It certainly seems reasonable to suspect that his decision to join the army represented another attempt at establishing a meaningful group membership, an attempted movement toward people in contrast to his earlier "loner" or social isolate role, and certainly this is a typical aspect of the identify process to which American males have been historically subjected. J.B.'s pattern of social behavior continued in much the same fashion during his first five years of active military duty. Although his eventual problem drinking behaviors were only now beginning to germinate, his degree of social interaction changed very little. One marked exception to this was the ability to initiate and maintain a relationship with another individual — his wife. While on leave at the age of twenty-four, J.B. met his future wife, five years his elder, and married her six months later. J.B.'s wife had grown up in a large city located close to his childhood home, attended college for two years and subsequently entered the work world. J.B. reported he had been drinking when he met his future wife and was continually intoxicated to various degrees during their period of relatively brief courtship. Although J.B. and his wife have experienced a relationship characterized by numerous ups and downs, including one extended separation, both have continued to feel a good deal of love and commitment to each other. Mr. and Mrs. J.B. have three children, two boys ages sixteen and fifteen, and an eleven-year-old daughter. In spite of J.B.'s extended struggle with alcohol, his entire family continued to support him. The feelings of anxiety, depression and guilt with which the alcoholic and problem drinker is continually confronted were a constant reality for both J.B. and his family.

Drinking History. J.B. reported that his earliest experiences with alcohol dated back as far as age fourteen. It was during the summer months of harvest that J.B. "developed" a taste for a few cold beers after a long day in the wheat fields. Parental awareness of J.B.'s beer consumption proved no problem, as J.B.'s first recalled experience of being drunk actually took place with his stepfather at the age of sixteen. It is apparent that J.B.'s drinking behaviors at this time (age fourteen to seventeen) were in many respects typical of those of most adolescent males. It was at this point that J.B. entered the army. Being a capable and well-motivated individual, J.B. found military life to his liking. He attended various training programs and fared well in making rank. Although he felt his first eight to ten years of military life involved a rather controlled drinking life-style, J.B. did indicate a general feeling that the military had in certain respects reinforced his drinking behaviors: "It seems like there's always a happy hour, a promotion or some reason to drink — where can you get cheaper booze?" At the same time J.B. was cognizant that the majority of individuals subjected to this same environment had not entered the ranks of the problem drinker; "Somehow I just couldn't accept the fact that it was me that had the problem with booze — it seems like a lot of other guys were drinking as much as I, but they weren't getting arrested, busted and ending up in jail like I was."

J.B.'s real problem drinking developed some eight years ago. It was at this point he first received treatment as a result of his drinking behaviors, that his job performance began to suffer and that his marital and family problems began to surface. From this time until his completion of active duty, May, 1972, J.B. was hospitalized numerous times for "drying out" and similar forms of medical treatment indicated for the alcoholic patient. More recent hospitalization involved overseas treatment in 1968, extended stateside hospitalization in 1969, 1970 and 1971, including withdrawal seizure treatment on three separate occasions. During June, 1970 the patient was air evacuated from Vietnam with a diagnosis of "chronic alcoholism and Wernicke's syndrome."

Although J.B. had been seen on numerous occasions by Mental Hygiene staff, as well as by Psychiatry staff, he terminated these contracts as quickly as possible, denying the fact that he was an alcoholic. He was consistently depicted by these professionals as extremely manipulative, friendly and cooperative, with a strong dependence upon denial and externalization defense mechanisms. The diagnosis of organicity remained in question. His company commanders consistently viewed J.B. as average or above intellectually, willing to work and accepting authority, but simultaneously noting that he used alcohol in excess, was nervous and exhibited "peculiar actions." It was in January, 1971 that J.B. first began to acknowledge his problem with alcohol and indicated some degree of initiative in the direction of working through his alcohol-related problem behaviors.

Rehabilitation Period. J.B. sporadically attended a group therapy program for alcoholics and problem drinkers initiated by the Mental Hygiene Service at Fort Gordon, Georgia, during the early part of February, 1971. J.B. avoided individual therapy and A.A. meetings, but did show up periodically for the group sessions which involved three or four patients at that time. He was asked more than once to leave these sessions as a result of his showing up completely intoxicated. His progress was certainly questionable at this point. In retrospect J.B.'s alcoholic behavior showed very little progress through September, 1971. He continued to deny that he was an alcoholic, remained intoxicated a good deal of the time and continued to be vocationally defunct. Realizing that he needed only one more year of active duty to retire, those involved in his case seemed satisfied to let him remain drunk for that final year. His CO had given up, his wife and family had moved back to her parents' home in March, and most importantly J.B. had resigned himself to the ranks of the uncurable.

In spite of this bleak picture, J.B. somehow continued to sporadically attend group therapy. It was during this same interval that J.B. experienced two Antabuse reactions. During the latter part of October and early November the rehabilitation staff began to notice what we felt to be some small, but nonetheless significant changes in J.B.'s drinking behavior. Instead of drinking for two weeks and staying sober two days he began to stay completely sober for two or three weeks at a time. He began to attend A.A. regularly, as well as continuing in group therapy on a regular, sober basis. It was rewarding for those of us who had been involved with J.B. for all those months to note his personality growth and change within the group. He became less manipulative, accepted his alcoholism problem, began to display genuine concern for himself as well as other group members and, to our pleasant astonishment, became quite insightful with regard to his overall behavior. At this juncture J.B. suggested that he was ready to terminate his Antabuse; "I'm ready to make it on my own."

After visiting a few days with the family six weeks later, it was decided by all involved in the case that another try at "making it" as a family would be appropriate. Upon relocating in this vicinity J.B.'s wife became actively involved in group therapy, A.A. and other activities designed to foster an understanding of her role in J.B.'s problem behaviors as well as a better understanding of herself emotionally. Within two months J.B. entered project transition and although supervisory reports were somewhat "shaky" at first, he was eventually able to successfully complete this program. As a matter of fact he became involved as a part of project transition with the Alcoholic Rehabilitation Unit of a major local medical facility and received the highest commendation for this work. His letter of recommendation from the coordinator of this unit was most impressive. Two months ago, J.B. completed twenty years of active service with the U.S. Army. At the time of separation from our rehabilitation center and the U.S. Army, J.B. had seven months of total sobriety. Instead of progressing to the depths of despair and oblivion J.B. was able to regain his self-confidence and personal esteem. Rather than becoming a burden upon society, his family and even himself, today J.B. is a functioning segment of society. Recent correspondence from J.B. indicated that he is currently employed with an alcoholic rehabilitation unit in a large hospital, in addition to pursuing further education.*

This case history is presented as an example of the good rehabilitation potential which many alcoholic patients manifest. Various aspects of the patient's personality, family constellation, drinking behavior and the rehabilitation process are discussed. It becomes increasingly apparent to those of us involved in the treatment of the alcoholic patient that these individuals can be helped to reestablish themselves as contributing and socially functional human beings. Certainly the process of recovery remains a struggle for all involved in the rehabilitation effort. Alcoholism remains a recondite topic for all; it is

---

*This case history was prepared in August, 1972; further correspondence with J.B. indicates his continued sobriety and personal growth. At this time (Second Edition) J.B. continues to be sober, employed with the same alcoholic rehabilitation unit, and he has completed an associate of arts degree.

only through our continued struggles, our innovations and creativity and our growing concern for investigation and research in this area of human behavior that we shall eventually be able to resolve the problem of alcoholism individually as well as collectively.

Chapter 21

CLINICAL IMPRESSIONS OF THE UNSUCCESSFULLY REHABILITATED ALCOHOLIC PATIENT

PROGNOSTIC criteria relative to the successful treatment of various clinical populations have remained less than satisfactory methods of speculation (Meltzoff and Kornreich, 1970). The emergent field of alcoholic rehabilitation seemingly suffers from this same lack of ability to predict which patients will or will not respond to therapeutic intervention. It has frequently been my experience that patients who initially seemed to manifest good rehabilitation potential proved eventually unsuccessful in the termination of their alcoholic pathology (Forrest, 1973). Indeed a number of these particular individuals met the proposed model of the "treatable patient" (Wolberg, 1967). In an even more disconcerting fashion, it has happened that patients manifesting the least satisfactory levels of rehabilitation potential have been highly successful in the resolution of their alcoholism.

It should be pointed out that I am equating successful rehabilitation of the alcoholic patient with the termination of alcohol ingestion; although there are certainly numerous other intrapersonal and interpersonnel dynamics specific to the "successfully" rehabilitated alcoholic patient, it is my feeling that global evaluation of alcoholic rehabilitation facilities very often revolves around the percentage of treated patients who either completely terminate their drinking behavior or significantly decrease their amount of alcohol ingestion following "treatment."

Avoiding the controversial issue of personality reorganization versus symptom reduction, it is my desire to point out some of my personal clinical observations relative to those alcoholic patients who proved unsuccessful in the resolution of their alcoholism. In general, these patients fell within the initially mentioned category; in spite of manifesting a number of characteristics felt to be essential to successful treatment, these particular patients were eventually labeled "therapeutic failures." Broadly speaking, these alcoholic male patients can be broken down into a married and an unmarried or divorced category.

Let me begin by discussing some clinical expressions of the unsuccessfully rehabilitated married male alcoholic. The patient population forming the basis for my impressions is that of an early forties age group within the military environment. These individuals typically have seventeen or more years of active military duty and have attained the rank of E-6 or E-7. Frequently they have been reduced in rank as a result of their alcohol-related behaviors. Perhaps the most impressive single characteristic of these individuals is simply their inability to talk. In spite of normal intelligence or above, and in the absence of psychotic thought disorder or other apparent marked psychopathology, these patients come across as being incapable of the most rudimentary forms of communication. Needless to say, individual counseling and psychotherapy with such patients proves a most difficult enterprise. This type of extremely limited verbal interaction applies to interpersonal behaviors with wives and family, other patients and the treatment staff as well. Fellow patients frequently report they are uncomfortable and at a loss to explain their inability to relate to these few individuals. Group therapy sessions provide an excellent arena in which to observe limited patterns of interaction and communication. Such patients respond to open-ended feeling types of material with a simple yes or no. Confrontation techniques by the therapist, as well as similar approach behaviors on the part of other patients, typically elicit a mere shrug of the shoulders or a similar type of uninvolved response. In my experience these patients can attend group therapy for weeks without active participation unless they are consistently and actively approached by both fellow patients and therapist. The net result of such approach behaviors upon the part of the therapist and other patients is of very little consequence. These stereotyped patterns of interaction remain fixed in spite of job losses, legal difficulties and similar environmentally related stresses which precipitate involvement and feeling behaviors for many alcoholic patients. At times it seems as though the most significant of interpersonal events are totally unrelated to the patient's experiential being.

Another group-related observation is that of seating position. Without exception I have found these patients to be seated on the "fringe" of the group. When encouraged to join the group circle they may outright refuse such a position. When they do attempt to move in this direction they invariably sit in the most removed position; it seems as though their seat is somehow always a foot or two removed from the group.

A temporal orientation toward never drinking again seems to predominate the unsuccessfully rehabilitated alcoholic patient's sober outlook. While other alcoholic patients often struggle with remaining sober today, the unsuccessful patient in my experience continually avows to "never touch the stuff again." This pattern relates to a drinking style which typically involves one or two months of total abstinence followed by a three- or four-week drinking episode which is frequently terminated by hospital admission.

A most significant pattern of interaction for the unsuccessfully rehabilitated alcoholic patient is that of the marital relationship. As has been noted extensively in literature (Fox, 1967; Blum and Blum, 1968; Milt, 1969) marital conflict, divorce and disturbed patterns of familial interaction are genetic to the problem of alcoholism. My experience readily confirms the reality of these patterns of interaction, but indicates two additional considerations specific to the unsuccessfully treated alcoholic patient. Aside from the "talk" or communication problem with the wife and family, these additional two symptoms frequently are among the most observable pathognomonic signs. Foremost is the trend toward prolonged marriage in spite of chronic gross marital discord. The unsuccessful patient, in my experience, has often experienced fifteen to twenty-five years of constant marital discord. In contrast to this pattern, the majority of problem drinkers and other alcoholics I have successfully worked with may have experienced two or three unsuccessful marital relationships. It is my opinion that the ability to terminate these pathological relationships may be a significant indication of growth or change potential. Unsuccessfully treated patients tend to "cling," and in other ways to continue their pathological patterns of marital dependence. It is readily apparent that any disruption of this relationship, in spite of all the emotional pain and pathology, is poorly tolerated by either spouse. Such disruptions create marked anxiety, depression and often basic personality disorganization. I suspect this emotional trauma may be one of the basic keys to the eventual resolution of a select alcoholic's alcohol dependency.

The second additional characteristic I would like to note is that of the intensity of the sadomasochistic flavor of these marriages. This variable has been discussed at some length in the literature and can certainly be related to the initially discussed pattern of prolonged marriages in spite of extreme discord; it is, nonetheless, a pattern of interaction I have observed over and again with patients eventually labeled "therapeutic failures." I'm quite certain that those with any experience in dealing with the alcoholic patient and his family are aware of the constant punitive nature of these family interactions. What I am attempting to get at is perhaps two standard deviations beyond the classic sadomasochistic relationship. With these particular unsuccessful cases, it is as if both spouses were actively attempting to destroy one another. The number of mutual beatings requiring hospitalization or medical treatment, the frequency of peace bonds and similar forms of legal intervention are more direct manifestations of this mutual need to punish one another. A more involved relationship with these couples reveals a constant punitive pattern of interaction. Often the behaviors of both husband and wife are akin to the preadolescent need to "get in the last punch." Perpetual belittling, sarcasm and ridicule have been an ever-present marital dynamic. One often gets the impression that the ultimate one-upmanship in these marriages is eventually determined by who survives. The death of one of the spouses seems to be unconsciously equated with victory. Needless to say, conditioning and learning theory can well be applied to these persistent patterns of extreme sadomasochistic behavior.

A somewhat humorous characteristic of the unsuccessfully rehabilitated patient within our treatment facility has had to do with using the fire escape as a means of entering and leaving the facility. This simple procedure has invariably been representative of an avoidance type of behavior. Patients entering and leaving the halfway house via the fire escape have usually been intoxicated and have, without exception, eventually proved failures in our program. This seemingly insignificant procedure has acquired increased meaning for staff as well as patients. It is of significance that fellow patients who have done well in our program and have remained active in the outpatient group therapy program are quick to identify such behavior as being indicative of resistance to the program.

Another characteristic which might be viewed as somewhat insignificant to the casual observer, but one which has nonetheless proved important in our program has to do with attitude toward psychometric evaluation. Patients who have outrightly refused or demonstrated marked resistance toward testing have fared poorly with our program. Obviously this is another denial mechanism whereby the patient says, "I'm not an alcoholic and I don't want any part of your rehabilitation program."

I have purposely avoided such areas as employability and vocational status as related to successful rehabilitation of the alcoholic patient. Certainly these are areas of major importance. However, it is my opinion that the reality of these factors has been relatively well established in the alcoholic-related literature. The purpose of this brief article was to share with the reader some of the more simplistic clinical observations I have experienced as meaningful. These reflections are for the most part made in retrospect. Hopefully they will provide those involved in the establishment and development of alcoholic rehabilitation treatment facilities with additional data which might prove meaningful. It would appear that an aggregate of prognostic indicators weighted toward a marked negative trend would indicate differential therapeutic management. It is my opinion that we must establish change-oriented treatment facilities adept at reaching those individuals who manifest poor rehabilitation potential. Surely the ability to identify these particular individuals is an essential step in the progress of establishing programs to reach "high risk" patients.

Chapter 22

SELF-DISCLOSURE AND SOBRIETY

PSYCHOTHERAPY theory and research emphasize the importance of patient transparency or self-disclosure within the therapeutic encounter. Clinical experience indicates the process of psychotherapy to be an interpersonal relationship characterized by increasing amounts of self-disclosure upon the part of both therapist and patient. Jourard (1964, 1968) has written extensively about the role of self-disclosure within the therapeutic context. In general, the facades and masks which we attempt to employ interpersonally are viewed by Jourard (1964, 1971) as neurotic. Numerous authors have indicated the importance of honesty, openness and authenticity within dyadic interpersonal encounters as well as collectively (Fromm, 1955; Mowrer, 1964; Bugental, 1965; Jourard and Jaffe, 1970; Bundza and Simonson 1973). One common aspect of all these theoretical postitions seems to focus on maladaptive behavior as a function of the patient's inability to be self-disclosing or transparent.

Research has indicated conflicting results regarding the role of self-disclosure in the successful therapeutic enterprise. Steele (1948) reported that more successful patients increasingly explore their problems more as therapy progresses. Similar findings have been reported by Seeman (1949), Jourard (1959, 1964) and Truax and Carkhuff (1963). Truax and Carkhuff (1967) report that as early as the second interview, level of patient self-disclosure provides a reasonably adequate prediction of final case outcome. Using the self-disclosure questionnaire (SDQ) (Jourard and Lasakow, 1958) as an index of initial patient transparency, Forrest (1970) and Hountras and Forrest (1970) found no relationship between initial transparency level and subsequent therapeutic outcome. These authors report that low scores on the self-disclosure questionnaire were significantly related to psychopathology within a psychiatric outpatient population. Low dislosing patients were significantly more disturbed on the MMPI clinical scales (Hountras and Forrest, 1970) than were high disclosing patients. Other researchers employing somewhat different methodologies and measures of self-disclosure report similar conflicting results (Anchor, Vojtisek and Patterson, 1973).

Quite recently we have begun to focus upon the problem of alcoholism and treatment modalities specific to dealing effectively with this patient population (Blane, 1968; Bennett, Bass, and Carpenter, 1969; Hoy, 1969; Forrest, 1973). Alcoholics Anonymous has historically been responsible for whatever "treatment" the vast majority of alcoholic patients have received (Milt, 1969). In fact, this organization is recognized by many as the most effective treatment modality to date for those individuals suffering from alcoholism and problem drinking (Milt, 1969). Realizing the A.A. model is predicated upon honesty and the admission that one is an alcoholic, it was felt an investigation of the relationship between initial level of self-disclosure and subsequent drinking behavior within an alcoholic outpatient population would be of benefit.

It was hypothesized that those alcoholic outpatients initially evidencing significantly higher levels of self-disclosure, as measured by the self-disclosure questionnaire (SDQ) (Jourard and Lasakow, 1958), would be more successful in the cessation of their alcoholic behavior than low scoring patients.

Method

The original research population consisted of fifty outpatient male alcoholics referred to the Fort Gordon Alcoholic and Drug Rehabilitation Center. From this number two groups were formed; the sixteen patients most successful in the termination of their drinking behavior formed Group One. Group Two was comprised of those sixteen patients least successful in the termination of their drinking behavior. All Ss functioned within the "normal" or above range of measured intelligence and ranged in age from twenty-three to forty-two years. The mean age for Group One was 36.38 (SD = 4.00). The mean age for Group Two was 32.49 (SD = 6.44). At the time of the investigation no subject was diagnosed as psychotic. Virtually all Ss had a history of previous hospitalization due to chronic alcoholism or alcohol-related behaviors. All Ss had a history of at least five years of problem drinking. All Ss were active duty military personnel. The mean number of years of active service for Group One was 15.19 and 12.60 for Group Two. T-values for both the age and number of years of active service variables were clearly nonsignificant (t = .52 for Group One and Group Two age comparision; t = .70 for Group One and Group Two number of years of active service comparison).

Instrument

A forty-item self-disclosure questionnaire (Jourard, 1964) was administered to fifty initially referred alcoholic outpatients seen at the Fort Gordon Alcoholic and Drug Addict Rehabilitation Center. The self-disclosure questionnaire was developed as a method for measuring the amount and content of self-disclosure directed at selected "target persons." Target persons in the present study were mother, father, male friend, female friend and spouse. The instrument inventories such areas of the self as attitudes and opinions, tastes and interests, work, money, personality and body. Reliability and validity data are provided by the author (Jourard, 1964). Total self-disclosure scores were employed in this investigation. Each item was scored as follows:

0—Have told the other person nothing about this item.

1—Have talked in general terms about this item.

2—Have talked in full and complete detail about this item.

—1—Have lied or misrepresented myself to the other person about this item.

Procedure

The self-disclosure questionnaire (Jourard, 1964) was administered to fifty newly diagnosed alcoholic patients referred to the Fort Gordon Alcoholic and Drug Addict Rehabilitation

Center. This particular instrument is administered to all patients during their initial contact with the treatment facility. Referrals are made directly to the center by the patient's company commander or immediate supervisor and are subsequently evaluated by the center treatment staff. Six months after initial contact with the Fort Gordon Alcoholic and Drug Addict Rehabilitation Center the fifty patient case histories were reviewed by the treatment staff. Continued patient contact and supervisor feedback indicated that certain Ss had improved in contrast to other Ss who had continued to remain intoxicated. In fact, a few Ss seemed to have deteriorated. With no knowledge of initial patient SDQ scores, the treatment staff differentiated a "most successful" and "least successful" group of Ss. Group One consisted of sixteen Ss who evidenced marked gain; during the six months interval these Ss suffered two or less "slips." In actuality eleven of these Ss had remained totally abstinent; the remaining five Ss had been intoxicated on one or two occasions of not more than a two-day duration. All Group One Ss had actively entered outpatient group psychotherapy and A.A. Group Two avoided treatment, remained intoxicated and in certain cases actually seemed to have deteriorated. A comparison of initial JSDQ scores for the most and least successful sixteen Ss of the original sample was completed.

Results

The means, standard deviations and t-value for the "most" and "least" successful groups of alcoholic outpatients are presented in Table 22-I. Most and least successful groups were established according to the sole criteria of sobriety.

It may be concluded from the data presented in Table 22-I that those patients (Group One) most successful in the cessation of their drinking behavior were initially more self-disclosing than those patients (Group Two) who were unable to terminate their drinking patterns. Patients in Group One were significantly more self-disclosing than patients in Group Two beyond the .001 level.

TABLE 22-I

INITIAL MEAN, STANDARD DEVIATION AND T-VALUE FOR "MOST"
AND "LEAST" SUCCESSFUL ALCOHOLIC OUTPATIENT
GROUP SDQ SCORES

Most Successful		*Least Successful*		*t-Value*
X	SD	X	SD	7.08*
164.62	75.0	118.31	68.0	

*p. < .001
1 tailed test

Discussion

The results of this investigation indicate that the SDQ
(Jourard and Lasakow, 1958) was related to the ability to terminate drinking patterns among an alcoholic outpatient population. Those alcoholics referred to an alcoholic treatment center
who were initially higher self-disclosers actively entered individual and group psychotherapy, A.A. and other treatment modalities deemed appropriate by center staff. In the process these
patients were able to maintain prolonged sobriety. In marked
contrast, those alcoholics who were initially significantly lower
self-disclosers were unable to become involved in the overall
rehabilitation program and subsequently remained intoxicated.
It was the staff consensus that three of these cases actually
deteriorated during the six-month interval. This finding lends
support to the opinion that patient self-disclosure or transparency is a crucial ingredient within the therapeutic encounter.
Moreover, it is suggested that perhaps a minimal level of self-
disclosure must be present before the patient is able to or ready
to actively enter any rehabilitation program. It should be noted
that this appears to be the case in spite of a good deal of
external pressure to enter treatment, seemingly internal conflict
and anxiety and other such variables which would seem to
facilitate the patient's involvement in some form of rehabilitation program.

It is of significance to note that the low disclosing group in the present investigation manifested a total disclosure score very similar to low disclosing groups within a random sample psychiatric outpatient population (Forrest, 1970; Hountras and Forrest, 1970). Although further investigation of this area is needed, it would seem that the finding that lower levels of self-disclosure within a psychiatric outpatient population was indicative of greater psychopathology, as measured by the MMPI (Forrest, 1970; Hountras and Forrest, 1970), might well be applicable to the present alcoholic outpatient population. Denial and other defense mechanisms specific to alcoholism and the personality of the long-term problem drinker are certainly pathological determinants which impede movement in the direction of seeking help. The low disclosing patients' movement in the direction of avoiding rehabilitation in the present study might be interpreted as being related to greater psychopathology, in contrast to the high disclosing patients' initiating and maintaining involvement with the rehabilitation center, which might be interpreted as being indicative of significantly better initial personality adjustment.

It should be noted that all Ss involved in the present study were active duty military personnel. Variables specific to the particular population may have facilitated the research findings; as such, further investigation of the self-disclosure variable with alcoholic patients of divergent environmental presses would be indicated.

It would also be of interest to assess change in level of self-disclosure as a function of the rehabilitation program. From these findings it would seem that a goal of the rehabilitation program would be that of increasing levels of self-disclosure. Another area of interest would be that of assessing change in levels of self-disclosure among those patients referred to the rehabilitation center, drop out after one or two contacts and subsequently enter treatment three or four months later.

It is the opinion of this author that the success of A.A. and A.A. oriented rehabilitation programs is contingent upon the reinforcement of self-disclosing types of behavior. Honesty, openness and authenticity are very much a part of the A.A. twelve steps. Certainly the present investigation is supportive of the position that self-disclosure or patient transparency is related to the problem of rehabilitating alcohol-dependent individuals. Patients capable of higher levels of self-disclosing behaviors appear to be the most amenable to treatment, and correspondingly seem to respond most favorably to treatment.

Chapter 23

THE EFFECT OF GROUP PSYCHOTHERAPY UPON LEVELS OF ANXIETY, DEPRESSION AND HOSTILITY WITHIN AN ALCOHOLIC POPULATION

ANXIETY, depression and hostility have been variables of primary consideration in both theoretical and research literature specific to alcoholism and problem drinking (Fox, 1967; Morgan, 1967; Blane, 1968; Weingold, Lachin, Bell and Coxe, 1969; Bennett, Bass and Carpenter, 1969). It is generally concluded that individuals experiencing symptomatic levels of these three variables are frequently diagnosed "alcoholic." Indeed, a large segment of any alcoholic population will readily acknowledge drinking as an escape from persistent feelings of anxiety and apprehension, chronic or acute depressive trends and long-term interpersonal difficulties relating to the control and expression of aggression and hostility.

Although psychotherapy as a global concept has received a good deal of scrutiny and criticism (Eysenck, 1960, 1965, 1967), Meltzoff and Kornreich (1970) recently concluded after extensive review that, "Far more often than not, psychotherapy of a wide variety of types and with a broad range of disorders has been demonstrated under controlled conditions to be accompanied by positive changes in adjustment that significantly exceed those that can be accounted for by the passage of time alone."

Group psychotherapy has attained rather widespread use as a treatment modality for alcoholism and problem drinking. Blane (1968) notes that group psychotherapy is particularly fashionable in treating alcoholics. Although group psychotherapy has become a *modus operandi* within many alcoholic

311

rehabilitation centers and other facilities involved in the treatment of the alcoholic patient, the effects of this approach remain controversial. Ends and Page (1957, 1959), investigating the effects of Rogerian Group Psychotherapy with alcoholics, found significantly greater change on self-ideal Q-sort measures for the therapy group than for the control group. Hoff (1968), McGinnis (1963), Rathod, Gregory, Blows and Thomas (1966) and Killings and Wells (1967) report similar positive outcomes as a function of group psychotherapy in the treatment of alcoholism. In contrast to these findings, Hoy (1969), Wolff (1967, 1968) and Hill and Blane (1967) were unable to demonstrate the effectiveness of group therapy in the treatment of the alcoholic.

In view of these conflicting results regarding the efficacy of group psychotherapy in the treatment of alcoholism, it was felt that further investigation of this area was needed. Moreover, the investigation of change in levels of anxiety, depression and hostility as a function of group psychotherapy was felt to be particularly appropriate as these variables have received considerable attention as being highly relevant to the problem of alcoholism.

It was hypothesized that patients receiving group psychotherapy would show significantly lower levels of anxiety, depression and hostility after treatment than those patients receiving no group psychotherapy.

Method

SUBJECTS: A total of thirty-five adult male alcoholics referred to the Fort Gordon Alcoholic Rehabilitation Center were selected: The Experimental Group (Group E), consisting of twenty Ss, received twenty-five hours of group psychotherapy. The Control Group (Group C), consisting of fifteen Ss, received no group psychotherapy. All Ss functioned within the "normal" or above range of measured intelligence, and ranged in age from twenty-five to forty-four years. The mean age for the group receiving psychotherapy (Group E) was 36.35 (SD = 5.26). The mean age for the group receiving no psychotherapy was 33.13 (SD = 5.81). This difference was nonsignificant. At the time of the investigation, no S was diagnosed as psychotic. All Ss had been previously hospitalized for chronic alcoholism and alcohol-related behavior problems. All Ss were determined to have had a history of at least five years of problem drinking. All Ss were active duty military personnel. The mean number of years of active service for Group E was 15.30 and 12.22 for Group C. This difference was found to be statistically nonsignificant.

INSTRUMENT: The Multiple Affect Adjective Check List (MAACL) was designed as a self-administered test to provide valid measures of three clinically relevant negative affects: anxiety, depression and hostility (Zuckerman and Lubin, 1965). The MAACL is brief, usually requiring five to ten minutes to administer. Two forms are available, A "General" form and a "Today" form. The "Today" form was employed in the present study. The Ss respond by checking words which describe how they are currently feeling; 132 words at or below an eighth grade reading level comprise the instrument. Considerable research and clinical data have been amassed demonstrating the acceptability of the reliability and validity of the MAACL. Prior to treatment, both groups functioned within the moderate-severe range of functioning on the MAACL Scales.

PROCEDURE: The Multiple Adjective Affect Check List (MAACL) (Zuckerman and Lubin, 1965) was administered to newly diagnosed alcoholic patients seen at the Fort Gordon Alcoholic and Drug Addict Rehabilitation Center during November and December, 1971. Referrals were made directly to the center by the patients' company commander or immediate supervisor and were subsequently evaluated by the center treatment staff. Only those patients meeting the requirements of (a) normal intelligence or above; (b) expressed desire to enter treatment for problem drinking; and (c) absence of psychotic thought disorder were referred to the outpatient group psychotherapy program. Of those patients referred to the outpatient· group psychotherapy program during this interval of time, twenty patients actively entered the program for a total of twenty-five hours of group psychotherapy, while fifteen patients failed to initiate group psychotherapy. These patients formed the experimental and control groups for the study. Ss were treated on an outpatient basis and remained vocationally functional during the experimental period. None of the Ss were receiving inpatient medical treatment specific to alcoholism during the investigation. Therapy was completed in approximately four months, at which time the experimental group and control group were retested with the MAACL. Control Ss received no group therapy during the four-month interval; follow-up evaluation with the MAACL was conducted via a phone contact with the S and subsequent testing at the center. The therapy time interval for Group E and the no-therapy time interval for Group C were carefully monitored in order to control for the possibility of MAACL change as a function of time.

Group psychotherapy consisted of weekly sessions of one hour and forty-five minutes duration for a period of approximately four months. Two therapists conducted all group sessions. The group leader was a doctoral level counseling psychologist, with three years of experience conducting group therapy. Leader training and therapy orientation could be characterized as a combination of Rogerian and analytic approaches. The co-therapist was a bachelor's degree level social worker with very limited prior experience or training in group work. Dynamically oriented group psychotherapy was directed at: (a) fostering some degree of insight into the underlying dynamics of the patient's drinking behavior; (b) confrontation with the destructiveness of such behaviors; and (c) maintaining a therapeutic atmosphere characterized by the presence of high level facilitative conditions (Truax and Carkhuff, 1967).

Results

In order to evaluate possible differences in levels of anxiety, depression and hostility, the t-test of significance was applied to initial experimental and control group MAACL scores. The means, standard deviations and t-values for experimental and control group MAACL anxiety, depression and hostility scales at the time of initial patient contact with the Fort Gordon Alcoholic and Drug Addict Rehabilitation Center are presented in Table 23-I.

TABLE 23-I

INITIAL MEAN, STANDARD DEVIATION AND T-VALUE FOR EXPERIMENTAL AND CONTROL MAACL ANXIETY, DEPRESSION AND HOSTILITY SCORES

| MAACL Variables | Group | | | | | |
| | Experimental | | Control | | |
	X	SD	X	SD	t-Value
Anxiety..........	10.00	5.10	12.30	2.23	-1.64
Depression.......	17.40	7.45	16.70	4.00	1.25
Hostility.........	7.70	3.90	8.80	2.80	- .84

It may be concluded from the data presented in Table 23-I that the experimental and control groups did not differ significantly with regard to initial levels of anxiety, depression and hostility as measured by the MAACL. Both groups functioned within the moderate-severe range of functioning on the MAACL scales (Zuckerman and Lubin, 1965). These results indicate that at the point of initial contact with the Fort Gordon Alcoholic and Drug Addict Rehabilitation Center all Ss were experiencing similar levels of anxiety, depression and hostility.

A comparison of the experimental group posttherapy anxiety, depression and hostility MAACL scores with the control group posttest anxiety, depression and hostility MAACL scores is presented in Table 23-II.

As can be seen in Table 23-II, Group E demonstrated significantly lower levels of anxiety, depression and hostility as measured by the MAACL than did Group C. In contrast to the control Ss the experimental Ss, at the completion of the investigation, were significantly less anxious, depressed and hostile.

TABLE 23-II

POST-TEST MEAN, STANDARD DEVIATION AND T-VALUES FOR
EXPERIMENTAL AND CONTROL GROUP MAACL ANXIETY,
DEPRESSION AND HOSTILITY SCORES

| MAACL | Group | | | | |
| | Experimental | | Control | | |
Variables	X	SD	X	SD	t-Value
Anxiety...........	7.60	3.60	13.60	2.20	5.45‡
Depression........	13.60	5.38	18.40	4.00	2.66†
Hostility..........	7.30	3.30	9.40	2.50	1.91*

*p. $< .05$
†p. $< .01$
‡p. $< .001$

At the end of treatment the experimental Ss functioned within the mild-moderate range of functioning on the MAACL scales, in contrast to the control Ss, who continued to function within the moderate-severe range of functioning (Zuckerman and Lubin, 1965).

In order to evaluate change within the experimental and control groups on the MAACL variables, Student t-ratio Direct Differences were computed for intragroup pre-post scores. The results of the within group MAACL pre-post comparisons are presented in Table 23-III.

As indicated by Table 23-III, Group E experienced significantly lower levels of anxiety and depression after twenty-five hours of group psychotherapy. Although change in level of hostility was in the direction predicted, it was clearly nonsignificant. In contrast to the improvement indicated for Group E, Group C deteriorated significantly on two of the three MAACL variables. Those Ss receiving no group psychotherapy became significantly more anxious and depressed. Control Ss approached significance on the MAACL hostility measure, indicating movement in the direction of deterioration on this variable as well.

TABLE 23-III

PRE-POST STUDENTS T-RATIO DIRECT DIFFERENCE COMPARISONS
FOR EXPERIMENTAL AND CONTROL WITHIN GROUP MAACL
ANXIETY, DEPRESSION AND HOSTILITY SCORES

MAACL *Variables*	Group	
	Experimental *t-Values*	*Control* *t-Values*
Anxiety..................................	3.26*	-3.40†
Depression.............................	3.07*	-2.16*
Hostility................................	.72	-1.51

*p. < .05
†p. < .01

Discussion

The results of this investigation indicate that group psychotherapy is an effective treatment modality in the rehabilitation of the alcoholic patient. Group psychotherapy significantly reduced levels of anxiety and depression as measured by the MAACL. Hostility, as measured by the MAACL, was not significantly modified by the group psychotherapy program. Alcoholic patients not receiving group psychotherapy, although initially experiencing levels of anxiety, depression and hostility quite similar to the psychotherapy group, showed no behavioral gain on the MAACL scales as a result of the passage of time. It should be noted that patients not receiving group psychotherapy actually became increasingly anxious, depressed and hostile. Although significant deterioration within the control group was limited to the MAACL anxiety and depression scales, this trend was clearly operational with regard to the hostility scale as well. This finding is in accord with Fox (1967) who notes that alcoholic behavior tends to become increasingly maladaptive.

It is interesting to speculate whether there is an age factor relative to this deteriorating effect with no treatment. In contrast to the Eysenck (1965) position that spontaneous remission is a function of time in the vast majority of neurotic disorders, the disease concept, as applied to alcoholism, would tend to predict a progressive psychological as well as physiological deterioration for the untreated alcoholic population. It would seem logical to assume that while the younger problem drinker or alcoholic might not be subject to the immediate psychological deteriorative effects of no treatment, the older, deteriorated alcoholic would progressively feel the effects of his continued intoxication to a more significant extent. From this perspective, deterioration within an older alcoholic population would be more easily assessed. This would certainly be a worthwhile area of future investigation.

A major point of concern with the present study has to do with the composition of the control group. Although both the control group and the experimental group appear to be homogeneous with regard to age, occupation, sex and initial levels of anxiety, depression and hostility, as measured by the MAACL, it is apparent that the experimental group manifested a significantly greater desire to terminate drinking than did the control group. Although all Ss expressed a desire to terminate their alcoholic behavior and were subsequently referred to the group psychotherapy program, only the experimental Ss actually followed up on the initial referral. Lack of a control group, as well as the appropriateness of control Ss has certainly been an area of major weakness relative to psychotherapy outcome studies.

Another point of importance related to the Ss involved in this study is the fact that all were active duty military personnel. This research project is but one facet of the current military awareness and intervention into social problems surrounding alcohol and drug abuse. Environmental variables specific to the Ss employed in the present study may or may not have helped facilitate the therapeutic outcome. A comparative study of the effects of group psychotherapy with alcoholics from various subcultures would be beneficial.

It is well to note at this point that approximately 65 percent of the experimental Ss remained totally abstinent during the treatment period. In contrast, not a single control *S* remained totally abstinent for the four-month interval (based upon self-report and supervisor feedback). It is also well to note that approximately 50 percent of both the experimental and control *S*s were initially prescribed Antabuse. At the end of the study 35 percent of the experimental group as opposed to none of the control group *S*s remained on Antabuse maintenance. The significantly greater percentage of experimental *S*s remaining totaly abstinent, in addition to the significantly greater percentage of experimental *S*s continuing Antabuse maintenance for the duration of the investigation, is interpreted as further evidence of the benefit of the group psychotherapy program.

A variable which may have helped facilitate gain within the experimental group was involvement with Alcoholics Anonymous. Although all *S*s were encouraged to participate in A.A., only four members of the control group attended a single A.A. meeting in contrast to thirteen experimental *S*s who attended A.A. weekly.

The major implications of this study are as follows: (1) group psychotherapy, on an outpatient basis, is effective both as a modifier of psychological assessment data and concrete behavioral data specific to an alcoholic population; and (2) alcoholic patients not receiving treatment of a psychological nature demonstrate psychological deterioration on assessment variables, as well as continuing to progress with their behavioral patterns of alcoholic consumption. Continued research is encouraged by the data. It would be worthwhile to evaluate the effects of a similar program of group psychotherapy conducted with control *S*s similar to those employed in the present study who were mandatorily placed in outpatient treatment. Perhaps the control *S*s employed in this study simply "weren't ready" to give up their drinking behaviors, or perhaps all that was needed was a bit more "nudging" in the direction of becoming involved in the therapy program. Assessment of the effects of group psychotherapy with a younger alcoholic population is indicated. It would be of interest to evaluate the relevance of the hostility variable more closely; the turning inward of hostility and aggression, as is so often seen in the self-destructive behavior of the chronic alcoholic, may also be subject to modification with more extended treatment. It should also be noted that the interaction effect of group psychotherapy, A.A. and Antabuse is a significant factor limiting the generalizability of the present findings.

Chapter 24

ALCOHOLIC REHABILITATION: FOR BETTER OR FOR WORSE?

AN area of major weakness in psychotherapy research has been that of adequate follow-up (Meltzoff and Kornreich, 1970). Indeed, this has been a point of criticism directed at the multiplicity of professional personnel and services involved in programs directed at the modification of human behavior. The recent emphasis upon alcoholism and alcoholic rehabilitation renders this area subject to similar criticism. Alcoholic rehabilitation programs are increasingly being confronted with the challenge of evaluating the effectiveness of their "treatment" approaches. Avoiding the controversial issue of treating symptoms as opposed to personality reconstruction, the particular pathology of alcoholism is in certain respects especially accessible to follow-up and outcome types of research. In dealing with many of the psychoneurotic and schizophrenic disorders, one is often confronted with an unending list of target symptoms or avenues of therapeutic approach. Although this is often the case with the alcoholic patient, we are nonetheless typically presented with the basic goal of extinguishing the patient's alcoholic behavior. While marital and family problems, depressive trends, anxiety features and other such clinical manifestations may be central to the patient's alcoholic pathology, it is my experience that we attempt to deal with these secondarily. Granted, comprehensive alcoholic rehabilitation centers do provide extensive individual and group psychotherapy, marital therapy, conjoint therapy and other measures appropriate to the modification of more than the specific target symptom of alcohol ingestion, but it is my feeling that the effectiveness of these programs is often evaluated solely in terms of the percentage of patients terminating their drinking behavior. This applies to the treatment staff, as well

321

as individual family members, the patient himself, affiliated professionals and even the community at large. When a particular individual's alcoholic pathology has progressed to the point of facilitating his active engagement with an alcoholic rehabilitation program it would appear that the termination of alcohol consumption has become one of the major issues at that point in his life space. Realizing this to mean, in effect, that we tend to evaluate ourselves as professionals in this area as well as being evaluated by the community at large in terms of the percentage of patients who successfully terminate their drinking behavior at the completion of our "treatment," we do have some concrete data relative to follow-up and outcome. While some might question the meaningfulness of these data, it is my impression that the successful resolution of the single target symptom — alcohol ingestion — might be one of the most significant events in the entire life space of the majority of patients treated within the alcoholic rehabilitation center milieu. It is my experience that while termination of drinking in no way solves or resolves many of the patients' basic conflicts, it does foster the ability to work on marital discord, it does help keep the patient out of jail, it does mean that he can become vocationally functional, and in numerous other pragmatic ways the termination of drinking behavior allows the patient the opportunity to enter the ranks of the simply more human.

It is with this underlying philosophy that the present follow-up investigation was conducted.

Method

In an earlier investigation of the effects of group psychotherapy upon levels of anxiety, depression and hostility within an alcoholic outpatient population (Forrest, 1973) it was found that treated alcoholics became significantly less depressed and anxious. In marked contrast, given a matched time interval of no treatment, a similar alcoholic outpatient population was found to deteriorate significantly on the anxiety, depression and hostility measures (Forrest, 1973). In order to evaluate the prolonged effectiveness of the treatment procedure employed in this particular investigation, a nine-month follow-up study was completed. It is well to note that Forrest (1973) reports behavioral data (continued intoxication versus termination of drinking behavior) were in accord with psychometric gain as evidenced by the experimental group and psychometric deterioration as evidenced by the control group in this earlier investigation.

Staff evaluation of the experimental and control group alcoholic Ss was conducted nine months after the termination of the original study. Based upon the sole criterion of alcohol consumption, each individual case was rated as (1) terminated drinking behaviors completely, (2) improved — significant decrease in drinking behavior, (3) no change — continuation of pattern of drinking behavior prior to investigation, and (4) deterioration — drinking behavior becoming more pathological based upon job loss, medical intervention as a result of alcohol consumption and legal difficulty as a result of drinking.

Results

The "treated" subjects, or the experimental subjects which received twenty-five hours of group psychotherapy, falling in each of the four follow-up categories are presented in Table 24-I.

TABLE 24-I

GROUP RECEIVING REHABILITATION
(TWENTY-FIVE HOURS OF GROUP PSYCHOTHERAPY)

| Totally Abstinent | 9-Month Follow-up Category | | |
	Improved	No Change	Deteriorated
9	6	3	2

N = 20.

As can be seen from the data presented in Table 24-I, nine, or 45 percent of the patient group receiving group psychotherapy, continued to remain totally abstinent nine months after the completion of the initial investigation. Seventy-five percent of the "treated" group continued to evidence behavioral gain at the end of the nine month follow-up interval. Five patients, or 25 percent of the groups receiving group psychotherapy either evidenced "no change" or seemed to have deteriorated psychologically.

The control subjects, or those patients receiving no group therapy falling in each of the four follow-up categories are presented in Table 24-II.

TABLE 24-II

GROUP RECEIVING NO REHABILITATION

Totally Abstinent	9-Month Follow-up Category		
	Improved	*No Change*	*Deteriorated*
0	1	8	2

N = 11.

It is readily apparent from Table 24-II that less than 10 percent of the control group evidenced behavioral gain. None of the control subjects remained totally abstinent. Eight patients, or approximately 75 percent of the control group subjects, fell within the "no change" category. Nearly 20 percent of the control population was rated as having deteriorated. It should be noted that adequate follow-up data were not available on four of the original control subjects. Although this is a typical problem area in follow-up research, the extent of subject shrinkage in the present investigation (27% of the original control sample) is felt to be a significant hinderance to the overall evaluation of behavioral data specific to this untreated alcoholic outpatient population.

Discussion

It is apparent from this data that the "treated" alcoholic outpatients involved in the present follow-up study did tend to maintain the behavioral gain evidenced at the completion of some twenty-five hours of group psychotherapy. Seventy-five percent of the outpatients receiving group therapy remained either totally abstinent for the nine month follow-up interval or were rated as significantly improved. In contrast to these findings the control group, or group receiving no group psychotherapy, was rated as basically unchanged; approximately 75 percent of this population was rated within the "no change" category.

Certainly a weakness of the present follow-up investigation was that of subject shrinkage within the control group. As these patients had never really established a relationship with the Fort Gordon Alcoholic and Drug Addict Rehabilitation Center, it was rather difficult to establish the reality of their drinking behavior during the nine month follow-up period. An exception was that of the one control patient rated as "improved." This patient had actively entered the rehabilitation program on his own accord some four months after the completion of the initial study. Presently this individual has approximately five months of total sobriety and is currently one of the most active individuals in the overall rehabilitation program. It should also be noted that data provided on four of the experimental patients were provided via phone conversation with the patient's job supervisor or company commander. As these particular patients had been shipped to other bases this was the only practical means of evaluation. This was felt to be a significant weakness by the staff involved in the present investigation as alcoholism is frequently "hidden" or covered up by those closest to the alcoholic, let alone supervisors and similar personnel involved in supervisory positions.

It was felt to be particularly significant to note "what happened" to the majority of the treated patients. As these patients experienced extensive contact with the rehabilitation center program and staff it was rather easy to evaluate specific drinking behaviors, as well as globally having an awareness of other significant aspects of the patient's behavior during the nine-month follow-up interval. Such was the case with sixteen of the patients receiving group psychotherapy. Of this number, ten continued to be actively involved in some form of program directed at the modification of alcoholic behavior. Four individuals had secured positions as staff within either alcoholic rehabilitation centers or similar facilities providing services for the alcoholic patient. With the exception of one patient who is currently being treated within a halfway house setting, these patients comprised the "totally abstinent" group in the follow-up study. Those patients rated as evidencing "no change" or "deteriorated" had totally disengaged themselves from the rehabilitation program. The one exception to this is currently involved in outpatient group therapy and marital therapy and has been sober three weeks.

Follow-up data pertaining to the untreated group of alcoholic outpatients simply indicated that these individuals, as a group, tended to continue their patterns of alcohol consumption. Staff contact with the supervisors and company commanders of these patients indicated continued poor job performance, continued absenteeism as a result of drinking and continued legal and marital problems central to the patient's alcohol ingestion. It would seem apparent from these data that in the absence of some form of intervention, one could rather accurately predict that these individuals will continue to remain intoxicated a good deal of the time and simultaneously experience the conflicts which have centered around their problem drinking for various periods of time. The passage of time alone did not precipitate positive behavioral gain in the present investigation.

It should again be emphasized that the patients involved in the present investigation were active duty military personnel. The results of this follow-up study may well be related in part to environmental or interpersonal variables specific to this particular population.

Although the sample employed in the present investigation was small and difficulties specific to accurate evaluation of follow-up status were encountered, the results are encouraging. Certainly, continued follow-up research efforts are indicated in the area of alcoholic rehabilitation. As is the case with other areas of "rehabilitation," we are in need of continued outcome and follow-up research. It is only by this method that we are able to grow and modify our own behaviors and programs so that we might provide more effective treatment modalities.

Five-year Follow-up Data

The data for this study were originally collected in October, November and December of 1972. Nine months after the completion of the study, it was quite apparent that the subjects who completed twenty-five hours of group psychotherapy were continuing to maintain treatment gain. As a group, the control subjects continued to drink pathologically.

After leaving the Fort Gordon Alcoholic Rehabilitation Center in November of 1973, I have maintained ongoing contact with eleven of the individuals who participated in the original group psychotherapy project. The ongoing contacts have been in the form of face-to-face interviews with the patients and their families. All of the eleven original patients have been seen annually, and in fact, three patients have been seen three or more times each year since 1972. Based upon five years of ongoing clinical contact with eleven of the original experimental subjects in the 1972 Fort Gordon Group Psychotherapy Research Project, I have constructed Table 24-III.

As shown in Table 24-III, at the time of this five-year follow-up study, five patients continued to be totally abstinent and four remained improved. In other words, over 85 percent of the experimental sample continued to manifest treatment gain at the five-year follow-up interval. In fact, almost half of the individuals in this sample had remained totally abstinent; the one subject in the "no change" category was in this same category at the time of the original investigation. The subject in the "deteriorated" category was previously in the "improved"

TABLE 24-III

FIVE-YEAR FOLLOW-UP FOR GROUP RECEIVING REHABILITATION
(TWENTY-FIVE HOURS OF GROUP PSYCHOTHERAPY)

Totally Abstinent	Improved	No Change	Deteriorated
5	4	1	1

N = 11

category. One of the subjects in the "totally abstinent" category died in April, 1977, from cancer. This man, according to his wife and family, had maintained total sobriety since the terminating of his group psychotherapy experience and through some eight months of being aware of his impending death.

A table for the five-year follow-up data relative to the original control group utilized in the investigation is not included. Only three of the original subjects in the control group have been followed during the five-year follow-up interval. It is significant that one of these subjects has been totally abstinent for nearly four years and one other for a period of two and one-half years. The third subject was killed in an automobile accident while intoxicated. Both of the abstinent control subjects attend Alcoholics Anonymous no less than twice a week and have done so for the duration of their sobriety.

The experimental subjects who fall within the "improved" category have continued to drink to the point of intoxication from time to time. Three of these subjects were, prior to treatment, chronically alcoholic to the extent of consuming roughly a fifth of vodka per day. All had a history of numerous hospitalizations due to alcoholism. The drinking style of three of the improved subjects involves four to eight months of total abstinence followed by a week to a month of chronic intoxication. Clearly, these subjects could benefit from further psychotherapeutic treatment. The fourth subject in this category drinks roughly two to eight drinks on three or four occasions per week. Prior to treatment, he was also roughly a "fifth a day" man, with a history of numerous hospitalizations specific to alcoholism. Every subject in the "improved" category has been vocationally and interpersonally functional since the completion of the original investigation.

With the exception of one subject, all of the "totally abstinent" experimental subjects have actively involved themselves with Alcoholics Anonymous. These subjects were involved with A.A. as a part of the Fort Gordon Rehabilitation Program at the time of the original study, and with the subsequent collapse of the group therapy phase of that program, they seem to have been "pushed" in the direction of A.A. involvement in order to maintain sobriety and other positive behavioral changes. One of the totally abstinent subjects appears to have "made it on his own." This individual does not attend Alcoholics Anonymous, he has not seen a therapist or been involved in group therapy since his termination with the Fort Gordon group, he has not joined the church, and he does not take Antabuse. He did get divorced some eight months after completing group therapy. I should note that this man has operated a tavern and night club for over three years. It would seem difficult for an alcoholic to remain sober and functional within such an environment, yet I am sure there are a number of psychodynamic variables operational in such an environment which could at least theoretically operate to reinforce abstinence. Three of the subjects involved in the study continue to be employed as counselors or staff in different alcoholic rehabilitation programs.

The sample in this five-year follow-up is very small. There is almost no data available on the control subjects employed in the original investigation. However, in view of the generally positive gain maintained by the experimental subjects over this extended period of time, I think counselors and clinicians working with alcoholic patients can better appreciate their efforts. It has been rewarding to see the two control subjects establish sobriety, especially in view of the fact that these alcoholic individuals had "refused" or rejected treatment some five years ago. In most military rehabilitation programs, with few exceptions, counselors simply never know what happens to their patients. I suspect that this datum may be telling us that many of our alcoholic patients do better than we suspect after treatment, and furthermore, those who do succeed in our rehabilitation programs have an excellent probability for actualizing continued growth potential. It is my continued clinical observation that, in the case of the chronic alcoholic, prolonged total abstinence is the most potent prognostic variable relating to the ongoing well-being and growth of the addicted person.

BIBLIOGRAPHY

Alcohol and Health, U.S. Department of Health, Education and Welfare. December, 1971.

Alcoholics Anonymous. New York, Alcoholics Anonymous World Services, Inc., 1939.

Alcoholism: New victims, new treatments. *Time*, April 22, 1974, pp. 75-81.

Anant, S. S.: A note on the treatment of alcoholics by a verbal aversion technique. *The Canadian Psychologist, 8a(1)*:19-22, 1967.

———. Treatment of alcoholics and drug addicts by verbal aversion techniques. *The International Journal of the Addictions, 33*:381-388, 1968.

Anchor, K. N., Vojtisek, J. E., and Patterson, R. L.: Trait anxiety, initial structuring and self-disclosure in groups of schizophrenic patients. *Psychotherapy: Theory, Research and Practice, 10(2)*:155-158, 1973.

Arbuckle, D. A.: The practice of the theories of counseling. *Counselor Education and Supervision, 13(3)*:214-222, 1974.

Astin, A. W.. A factor study of the MMPI Psychopathic Deviate Scale. *Journal of Consulting Psychology, 23*:550-554, 1959.

Bales, R. F.: Cultural differences in rates of alcoholism. *Quart J Stud Alc, 6*:480-499, 1946.

Bandura, A.: *Principles of Behavior Modification.* New York, Holt, Rinehart and Winston, 1969.

Bandura, A., and Walters, R. H.: *Social Learning and Personality Development.* New York, Holt, Rinehart and Winston, 1963.

Bateson, G., Jackson, D. D., Haley, J., and Weakland, J.: Toward a theory of schizophrenia. *Behavioral Science, 1*:251-264, 1956.

Beaubrum, M. H.: Treatment of alcoholism in Trinidad and Tobago. *Brit J Psychiat, 113*:643-658, 1967.

Bennett, R. M., Bass, A. H., and Carpenter, J. A.: Alcohol and human physical aggression. *Quart J Stud Alc, 30*:870-876, 1969.

Berne, Eric: *Games People Play.* New York, Grove, 1964.

Blake, B. G.: The application of behavior therapy to the treatment of alcoholism. *Behavior Research and Therapy, 5*:89-94, 1967.

Blane, H. T.: *The Personality of the Alcoholic.* New York, Harper and Row, 1968.

Bleuler, M.: Familial and personal background of alcoholics. In Diethelm, O.: *Etiology of Chronic Alcoholism.* Springfield, Thomas, 1955.

Blum, E., and Blum, R.: *Alcoholism: Modern Psychological Approaches to*

Treatment. San Francisco, Jossey-Bass, 1969.

Bugenthal, J. F. T.: *The Search for Authenticity.* New York, Holt, Rinehart and Winston, 1965.

Bundza, K. H., and Simonson, W. R.: Therapist self-disclosure: Its effect on impressions of therapist and willingness to disclose. *Psychotherapy: Theory, Research and Practice, 10(3)*:215-217, 1973.

Burch, G. E., and Giles, T. D.: Editorial: alcoholic cardiomyopathy. Concepts of the disease and its treatment. *Am J Med, 40*:141-145, 1971.

Burch, G. E., and DePasquale, N. P.: Alcoholic cardiomyopathy. *Am J Cardiol, 23*:723-731, 1969.

Cahalan, D., Cisin, I. H., and Crossley, H. M.: *American Drinking Practices: A National Study of Drinking Behavior and Attitudes.* Monograph No. 6. New Brunswick, Rutgers Center of Alcohol Studies, 1969.

Cahill, C. A.: Safety of disulfiram. *New Engl J Med, 287*:935-936, 1972.

Caster, D. U.: *Tailoring treatment modalities to brain function in sobering alcoholics.* Lecture presented at Psychotherapy Associates Fourth Annual Winter Treatment and Rehabilitation of the Alcoholic Workshop, Colorado Springs, Colorado, February 2, 1978.

Catanzaro, R. J.: *Alcoholism: The Total Treatment Approach.* Springfield, Thomas, 1968.

Cautela, J. R.: The treatment of alcoholism by covert sensitization. *Psychotherapy: Theory, Research and Practice, 7(2)*:86-90, 1970.

Cheek, F. and Mendelson, M.: Developing behavior modification programs with emphasis on self-control. *Hospital and Community Psychiatry, 24*:410-415, 1973.

Clinebell, H. J., Jr.: *Understanding and Counseling the Alcoholic.* Nashville, Abingdon, 1956.

Coleman, J.: *Abnormal Psychology and Modern Life.* Glenview, Scott, Foresman and Co., 1976.

Conger, J. J.: The effects of alcohol on conflict behavior in the albino rat. *Quart J Stud Alc, 12*:1-29, 1951.

Crowley, T. J., Chesluk, D., Dilts, S., and Hart, R.: Drug and alcohol abuse among psychiatric admissions. *Arch Gen Psychiat, 30(1)*:13-20, 1974.

Curlee, J.: Alcoholic blackouts; some conflicting evidence. *Quart J Stud Alc, 34*:409-413, 1973.

Cutter, H. S. G., Key, J. C., Rothstein, E., and Jones, W. C.: Alcohol, power and inhibition. *Quart J Stud Alc, 34*:381-389, 1973.

Cutter, H. S. G., Schwaab, E. L. Jr., and Nathan, P. E.: Effects of alcohol on its utility for alcoholics and nonalcoholics. *Quart J Stud Alc, 31*:369-378, 1970.

Dahlstrom, W. G., and Welsh, G. S.: *An MMPI Handbook.* Minneapolis, U of Minn Pr, 1960.

Davison, R. S.: Moderation of alcoholic behavior. *Newsletter for Research in Psychology, 14(1)*:30-34, 1972. (Published by Veterans Administration Center, Bay Pines, Florida.)

Delint, J.: The status of alcoholism as a disease: A brief comment. *Br J Addict, 66*:108-109, 1971.

Dollard, J., and Miller, N. E.: *Personality and Psychotherapy.* New York, McGraw-Hill, 1950.

Dreiling, D. A., Richman, A., and Franklin, N. F.: The role of alcohol in the etiology of pancreatitis: A study of the effect of intravenous ethyl alcohol on the external excretion of the pancreas. *Gastroenterology, 20*:636-646, 1952.

Edwards, G.: The status of alcoholism as a disease. In Phillipson, K. V. (Ed.): *Modern Trends in Drug Dependence and Alcoholism.* New York, Appleton-Century-Crofts, 1970, pp. 140-163.

Elkins, R. L.: Aversion therapy for alcoholism: Chemical, electrical or verbal-imagery? *International Journal of the Addictions, 8*:6, 1973.

Ellis, A., and Harper, R.: *A Guide to Rational Living.* Englewood Cliffs, Prentice-Hall, Inc., 1961.

Ends, E. J., and Page, C. W.: A study of three types of group psychotherapy with hospitalized male inebriates. *Quart J Stud Alc, 18*:263-277, 1957.

―――. Group psychotherapy and concomitant psychological change. *Psych Mono, 73*:480, 1959.

Erickson, G. D., and Hogan, T. P.: *Family Therapy: An Introduction to Theory and Technique.* New York, Aronson, Jason, Inc., 1976.

Evans, J. H.: *A Scientific Examination of the "Disease Concept" of Alcohol Dependency.* Paper presented at the Annual Psychotherapy Workshop, Colorado Springs, Colorado, 1977.

Expert Committee on Mental Health, Alcoholism Subcommittee, Second Report, *WHO Tech Rep Series, No. 48,* August, 1952.

Eysenck, H. J. (Ed.): *Behavior Therapy and the Neuroses.* New York, Pergamon, 1960.

―――. The effects of psychotherapy. *Int J Psychiat, 1*:97-178, 1965.

―――. New ways in psychotherapy. *Psychology Today, 1*:39-47, 1967.

Eysenck, H. J., and Rackmann, S.: *The Causes and Cures of Neurosis.* London, Routledge and Kegan Paul, 1965.

Fahlgren, H., Hed, R., and Lundmark, C.: Myonecrosis and myoglobinuria in alcohol and barbiturate intoxication. *Acta Med Scand, 158*:405-412, 1957.

Fiedler, F. E.: The concept of an ideal therapeutic relationship *Journal of Consulting Psychology, 14*:239-245, 1950.

―――. Factor analysis of psychoanalytic, nondirective and Adlerian therapeutic relationships. *Journal of Consulting Psychology, 15*:32-38, 1951.

Forrest, G. G.: *Alcoholism As An Interpersonal Process.* Text in press, 1978.

―――. *A Model For Training Addiction Counselors.* Paper presented at the Rocky Mountain Counselor Education and Supervision Convention, Denver, Colorado, Oct. 3, 1976.

Forrest, G. G.: *Alcoholism and Family Psychodynamics II.* Lecture presented at Psychotherapy Associates Fourth Annual Winter Treatment and Rehabilitation of the Alcoholic Workshop, Colorado Springs, Colorado, February 1, 1978.

————. Personality characteristics of the military drug abuser entering a halfway house treatment facility. Fort Gordon, Georgia, Alcohol and Drug Rehabilitation Center, 1973.

————. Resolution of the Alcoholic Power Fantasy. Conversation Hour, Division of Psychotherapy, American Psychological Association Convention, New Orleans, September 2, 1974.

————. *The Diagnosis and Treatment of Alcoholism*, 1st ed. Springfield, Thomas, 1975.

————. The effect of group psychotherapy upon levels of anxiety, depression and hostility within an alcoholic population. Fort Gordon, Georgia, Alcohol and Drug Rehabilitation Center, 1973.

Forrest, G. G.: *Group psychotherapy techniques in the treatment of alcoholism.* Lecture presented at Psychotherapy Associates First Annual Southeastern Treatment and Rehabilitation of the Alcoholic Workshop, Savannah, Georgia, October 4, 1977.

————. *Transparency as a Prognostic Variable in Psychotherapy.* Unpublished doctoral dissertation, University of North Dakota, 1970.

Fox, R.: *Alcoholism Behavioral Research; Therapeutic Approaches.* New York, Springer, 1967.

Franks, C.: Behavior modification and the treatment of the alcoholic. In Fox, Ruth (Ed.): *Alcoholism, Behavioral Research; Therapeutic Approaches.* New York, Springer, 1967.

Franks, C. M.: Conditioning and conditioned aversion therapies in the treatment of the alcoholic. *International Journal of the Addictions,* *1*:61-98, 1966.

Freud, S.: Analysis terminable and interminable. In *Collected Papers,* Vol V. London, Hogarth, 1952, pp. 313-357.

————. *New Introductory Lectures on Psychoanalysis.* New York, W. W. Norton and Co., 1933.

————. The future prospects of psychoanalytic therapy. In *Collected Papers,* Vol. II. London, Hogarth, 1953, pp. 285-296.

Fried, R.: Essentials of electroshock and electroshock devices. *Newsletter, Assoc Adv Behav Ther,* *2*:3-4, 1967.

Fromm, E.: *The Sane Society.* New York, Holt, Rinehart and Winston, 1955.

Gilberstadt, H., and Duker, J.: *A Handbook for Clinical and Actuarial MMPI Interpretation.* Philadelphia, Saunders, 1965.

Gilbert, J. G., and Lombardi, D. N.: Personality characteristics of young male narcotic addicts. *Journal of Consulting Psychology,* *31*:536-538, 1967.

Glasser, W.: *Reality Therapy: A New Approach to Psychiatry.* New York, Harper and Row, 1965.

Goodwin, D. W., Hill, S. Y., Powell, B., and Viamontes, J.: Effect of alcohol on short-term memory in alcoholics. *Brit J Psychiat,* *122*:93-94, 1973.

Goslinga, J. J.: Biofeedback for chemical-problem patients: a developmental process at the V.A. Hospital in Topeka. *Journal of Biofeedback, 2(4):*17-27, 1975.

Green, E. F.: *Autogenic-Feedback Training for Anxiety Tension Reduction.* Annual meeting of the National Council on Alcoholism, Washington, D.C., April, 1973.

Green, E. F., Green, A. W., and Walters, E. D.: Biofeedback training for anxiety tension reduction in the person with alcoholism. *Annals of Academy of New York Sciences.* 233, 1974.

Gurman, A. S., and Rice, D. G.: *Couples In Conflict.* New York, Aronson, Jason, Inc., 1975.

Haggard, H. W.: Critique of the allergic nature of alcohol addiction. *Quart J Stud Alc, 4:*233-241, 1944.

Haley, J.: Marriage therapy. *Arch Gen Psychiatry, 8:*213-224, 1963.

Harris, T.: *I'm OK--You're OK: A Practical Guide to Transactional Analysis.* New York, Harper and Row, 1969.

Hilgard, E., and Bower, G.: *Theories of Learning.* New York, Meredith Co., 1966.

Hill, H. E., Haertzen, C. A., and Davis, H.: An MMPI factor analytic study of alcoholics, narcotic addicts and criminals. *Quart J Stud Alc, 23:*411-431, 1962.

Hill, M., and Blane, H.: Evaluation of psychotherapy with alcoholics: A critical review. *Quart J Stud Alc, 23:*160-194, 1967.

Hindman, M.: Rational emotive therapy in alcoholism treatment. *Alcohol Health and Research World,* 14-16, Spring, 1976.

Hoff, E. L.: Group therapy with alcoholics. *Psychiatric Residency Report, 24:*61-70, 1968.

Horsey, W. J., and Akert, K.: The influence of ethyl alcohol on the spontaneous electrical activity of the cerebral cortex and subcertical structure of the cat. *Quart J Stud Alc, 14:*363-377, 1953.

Hountras, P. T., and Forrest, G. G.: Personality characteristics and self-disclosure in a psychiatric outpatient population. *College of Education Record,* University of North Dakota, *55:*206-213, 1970.

Hoy, R. M.: The personality of inpatient alcoholics in relation to group psychotherapy, as measured by the 16-PF. *Quart J Stud in Alc, 30:*401-407, 1969.

Irgens, E. M.: Most parents' attitudes become modified in order to bring about adjustment in problem children. *Smith College Student Social Work, I:*17-45, 1936.

Jellinek, M. E.: *Phases of Alcohol Addiction, Society, Culture and Drinking Patterns.* Pittman and Snyder, 1962, pp. 356-368.

———. Heredity and alcohol, science and society. *Quart J Stud Alc,* 104-113, 1945.

Jellinck, N. V.: *The Disease Concept of Alcoholism.* New Haven, Hill House Press, 1960.

Jourard, S. M., and Jaffe, P.: Comments on Black and Goodstein's comments on the paper, "Influence of an interviewer's disclosure on the self-disclosing behavior of interviewers." *J of Cons Psych, 18*:598-600, 1971.

Jourard, S. M.: *Disclosing Man to Himself.* Princeton, Van Nostrand, 1968.

———. *Self-Disclosure: An Experimental Analysis of the Transparent Self.* New York, Wiley, 1971.

———. Self-disclosure and other cathexis. *J of Abnormal and Social Psych, 59*:428-431, 1959.

Jourard, S. M., and Lasakow, P.: Some factors in self-disclosure. *J of Abnormal and Social Psych, 56*:91-98, 1958.

Jourard, S. M.: *The Transparent Self.* Princeton, Van Nostrand, 1964.

Kantorovich, N. V.: An attempt of curing alcoholism by association reflex conditioning. Cited by Razran, G. H. S.: Conditioned withdrawal responses with shock as the conditioning stimulus in adult human subjects. *Psychological Bulletin, 31*:111-143, 1934.

Keller, M.: The oddities of alcoholics. *Quart J Stud Alc, 33*:1147-1148, 1972.

Killins, C. G., and Wells, C. L.: Group therapy of alcoholics. *Current Psychiatric Therapy, 7*:174-178, 1967.

Kissin, B., and Begleiter, H. (Eds.): *The Biology of Alcoholism.* Vol 2: *Neurophysiology and Behavior.* New York, Plenum Pr., 1972.

Knanert, A. P.: *The Alcoholic Personality: Myth or Reality?* Lecture presented at Psychotherapy Associates Fourth Annual Winter Treatment and Rehabilitation of the Alcoholic Workshop, Colorado Springs, Colorado, January 30, 1978.

Knanert, A. P.: *Alcoholism and Brain Damage.* Lecture presented at Psychotherapy Associates Third Annual Winter Treatment and Rehabilitation of the Alcoholic Workshop, Colorado Springs, Colorado, January 31, 1977.

Knox, W. J.: Attitudes of psychiatrists and psychologists toward alcoholism. *Amer J Psychiat, 127*:1675-1679, 1971.

Kramer, K., Kuller, L., and Fisher, R.: The increasing mortality attributed to cirrhosis and fatty liver in Baltimore (1957-1966). *Ann Int Med, 69*:273-282, 1968.

Kurtz, P. S.: Treating chemical dependency through biofeedback. *Hospital Progress, 55(3)*:68-70, 1974.

Lazarus, H. A.: Towards the understanding and effective treatment of alcoholism. *South African Medical Journal, 39*:736-741, 1965.

Leslie, G. R.: Conjoint therapy in marriage counseling. *Journal of Marriage and the Family, 26*:65-71, 1964.

Lemere, F., and Voegtlin, W. L.: An evaluation of the aversion treatment of alcoholism. *Quart J Stud Alc, 11*:199-204, 1950.

Levitt, B. E.: The results of psychotherapy with children: An evaluative. *Journal of Consulting Psychology, 21*:189-196, 1957.

Lidz, T., Cornelison, A. R., Fleck, S., and Terry, D.: Schism and skew in families of schizophrenics. *Am J Psychiatry, 64*:241-248, 1957.

Lieber, C. S.: Liver adaptation and injury in alcoholism. *New Engl J Med, 288*:356-362, 1973.

Lieber, C. S., and Rubin, E.: Alcoholic fatty liver. *New Engl J Med, 280*:705-708, 1969.

Lisman, S. A.: Alcoholic "blackout": State dependent learning? *Arch Gen Psychiat, 40(1)*:46-53, 1974.

Louhija, A.: Cardiovascular effects of alcohol. *Duodecim, 88*:292-299, 1972.

Maddox, G. L., and Borinski, E.: Drinking behavior in Negro collegians. *Quart J Stud Alc, 25*:651-668, 1964.

Mass, H. S., et al.: Socio-cultural factors in psychiatric clinic services for children. *Smith College Student Social Work, 25*:1-90, 1955.

Masserman, J. H., Jacques, M. G., and Nicholson, M. R.: Alcohol as a preventative experimental neurosis. *Quart J Stud Alc, 6*:281-299, 1945.

Matz, P. B.: Outcome of hospital treatment of exservice patients with nervous and mental disease in the U.S. Veterans Bureau. *U.S. Veterans Bureau Medical Bulletin, 5*:829-842, 1929.

May, Rollo: Psychotherapy and the daimonic. In Mahrer, A. and Pearson, L. (Eds.): *Creative Developments in Psychotherapy.* New York, Aronson, 1973.

McCance, C., and McCance, P. F.: Alcoholism in north-east Scotland: Its treatment and outcome. *Br J Psychiat, 115*:189-198, 1969.

McClelland, D. C.: The power of positive drinking. *Psychology Today, 4(8)*:40-41, 1971.

McClelland, D. C., Davis, W. N., Kalin, R., and Wanner, E.: *The Drinking Man.* New York, Free Press, 1972.

McClelland, D. C., Davis, W. N., Wanner, E., and Kalin, R. A.: Cross-cultural study of folktale content and drinking. *Sociometry, 29*:308-333, 1966.

McCord, W., and McCord, J.: *Origins of Alcoholism.* Stanford U Pr, 1960.

McCord, J.: Etiological factors in alcoholism; family and personal characteristics. *Quart J Stud Alc, 33*:1020-1027, 1972.

McGinnis, C. A.: The effect of group therapy on the ego-strength scale scores of alcoholic patients. *J of Clin Psych, 19*:346-347, 1963.

Meltzoff, J., and Kornreich, M.: *Research in Psychotherapy.* New York, Atherton Pr, 1970.

Meyer, V., and Chesser, E. S.: *Behavior Therapy in Clinical Psychiatry.* New York, Science House, 1970.

Mezey, E., Jow, E., Slavin, R. E., and Tobon, R.: Pancreatic function and intestinal absorption in chronic alcoholism. *Gastroenterology, 59*:657-664, 1970.

Miller, E. C., Dvorack, B. A., and Turner, D. W.: A method of creating aversion to alcohol by reflex conditioning in a group setting. *Quart J Stud in Alc, 21*:424-431, 1960.

Miller, E. D., Dvorak, A., and Turner, D. W.: A method of creating aversion to alcohol by reflex conditioning in a group setting. *Quart J Stud Alc, 21*:424-431, 1950.

Miller, M. M.: Treatment of alcoholism by hypnotic aversion. *JAMA*, *1959:*1492-1495, 1971.

Milt, H.: *Basic Handbook on Alcoholism.* New Jersey, Scientific Aids Publications, 1969.

Morgan, W. P.: *Selected Physiological and Psychomotor Correlates of Depression in Psychiatric Patients.* Doctoral dissertation, University of Toledo, 1967.

Morgenstern, F., Pearce, J., and Davis, B.: The application of aversion therapy to tranvestism. In Franks, D. M.: *Behavior Therapy: Appraisal and Status.* New York, McGraw-Hill, 1969.

Mowrer, O. H.: *The New Group Therapy.* New York, Van Nostrand, 1964.

Mulford, H. A.: Drinking and deviant behavior, U.S.A., 1963. *Quart J Stud Alc, 25:*634-650, 1964.

Myerson, R. M., and Lafair, J. S.: Alcoholic muscle disease. *Med Clin N Amer, 54:*723-730, 1970.

Naitoh, P.: Value of electroencephalography in alcoholism. *Annals of the New York Academy of Sciences, 215:*303-320, 1973.

National Council on Alcoholism, Criteria Committee: Criteria for the diagnosis of alcoholism. *Am J Psychiat, 129:*127-135, 1972.

Negrete, J. C.: Cultural influences on social performance of alcoholics; A comparative study. *Quart J Stud Alc, 34:*905-916, 1973.

Olson, D. H.: A critical overview. In Gurman, A. S., and Rice, D. G. (Eds.): *Couples in Conflict.* New York, Aronson, Jason, Inc., 1975.

Olson, R. W.: MMPI sex differences in narcotic addicts. *J of Gen Psych, 71:*257-266, 1964.

Pader, E.: Clinical heart disease and electrocardiographic abnormalities in alcoholics. *Quart J Stud Alc, 34:*774-785, 1973.

Pennington, L. A.: Psychopathic and criminal behavior. In Pennington, L. A., and Berg, I. A. (Eds.): *An Introduction to Clinical Psychology.* New York, Ronald Pr, 1954.

Perkhoff, G. T.: Alcoholic myopathy. *Ann Rev Med, 22:*125-132, 1971.

Rachman, S. J., and Teasdale, J.: Aversion therapy: An appraisal. In Franks, C. M. (Ed.): *Behavior Therapy: Appraisal and Status.* New York, McGraw-Hill, 1969(a), pp. 279-320.

———. *Aversion Therapy and Behavior Disorders: An Analysis.* Coral Gables, University of Miami Press, 1969(b).

Rathod, N. H., Gregory, E., Blows, P., and Thomas, G. H.: A two-year follow-up study of alcoholic patients. *Brit J Psychiat, 112:*683-692, 1966.

Razran, G. H. S.: Conditioned withdrawal responses with shock as the conditioning stimulus in adult human subjects. *Psychological Bulletin, 31:*111-143, 1934.

Reich, Wilhelm: *The Murder of Christ.* Orgone Institute Press, 1953.

Reynold, G. S.: *A Primer of Operant Conditioning.* New York, Scott, Foresman, 1968.

Robin, L. N., Bates, W. W., and O'Neal, P.: *Adult Drinking Patterns of Former Problem Children, in Society, Culture and Drinking Patterns.* Pittman and Snyder, 1962, pp. 395-412.

Roe, A.: Children of alcoholic parents raised in foster homes. Alcohol, Science and Society, *Quart J Stud in Alc,* 115-128, 1945.

Rogers, C. R.: *Client-Centered Therapy.* Boston, Houghton Mifflin, 1952.

Rohan, W.: A Comparison of two aversion conditioning procedures for problem drinking. *Newsletter,* Research in Psychology, *12(4)*:14-15, 1970. (Published by Veterans Administration Center, Bay Pines, Florida.)

Ross, T. A.: *An Inquiry into Prognosis in the Neurosis.* London, Cambridge U Pr, 1936.

Rubington, E.: The hidden alcoholic, *Quart J Stud Alc, 33*:667-683, 1972.

Sanderson, R. E., Campbell, D., and Laverty, S. G.: An investigation of a new aversive conditioning treatment for alcoholism. *Quart J Stud Alc, 24*: 261-275, 1963.

Satir, V.: *Conjoint Family Therapy: A Guide to Theory and Technique.* Palo Alto, Science and Behavior Books, 1964.

Schuckit, M. A.: Alcoholism and sociopathy — diagnostic confusion. *Quart J Stud Alc, 34*:157-164, 1973.

Seeman, J. A.: Study of the process of nondirective therapy. *Journal of Consulting Psychology, 13*:157-168, 1949.

Shapiro, J. L., and Gust, T.: Counselor training for facilitative human relationships. *Counselor Education and Supervision, 13*:198-206, 1974.

Shore, J. H., and Von-Fumetti, B.: Three alcohol programs for American Indians. *Am J Psychiat, 128*:1450-1454, 1972.

Smith, J. J.: The endocrine basis of hormonal therapy of alcoholism. *N Y State J of Med, 50*:1704-1706, 1711-1715, 1950.

———. The effect of alcohol in the adrenal ascorbic acid and the cholesterol of the rat. *J Clin Endocrin, 11*:792, 1951.

Sobell, M., and Sobell, L. Individual behavior therapy for alcoholics. *California Mental Health Research Monograph, 13,* 1972.

Sobell, M., and Sobell, l.: *Training Responsible Drinking with State Hospital Alcoholics.* Paper presented at the American Psychological Association annual meeting, Chicago, 1975.

Spelt, D. K.: The conditioning of the human fetus in utero. *J Exp Psychol, 38*:338-346, 1948.

Steele, B. C.: *The Amount of Exploration into Causes, Means, Goals and Agent: A Comparison of Successful and Unsuccessful Cases in Client-centered Therapy.* Unpublished master's thesis, University of Chicago, 1948.

Steffen, J. Electromyographically induced relaxation in the treatment of alcohol abuse. *J Consult Clin Psychol, 43(2)*:275, 1975.

Steiner, C.: *Games Alcoholics Play.* New York, Grove, 1971.

Steinback, A., and Blumenthal, M.: Alcohol addiction and body build. *Acta*

*Psychiat Scand, 46:*224-231, 1970.

Strupp, H.: *Psychotherapy: Clinical, Research and Theoretical Issues.* New York, Aronson, 1973.

Sutker, P. B.: Personality differences and sociopathy in heroin addicts and nonaddict prisoners. *J of Abnormal Psych, 78:*247-251, 1971.

The Little Red Book. Center City, Hazelden, 1957.

Trice, H.: The job behavior of problem drinkers. In Pittman, D. and Snyder, C. (Eds.): *Society, Culture and Drinking Patterns.* New York, Wiley, 1962.

Truax, C. B., and Carkhuff, R. R.: *Client and Therapist Transparency in the Psychotherapeutic Encounter.* Invited paper, Symposium: The Transparent Self, American Psychological Association, Philadelphia, August 29, 1963.

———. *Toward Effective Counseling and Psychotherapy: Training and Practice.* Chicago, Aldine, 1967.

Truax, C. B., and Lister, J. L.: Effects of short-term training upon accurate empathy and nonpossessive warmth. *Counselor Education and Supervision, 10:*120-125, 1971.

Truax, C. B., and Wargo, D. G.: *Antecedents to Outcome in Group Psychotherapy with Juvenile Delinquents: Effects of Therapeutic Conditions, Alternate Sessions, Vicarious Therapy Pretraining and Patient Self-exploration.* An unpublished manuscript, University of Arkansas, Arkansas Rehabilitation Research and Training Center, 1966.

Truitt, E. B. Jr.: Is there a biochemical lesion in the disease of alcoholism? *Ohio State Med J, 66:*681-683, 1970.

Ullman, L., and Krasner, L.: *A Psychological Approach to Abnormal Behavior.* Englewood Cliffs, Prentice-Hall, 1969.

Uraa, C. W.: *Alcoholism and the Treatment of Sexual Dysfunction.* Lecture presented at Psychotherapy Associates Fourth Annual Winter Treatment and Rehabilitation of the Alcoholic Workshop, Colorado Springs, Colorado, February 3, 1978.

Voegtlin, W.: The treatment of alcoholism by establishing a conditioned reflex. *Am J Med Sci, 199:*802-809, 1940.

Voegtlin, W. L., and Lemere, R.: An evaluation of the aversion treatment of alcoholism. *Quart J Stud Alc, 11:*199-204, 1950.

Vogler, R. E., Lunde, S. G., Johnson, F. R., and Martin, P. L.: Electrical aversion conditioning with chronic alcoholics. *Journal of Consulting and Clinical Psychology, 34:*302-307, 1970.

Von Wartburg, J. P.: Addiction — A biological problem? *Alcoholgia, 2:*49-53, 1971.

Walker, S. H.: Personal communication. Pikes Peak Psychological Center, Colorado Springs, Colorado, March, 1977.

Warkov, S., Bacon, S., and Hawkins, A.: Social correlates of industrial problem drinking. *Quart J Stud Alc, 26:*58-71, 1965.

Weiner, S., Tamerin, J. S., Steinglass, P., and Mendelson, J. H.: Familial patterns in chronic alcoholism; A study of a father and son during experimental intoxication. *Amer J Psychiat, 127:*1646-1651, 1971.

Weingold, H. P., Lachin, J. M., Bell, A. H., and Coxe, R. C.: Depression as a symptom of alcoholism: Search for a phenomenon. *J. of Abnormal Psych, 73:*195-197, 1968.

Wellman, L.: *A Learning Theory Approach to the Treatment of Substance Abuse.* Paper presented at the Summer Institute of Drug Abuse, Colorado Springs, Colorado, 1977.

Whitehorn, J. C., and Betz, B. J.: A study of psychotherapeutic relationships between physicians and schizophrenic patients. *Amer J of Psychiat, 3:*321, 1954.

Winaker, S. J., Bejar, J., McCray, R. S., and Zamcheck, N.: Hemorrhagic gastritis: importance of associated chronic gastritis. *Arch Inter Med, 127:*129-131, 1971.

Wolberg, L.: *The Technique of Psychotherapy,* Part One. New York, Grune and Stratton, 1967.

Wolff, K.: Group therapy for alcoholics. *Mental Hygiene, 51:*549-551, 1967.

―――. Hospitalized alcoholic patients: Motivating alcoholics through group psychotherapy. *Hospital Community Psychiatry, 19:*206-209, 1968.

Wolpe, J. Objective psychotherapy of the neuroses. *South African Medical Journal, 26:*825, 1952.

Wolpe, J.: *Psychotherapy by Reciprocal Inhibition.* Stanford, Stanford U Press, 1958.

Wolpe, J.: *The Practice of Behavior Therapy.* Englewood Cliffs, Prentice-Hall, 1969.

Wooddell, W. J.: *Alcohol and the Liver.* Lecture presented at Psychotherapy Associates Fourth Annual Winter Treatment and Rehabilitation of the Alcoholic Workshop, Colorado Springs, Colorado, February 2, 1978.

Zuckerman, M., and Lubin, B.: *Manual for the Multiple Affect Adjective Check List.* San Diego, Educational and Industrial Testing Service, 1965.

Zuk, G. H.: Family therapy. *Arch Gen Psychiatry, 16:*71-79, 1967.

INDEX

A

Akert, K., 154
Al-Anon, 109, 123, 124, 172
Ala-Teen, 123, 124, 172
Ala-Tot, 172
Alcohol addiction, developmental stages of, 12-24
Alcoholic marital relationship, 173-182
Alcoholic, definition of, 5, 8
Alcoholics Anonymous, 112-125, 172, 212-215, 238-240, 305, 307-309
Alcoholic, chronic developmental stage, 21-24
Alcoholism, diagnosis of, 57-72
Alcoholism, sociological aspects, 25-39
Allergy, theory of alcohol addiction, 218
Anant, S. S., 145
Anchor, K. N., 305
Anger, 46, 47
Antabuse (disulfiram), 146, 147, 319
Anxiety, 43, 44, 220-221, 311-320
Arbuckle, D. S., 89
Assertive training, 156, 157, 166
Astin, A. W., 55
Aversion therapy
chemically based, 140-142
electric shock-noxious faradic stimulation, 142-144
verbally based, 144-146

B

Bacon, S., 254
Bales, R. F., 31
Bandura, A., 141, 148, 157, 165, 167
Basic trust, 91
Bass, A. H., 305, 311
Bateson, G., 179
Beaubraum, M. H., 141
Begleiter, H., 37

Behavior therapy, techniques in the treatment of alcoholism, 139-167
Bejar, J., 36
Bell, A. H., 311
Bennett, R. M., 305, 311
Berne, E., 224
Bernstein, 155
Betz, B. J., 78, 79
Biofeedback, 158, 159
"Blackout," definition of, 16, 17
Blake, B. G., 143
Blane, H. T., 95, 305, 311, 312
Bleuler, M., 217
Blows, P., 312
Blum, E. and Blum, R., 200
Blumenthal, M., 222
Bower, G., 148
Bugental, J. F. T., 304
Bundza, K. H., 304
Burch, G. E., 35

C

Cahalan, D., 26
Cahill, C. A., 146
Cardiac, effects of alcoholism, 35
"Career," alcoholic, 136, 137
Carkhuff, R. R., 79, 80, 88, 93, 111, 304, 314
Carpenter, J. A., 305, 311
Case histories, alcoholic, 9, 10, 264-269, 291-296
Catanzaro, R. J., 157
Cautela, J. R., 144, 145
Character armor, 247-253
Cheek, F., 159
Chesluk, D., 60
Chesser, E. S., 139-140
Cisin, I. H., 26
Clinebell, H. J. Jr., 157
Clinical readings in the treatment of al-

343